ALSO BY DONNA L. FRANKLIN

Ensuring Inequality:
The Structural Transformation of the African-American Family

What's Love Got to Do with It?

Understanding and Healing the Rift
Between Black Men and Women

Donna L. Franklin

SIMON & SCHUSTER

New York London Toronto Sydney Singapore

SIMON & SCHUSTER
Rockefeller Center
1230 Avenue of the Americas
New York, NY 10020

Manufactured in the United States of America

1   3   5   7   9   10   8   6   4   2

Library of Congress Cataloging-in-Publication Data

Franklin, Donna L.
What's love got to do with it? : understanding and healing the rift between Black men
and women / Donna L. Franklin.
p. cm.
Includes bibliographical references and index.
1. Man-woman relationships. 2. Afro-American women. 3. Afro-American men.
I. Title.
HQ801.F76 2000
306.7'089'96073—dc21   00-032984

ISBN 0-684-81851-5

The author gratefully acknowledges permission from the following sources
to reprint material in their control:
Africa World Press for Robert Lewis and Patrick Bryan, eds.,
Garvey: His Work and Impact. Copyright © 1991.
Princeton University Press for graphs from William G. Bowen and Derek Bok,
*The Shape of the River: Long-Term Consequences of Considering Race in College
and University Admissions.* Copyright © 1998.

Acknowledgments

Words seem woefully inadequate to express my deepest gratitude to all of the individuals who provided encouragement and support as the manuscript took shape. I owe the greatest debt to Faith Childs, my fearless literary agent, for her vision and her tireless work to make this book a reality. I also owe a great deal to the following individuals: Dominick Anfuso for his forbearance and belief in this project. John Bergez for his skillful editing of the manuscript to improve its readability for a more general audience—working with John was truly a godsend. Emily Remes for the attention and scrutiny she gave to my manuscript—her contributions were indispensable in the enhancement of the manuscript as a whole. Isolde C. Sauer for going above and beyond the call of duty in supervising the copyediting work on the book. Pamela Lusby-Bailey for her generosity and for conducting the comprehensive online search for relevant research studies, surveys, and many of the references found in the book. Dana Gamble for his willingness to respond expeditiously and amiably to my unwieldy requests. Dana drafted the diagrams and charts found in the appendix.

There were many friends and colleagues who were also a part of this project, offering attentive listening and ideas. Elizabeth Alexander for taking time from her family commitments to give me invaluable literary input and emotional support. Jessie Combre for her probing questions and piercing analysis. Pat Bates for transferring her expertise in the electronic media to a print project. Kristal

Zook, J. R. Murray, and Donna DeBruhl-Hemer for thought-provoking discussions and for being available when I needed someone to lend an ear. Barbara Solomon for her unwavering support and perceptiveness; Clarice Walker for her wisdom; Shirley Peppers for her tutelage regarding development issues. To my colleagues at the Council for Contemporary Families, especially Connie Ahrons, Stephanie Coontz, Phil and Carolyn Cowan, and William Julius Wilson for joining forces with the Council. To my colleagues at Smith College, especially Carolyn Jacobs, Edith Fraser, and Joyce Everett. Regan Jordan and Jenny Quan for guidance and illumination on matters related to mind, body, and spirit.

I was also nurtured by my family's embrace. My sister and brother-in-law, April and Matthew, for their gracious hospitality whenever I needed to take a break from my writing. I also want to extend my appreciation to other family members for cheering me on and being there when I wavered, especially Vicki and Stephani.

For Myisha,
The Most Extraordinary Gift—

Here's hoping the men and women of your
generation can know what possibilities the future
will hold for them if they build and maintain trusting
and harmonious relationships with one another.

If we do not know our history, we are doomed to live it as though it were our private fate.

—Hannah Arendt

One of the most characteristic features of our community is the antagonism between our men and women.

—Toni Cade Bambara

Contents

What's Love
Got to Do with It?

1

Breaking the Silence

Black people are big on keeping race secrets. It's as if
the bond of our skin color demands that we keep at
least a façade of monolithic solidarity, even when doing
so cripples and disenfranchises us. . . . The men are
always more important than the women, and, when it
comes to issues particular to women, there's not much
difference between a black or white patriarch.

— JILL NELSON, *Straight, No Chaser: How I
Became a Grown-up Black Woman*

RELATIONSHIPS BETWEEN black men and women in
America are in crisis. Black women and men know this well, for
they experience it in their attempts to date, to forge relationships,
to marry, and to stay together. More often than ever before, their
attempts end in mutual misunderstandings and mutual recrimina-
tions.

Although forming satisfying and lasting bonds in today's society is a challenge for men and women of every racial background,
the challenge is greatest for African Americans. Perhaps no group
feels the problem more acutely than young, educated black women.
A public school administrator with the District of Columbia has

expressed the frustrations and disappointments shared by many black women:

> Have you met this woman? She has a good job, works hard, earns a good salary. She went to college, got her master's degree; she is intelligent. She is personable, articulate, well read, interested in everybody and everything. Yet, she's single.
>
> Or perhaps you recognize the community activist. She's a black lady—or, as she prefers, an African-American woman—on the move. She sports a short natural, sometimes cornrow braids, or even dreadlocks. She's an organizer, a motivator, a dynamo. Her work for her people speaks for itself—organizing women for a self-help collective, raising funds for a community cause, educating others around a new issue in South Africa. Black folks look up to her, and white folks know she's a force to be reckoned with. Yet once again, the men leave her alone. What do these women have in common? They have so much; what is it they lack? Why is it they may be able to hook a man but can't hold him?
>
> The women puzzle over this quandary themselves. They gather at professional clubs, at sorority meetings, or at the office over coffee and wonder what's wrong with black men. They hold special prayer vigils and fast and pray and beg Jesus to send the men back to church. They find the brothers attending political strategy sessions or participating in protests, but when it comes time to go home, the brothers go home to someone else. I know these women because I am all of these women.[1]

The problem that black women like this one confront in finding black men to date and marry is exacerbated by the shrinking pool of available candidates. The ratio of black women to men is highly imbalanced and has been for generations. Although the gender ratios in the African-American community were balanced at the turn of the century, the ratios of men to women fell continuously and sharply until 1990 when the marital opportunities index fell below 65—meaning that there would be less than 65 men available to marry for every 100 women.[2] For professional black women, the pool of eligible black men shrinks even further because so many black men face uncertain economic futures.

But attention to these demographic factors can obscure the deeper problem of the distressed state of gender relations in the African-American community. The data on relational patterns among African Americans are nothing short of alarming:

- The current divorce rate for blacks is four times the 1960 level and double that of the general population.[3]

- Interracial marriages have risen from a reported 51,000 in 1960 to 311,000 in 1997. Even though marriageable black females outnumber black males, twice as many black men as women marry outside the race. Among sexually active African Americans, 23 percent of the black men had had white partners, compared with only 6 percent of black women.[4]

- Both black men and women are significantly less desirous of marriage than their white counterparts. Of all these groups, black men are the least desirous of marriage.[5]

- The rates of violence between black men and women are higher than those for other races. Not only are black wives more likely to kill their husbands than wives of other races, but the majority of the women killed by husbands or boyfriends are also black. Paradoxically, white women have been more likely to push for tougher laws against domestic violence and for shelters for battered women.[6]

- For couples in long-term marriages, 72 percent of the African-American husbands reported using a confrontational style of dealing with marital conflict, compared with 25 percent of Mexican-American husbands and 18 percent of white husbands.[7]

- Forty-four percent of married black men admit to having been unfaithful to their wives, almost double the percentage for whites. In contrast, the differences between black women and white women were minuscule—18 percent and 15 percent respectively.[8]

- If these patterns of infidelity are multigenerational, they could be one explanation for the findings of a nationwide survey of black women. This survey found that 77.1 percent of black mothers gave negative messages to their daughters about black men.[9]

Why do the marriage and relationship experiences of African Americans differ so markedly from those of other Americans? How are we to explain the high levels of tension and conflict between black men and women? What are the root causes of their turbulent relationships?

In reflecting on her own experiences, the public school administrator points a finger squarely at herself and other black women:

After asking over and over again, "What's wrong with these men?" it finally dawned on me to ask the question, "What's wrong with us women?" What I have found, and what many of these women have yet to discover, is that the skills that make one successful in the church, community or workplace are not the skills that make one successful in a relationship.

Being acknowledged as the head of the household is an especially important thing for many black men, since their manhood is so often actively challenged everywhere else. Many modern women are so independent, so self-sufficient, so committed to the cause, to the church, to career—or their narrow concepts of same—that their entire personalities project an "I don't need a man" message. So they end up without one. An interested man may be attracted, but he soon discovers that this sister makes very little space for him in her life.

Going to graduate school is a good goal and an option that

previous generations of blacks have not had. But sometimes the achieving woman will place her boyfriend so low on her list of priorities that his interest wanes. Between work, school and homework, she's seldom "there" for him, for the preliminaries that might develop a commitment to a woman. She's too busy to prepare him a home-cooked meal or to be a listening ear for his concerns because she is so occupied with her own.

Like many discussions of the dating challenges facing black women, this administrator's remarks place most of the responsibility on black women themselves. They echo the common idea that black women are simply too strong, too independent, and too self-sufficient for their own good or for the good of their relationships. As with male and female relationships, little attention is given to the attributes of black men that are problematic in relationships. When black men are discussed, it is usually within the context of how their manhood is constantly being challenged or how much more difficult life is for them than it is for black women. If a black woman is to have a harmonious relationship with a black man, she will have to learn to provide more nurturance by preparing home-cooked meals and offering a listening ear in an effort to offset his pain. Rarely is anything mentioned about the importance of her mate providing her with reciprocal care.

In part, this common way of thinking is an outgrowth not just of the black experience in America but of attitudes about gender roles in society at large. Despite the efforts of the women's movement and the entry of most women into the workforce, the images of men as providers and women as nurturing partners continue to persist. Genuine equality and mutuality in relationships remain an elusive goal for many men and women, not just African Americans. But for black Americans, these issues are compounded by the distinctive character of the black experience in America.

The perceptions black women have of themselves mirror societal perceptions and are not always aligned with the facts. For example, shortly after Daniel Patrick Moynihan characterized the black family as "matriarchal," asserting that black women fared better interpersonally and economically than black men, a study found that black women were the least likely of all race/gender groups to be employed in male-dominated professions.[10] During this same time frame, an analysis of trends in higher education among blacks found that although a greater proportion of black women were enrolled in colleges and universities, black men were more likely than black women to obtain graduate degrees beyond the master's level. Moreover, 91 percent of the professional degrees granted in the combined fields of medicine, dentistry, law, veterinary medicine, and theology went to black men. Specifically, 85.6 percent of the M.D.s conferred on blacks went to black men and 90.4 percent of the law degrees went to black men.[11] In addition, two analyses of blacks with doctorates in all fields from all institutions in 1969 and 1970 found that black women held roughly 21 percent of the advanced degrees. By the mid-1980s, for the first time, black women received more than half of all doctorates, including science and engineering. Only 6 percent of all science degrees awarded to black women were in the higher paying and more prestigious areas of engineering, mathematics, and physical science. Black men were predominant in these areas. Black women, on the other hand, were dominant in the less lucrative social/behavioral sciences.[12] In short, the major oversight in the Moynihan Report was that he misread the absence or marginalization of black fathers in poor families as the black woman's economic and interpersonal dominance in the black community at large—and this misperception persists to this day.

Although both sexes have been shaped and scarred by prejudice and discrimination, the damage inflicted on the black male psyche is perceived as penetrating more deeply than the injustice inflicted on black women. This perception is due in part to the fact that being a man in American society means having a stable job and being able to provide adequately for oneself and one's family. In view of this, being unemployed or being employed in jobs that are demeaning, neither of which offers a sense of accomplishment or provides a living wage, may be especially damaging for black men.

Although the objective economic position of black women is more tenuous than that of white men, white women, or black men, it is the black man who is placed in the hapless position of proving his "manhood" while being systematically denied access to the tools with which to do so. Ben, a forty-two-year-old city government employee, reports, "I have had to work hard 'cause as a black man in white society, I have coped with more obstacles than the average white man 'cause opportunities are still marked for whites only." Jim, a forty-year-old auto mechanic, explains, "As a black man, most whites viewed me as a threat. Thus my job has never gone smooth and my chances for advancement have not been great, but I've worked hard, like two and three jobs for years. I've relied on my own strength to survive in American society." Robert, a forty-three-year-old bus driver, states, "As a black man, I was foolish to think that my marriage would be a fair relationship because society makes black men feel like second-class citizens. I've had to depend only on my own abilities and worked overtime with a part-time job to make it in American society. Indeed, I've had to make a way out of no way."[13]

The difficulties faced by black men in a white-dominated society are real, and they have been amply documented. In fact, so much attention has been paid to the challenges facing the black *man* that he has become the symbolic representation of the victims of racial injustice. By comparison, the black *woman* is lost in shadow. Yet she, too, faces profound challenges—challenges that are further complicated by her gender. Moreover, she, too, has been shaped by her history. The image of black women as strong to the point of overbearing is no less a legacy of the African-American experience than the image of the "emasculated" black man. Given these images of the two sexes, it is little wonder that even black women may conclude that they bear the responsibility of going more than halfway in making their relationships work. Yet such a "solution" only perpetuates the dysfunctional patterns that are the common legacy of slavery and its aftermath for black men and women alike.

When black men and women try to relate to one another today, their starting point is fixed by experiences of injustice and oppression that have affected them in ways that are both similar and profoundly different. These experiences have interacted in complex ways with larger trends in society to shape their self-concepts, their images of each other, the values and expectations they bring to their relationships, and their views of what it means to be a man or woman—let alone a *black* man or a *black* woman. To understand the tensions and turmoil in the relationships of black men and women today, we must come to grips with the distinctive relational patterns whose roots extend deep into the history of blacks in America.

In so doing we must acknowledge that the "problem" of black relationships is not a new development. Black men and women have faced distinctive challenges in their relationships ever since slavery. These challenges have taken different forms over time, but they are unique in being created in a vortex resulting from racial discrimination and injustice.

We must be willing to bring these issues into the light of open and candid discussion. Although the turbulence in gender relations in the African-American community is common knowledge, the popular media have given it little attention. One of the primary reasons for this silence is that African Americans, especially African-American women, have been unwilling to expose any internal conflict that might reflect negatively on the black community. Historian Darlene Clark Hine describes the defense mechanism black women have had to create as a "culture of dissemblance." In Hine's view, this culture is maintained by the "behavior and attitudes of black women that created the appearance of openness and disclosure but actually shielded the truth of their inner lives and selves from their oppressors."[14]

The reticence of black women (and men) in discussing the "truth of their inner lives" is understandable. But we cannot hope to resolve the dilemmas that beset our relationships until we are willing to speak about them frankly. The problems are there. The crisis is palpable. We cannot afford to ignore the toll it is taking on us and the toll it will take on our children. It is time to break the silence.

This book is intended to be a contribution to a much-needed dialogue about the issues in gender relations in the African-American community. It traces these issues to their roots in slavery and the efforts of generations of black men and women to find their way in a free but manifestly unequal society. It is written from the perspective of a social scientist and a black woman. As such, it emphasizes the interplay of social, economic, and cultural factors, and it departs from prior discussions in focusing equal attention on the injuries that have been imposed on African-American women. Doing so is one step toward achieving a more comprehensive understanding of the issues black men and women face in their relationships today.

Taking a comprehensive view of gender relations among African Americans will lead us well beyond such simplistic analyses as those which suggest that black men need to get on their feet and black women need to be more pliant and deferential to their men. By the same token, it will take us beyond pointing fingers at each other for causing the failures in our relationships. Before the healing begins, black males and females must stop the blame game—and the victim game, too. Both must take full responsibility for the current state of their relationships. Both must be willing to examine their relational patterns as well as their role in perpetuating them. Both must be willing to change.

The challenge is formidable, but it will be made easier if we understand how we came to be where we are. Understanding is the first step on the path to healing.

2

The Past Is Prologue: Slavery and Its Aftermath

There exists, indeed, a profound and natural antipathy between the institution of marriage and that of slavery. A man
does not marry when he cannot exercise marital authority,
when his children must be born his equal, irrevocably destined
to the wretchedness of their father; when, having no power
over their fate, he can neither know the duties, privileges,
the hopes, nor the cares which belong to the paternal relation.
It is easy to perceive that every motive which incites the
freedman to a lawful union is lost to the slave
by the simple fact of his slavery.

—ALEXIS DE TOCQUEVILLE

White folks got a heap to answer for the way
they've done to colored folks! So much they won't
never pray it away!

—A FORMER SLAVE

ONE OF THE COMMENTATORS
who have broken the silence
surrounding current tensions between black men and women is
writer Maya Angelou. Angelou's heartfelt words echo the anguish
felt by many African Americans today:

There is a schism which exists between black men and women, and it's really painful and frightening because we were taken together from the African continent. We lay spoon fashion, back to belly, in the filthy hatches of slave ships, and in our own and each other's excrements and urine. We stood up at the auction block together. We were sent to work before sunrise, came back after sunset together. We have been equals and we are in danger if we lose that balance because if women begin to feel, "The black woman is the strongest—," then where is the man? If the man begins to feel, "I have no place in her life," then there's no balance, and all people will have paid all of those dues for nothing.[1]

Angelou is correct in characterizing the deep divide between black men and women as nothing less than a "schism." What she fails to note, however, is that this schism was not created in the last two decades or even in the past half-century. Moreover, in implying that black men and women were once equals united by the experience of enslavement, Angelou's analysis overlooks the destructive effects of slavery on black family life in general and on gender relations in particular. Far from uniting black men and women as equal partners sharing a common fate, slavery drove a wedge between them. We are still trying to find our way across that divide today.

The thesis of this book is that the relationships between African-American men and women are the result of a distinctive set of experiences they have had in this country. These experiences have been created as African Americans' values and self-understanding have interacted with societal institutions and historical circumstances. If we want to understand the schism Angelou describes, we must go back to its origins in the formative experience of slavery and its immediate aftermath in the era of Reconstruction.

The "Peculiar Institution"

For more than three centuries the all-embracing system of American slavery was the defining experience of the vast majority of blacks in the United States. Slavery destroyed the customs the slaves had known as a free people and substituted a way of life that was geared to the convenience of the slaveholders. In the process, slavery weakened the family unit, disrupting and redefining marriage and family roles. It also inflicted profound indignities on the slaves that compelled them to respond and cope in ways that would deeply influence their views of their roles as men and women long after emancipation.

Slaveholders' absolute control over the intimate lives of the slaves began with their authority to select a slave's marital partner. On some plantations "marriages" were forced on men and women who had spouses in other places. Slave masters could insist that their slaves form partnerships with other slaves regardless of compatibility or depth of affection.

> I myself had my wife on another plantation. The woman my master gave me had a husband on another plantation. Everything was mixed up. My other wife had two children for me, but the woman master gave me had no children. We were put in the same cabin, but both of us cried, me for my old wife and she for her old husband. As I could read and write I used to write out passes for myself, so I could go and see my old wife, and I wrote passes for the other men on the place, so they could go see their wives that lived off the place.[2]

Slaveholders also had the power to decide the length of time married couples could stay together. According to some accounts, marital relationships were forcibly broken up with enough regularity to depreciate the meaning of the ceremony.

One night a couple married an' de next mornin' de boss sell de wife. Ma got de gal in de street an' cursed de white woman fur all she could find. She said: "dat damn white, pale-face bastard sell my daughter who jus' married las' night," as other t'ings.

The married woman's mother was so distraught the police had to be summoned to restrain her. She was transported to the local workhouse.[3]

The forced separation of families was also not uncommon. These disconnections often occurred at early ages. Frances Berry, an ex-slave, describes one particularly appalling incident:

Two or three of dem gals had young babies taken with 'em. Poor little things. As soon as they got on the train this ol' new master had [the] train stopped an' made dem poor mothers take off and laid dem precious things on de groun' and left dem behind to live or die. . . . Master who bought de mothers didn't want gals to be bothered with these chillun 'cause he had cotton fields fer new slaves to work.[4]

The roots of black gender conflict can be traced to this experience of powerlessness during slavery. Stripped of the most fundamental control over their family lives, slaves could not ordinarily choose how to fulfill the human roles of husbands and wives, fathers and mothers, sons and daughters. As we will see, this destruction of family roles would have far-reaching effects. But the indignities of slavery cut even more deeply than this. Male and female slaves were subject to distinctive assaults on their freedom and dignity that went to the heart of their identities as men and women. This dismantling of black manhood and womanhood would profoundly affect their views of themselves and one another long after emancipation.

The Dismantling of Black Manhood and Womanhood

Slavery's destruction of the basic family unit had damaging effects on both males and females. However, the impact on males was particularly devastating. Most of the slaves brought to the United States were from West Africa, where the socially constructed concept of manhood entailed the fulfillment of the male's sociofamilial roles as husband, father, and warrior. Slavery systematically stripped a West African man of the roles that defined for him what it meant to be a man.

Most West African communities were patriarchal, and male children were more valued than female progeny.[5] The birth of a boy was commemorated by celebrations in most villages. Prior to becoming a man, a young boy was initiated into several rites of passage. Although the particular ceremonies and rituals differed from one West African village to the next, there was a common theme in all of them. The status of manhood was generally attained in four successive stages: rites of passage from a boy to an adolescent; exhibition of his physical prowess as a warrior; achieving the status of husband; and finally fatherhood. Only after the male experienced these sequential stages of maturation was he considered a man by his community.

Of these four stages of manhood, the final and most important role that could be conferred on a man was that of fatherhood. Children were viewed as gifts from God; therefore, to have children was to be blessed by God. It was the importance of fathering children, together with the patriarchal nature of the society, that permitted the sanctioning of polygamy. Having multiple wives was perceived as a safeguard against childlessness.

The experience of enslavement effectively destroyed the black man's ability to fulfill any of the duties he had been socialized to discharge as a male citizen of a West African community. Captivity alone meant that he no longer enjoyed the status of warrior, and even a married male slave could not meaningfully fill the roles of husband and father. One scholar on slavery put it this way:

> When the male slave lived on the same plantation with his mate, he could rarely escape frequent demonstrations of his power-lessness. The master, not the male slave, furnished the cabin, the clothes, and the minimal food for his wife and children. Under such a regime slave fathers had little or no authority.[6]

There is no question that slavery had a devastating impact on the black man's psyche. The personality traits associated with being a "good slave" were diametrically opposed to his West African concept of manhood. The primary characteristics of manhood in West Africa were bravery, fearlessness, and gallantry, and West African communities were very clear about how a male should comport himself. How could a male slave reconcile the contradictory demands of his heritage and his circumstances?

Historians who have evaluated the effects of slavery on black men have identified three distinct personality types that emerged from slavery. One was Nat, the openly rebellious insurrectionist. He was the incorrigible runaway who, in the minds of whites, ravaged white women and attacked and killed other whites. The other two types were Sambo, the slave who adopted the pose of "fawning dependence," and Jack, the "trickster." Jack was called a trickster because he fooled many planters. Although he worked steadily as long as he was treated fairly, he often worked in alliance with other slaves to resist the white man's cruelty and domination. The common theme in Sambo's and Jack's behavior is that their survival among whites was based on their ability to hide their real feelings—their hunger for freedom, their discontent, and their disdain for whites. Ultimately, the traits they hid from whites were those generally associated with manliness.[7]

Although slave men may not have internalized the roles they played, this role-playing was demeaning and psychologically destructive. It is not uncommon for members of a subgroup to adhere simultaneously to the values of that subgroup and the majority group. Psychological damage occurs when there is dissonance between internal beliefs and outward behavior. The greater the conflict, the greater the toll. Male slaves who worked on large plantations in gang systems were able to deviate more freely from the majority group's role expectations in that they did not have as much daily contact with whites. Thus dissonance may have been the greatest for slaves on smaller plantations.[8]

If slavery was a direct assault on black manhood, it also did violence to black womanhood. Not only did black women lack the "protection" of marriage, but they had no protection under the law whatsoever. If they were raped, they had no legal recourse. Slave women could be forced into having illicit liaisons with white men and even bearing their children, but laws commonly prohibited interracial marriages. As Alice Walker has pointed out, from the moment black women entered slavery "they were subjected to rape as the 'logical' convergence of sex and violence. Conquest, in short."[9]

For example, in 1792, Virginia legislation was passed that stipulated a six-month prison term as well as a fine for whites who intermarried with blacks.[10] The net effect of this kind of legislation was that it contributed further to the vulnerability of black women and their progeny. Often, the father of a slave child was the slaveholder himself— who had no legal or financial responsibility for his biological descendants.[11]

This kind of legislation allowed white men to continue to sexually exploit black women even after slavery was prohibited, without suffering any consequences for their actions. One former slave discussed his experiences after he and his wife signed a ten-year contract to work on a very large cotton plantation that also had two big sawmills. He described the differences in the way he and his wife were treated:

My wife fared better than I did, as did the wives of some of the other Negroes, because the white men about the camp used these unfortunate creatures as their mistresses. When I was first put in the stockade my wife was still kept for a while in the "Big House." . . . When I left the camp my wife had had two children by some of the white bosses, and she was living in a fairly good shape in a little house off to herself. . . . Of the first six women brought to the camp, two of them gave birth to children after they had been there more than twelve months—and the babies had white men for their fathers.[12]

Although black women were forced to endure the sexual assaults of white men with no protection from the law or from their husbands or fathers, most black women retained the most vital role from their West African heritage—that of motherhood. As Deborah Gray White put it,

Giving birth was a life-affirming action. It was, ironically, an act of defiance, a signal to the slave owner that no matter how cruel and inhumane his actions, African Americans would not be utterly subjected or destroyed.[13]

If childbearing was a "life-affirming action" for slave women, it was of necessity a profoundly ambiguous affirmation and one that was experienced at great cost. Frances Kemble, a distinguished British actress, observed firsthand the hardship endured by slave mothers. After marrying slaveholder Pierce Butler and spending a season on his Georgia plantation, she concluded: "In considering the whole condition of the people on this plantation, it appears to me that the principal hardships fall on the lot of women." During her stay on the plantation, Kemble spoke with many slave women and observed that "there was hardly one of these women . . . who might not have been a candidate for a bed in a hospital, and they had all come to me after working all day in the fields." The slave women's biggest complaint, she recorded, was that they were not

32

allowed the customary four weeks of rest after they had given birth.

The most dismal story told to Kemble came from a woman who had sixteen children, fourteen of whom were dead. She had had four miscarriages. One had been caused when she fell down while carrying a very heavy burden on her head, and another when she received a lashing. The woman described the lashing. She said her hands were tied together and drawn up to a tree or post. Her clothes were rolled around her waist and a man then whipped her with cowhide strips. Kemble was amazed that the slave did not speak of this as anything "strange, unusual, or especially horrid and abominable." Kemble wrote in her journal, "I remember choking with indignation and grief long after they had all left me to my most bitter thoughts."[14]

Slave women's role as mothers was distorted not only by the hardships of their lives as slaves but also by the way the system of slavery fostered unnaturally high birthrates. The American system of slavery was the only one in the world where fertility rates were so high that over time there was no need to import new slaves. Between 1620 and 1860 the growth rates among slave populations in North America were much higher than in any other slave society.[15]

These high fertility rates eventually contributed to the image of black women as indefatigable breeders of children. One of the clearest indicators that the fertility rates of childbearing were linked to the institution of slavery rather than the result of personal choice emerged after the slaves were emancipated. Between 1880 and 1940 the birthrate among black women in the United States dropped by one-half. Demographers generally agreed that this decline for blacks was sharper, both absolutely and relatively, than that for whites.[16]

How did the American system of slavery achieve its high growth rates? There were few slave women who did not have to endure sexual assaults as an integral feature of their daily lives.

Defined as chattel, slave women were violated by any white man, including their masters, with impunity. Whenever black women resisted a white man's sexual encroachments, they did so at the risk of being either beaten or sold and separated from their children.

When slave women were placed on the auction block, the slave traders could get top dollar for the slave women who had the highest fertility rates. These women were generally referred to as "breeders."[17] Breeders were the women who began having children at an early age and during their childbearing years had offspring in rapid succession.

One former slave recalled the special consideration given to "breeder women" by slave masters:

> Lawdy, lawdy, them was tribbolashuns! Wunner dese womans was my Antie en she say dat she skacely call to min' he e'r whoppin' her, 'case she was er breeder woman en' brought in chillun ev'y twelve mont's jes lak a cow bringin' in a calf. . . . He orders she can't be put to no strain 'casen uv dat.[18]

The value of "breeders" only increased after the importation of slaves from abroad was banned in 1808. At this point new slaves would have to be "home grown." Slaveholders in the most northerly slave states did a profitable business exporting slaves and their offspring to states in the Deep South, where the invention of the cotton gin had made massive plantations worked by slave labor economically viable. Slave traders regularly traveled between the regions, marching slaves long distances or conveying them on boats to markets where the price per head at least quadrupled between 1800 and 1860.[19] For the fortunate owners of "breeders," slaves were a form of cash crop.

These economic dynamics contributed not only to high birthrates among slave women but to the breakup of slave families. While to some degree it was in the planters' interest to encourage stable relationships between slave men and women—as well as large broods of children—the internal traffic in slaves meant that at any time fathers, mothers, or children might be sold to other owners. The threatened loss of family roles, not to mention loved ones, was another aspect of the dismantling of black manhood and womanhood.

The Challenges of Love and Commitment

Although slaves were not allowed a legal marriage, committed relationships were sacrosanct in slave society. Once again, this was a continuity of the slaves' West African heritage. Many planters were likewise committed to these settled relationships, because they understood that a committed relationship to one woman deterred male slaves from seeking their freedom.[20] Of course, black men shared this understanding. Although they valued the companionship and camaraderie that a committed relationship ideally could provide, the realities of these relationships under the institution of slavery represented a burden and an impediment to freedom.

Thus many male slaves viewed the responsibilities of having a wife and children as something to be avoided if one truly wanted to be free. If a slave man committed to one woman and married her, he was in effect giving up his freedom. Conversely, being free seemed to be a condition of fulfilling family responsibilities. For example, when asked if they planned to marry, many slave men replied that they would never marry until they were free. When asked if he had a wife and child, William Wells Brown replied, "If I should have a wife, I should not be willing to leave her behind; and if I should attempt to bring her with me, the chances would be difficult for success."[21] For slave men, staying single and uncommitted was the price of the chance for freedom.

At the time of life when white males were marrying and starting their families, the black male slave was struggling to attain his freedom. The best way to do so was to become a runaway. According to John Hope Franklin and Loren Schweninger in *Runaway*

Slaves, males constituted 81 percent of those who were classified as runaways; of those, 78 percent were between the ages of thirteen and twenty-nine. Those who married sometimes took their loved ones with them, but in most cases they were forced to leave wives and children behind.[22]

When slave couples did form committed attachments, they faced formidable challenges that stemmed from the fact that they were far more independent of each other than most spouses who live in sovereignty. Some historians have argued that slave couples survived all sorts of difficulties and that the breakup of marital unions through the sale of one of the partners was not the rule. However, a recent study that rigorously analyzed the residential patterns of slaves points to considerable disruptions of slave marriages. The findings suggest that most slave men did not live with their wives and children even when they were on the same plantation. For example, among George Washington's slaves, 71 percent of the slave mothers lived with their children but had no husband present. Similarly, among the slaves of other planters in Virginia, slave men were much more likely than not to live outside family units that included women and children.[23]

When former slaves were interviewed, 82 percent reported the presence of their mothers during their early childhood years, whereas only 42 percent remembered having contact with their fathers. About one-third of those who mentioned the presence of a father during childhood also noted that these men did not live with their family on the same plantation.[24]

The black male was marginalized from the family because planters and slave traders frequently perceived the black family as consisting of just the slave mother and her children. As sales were negotiated, husbands and fathers were often not included as part of the deal but were "unbundled"—like a commodity—from the family unit. Not only did wives lose husbands but husbands lost wives and their children. The forced (or threatened) dissolution of not only marital but familial relationships meant that slaves could not develop the interdependency that characterized most marital relationships; they could be separated and sold away from each other at any time.

Moreover, slave wives could not rely on their husbands for the care and protection that was almost universally expected of men at the time; nor could slave men provide them. This was likely the most frustrating aspect of slavery's effects on gender relations, and it laid the foundation for the anger and distrust that persist between black men and women to this day.

Henry Bibb, a fugitive slave, articulated the feelings of numerous slave husbands when he asserted: "I don't want any man to meddle with my wife."[25] Yet Bibb was often compelled to witness the abuse of his wife and children. Like Bibb, most male slaves were powerless to defend their wife's honor. Those who tried were harshly disciplined. Josiah Henson, for example, fearlessly came to the defense of his wife. As a result, he was mercilessly beaten. Henson subsequently underwent a personality change. Previously light-hearted and easygoing, he became gloomy and irascible. Displaying drastic changes in his moods and his state of mind, Henson became uncontrollable and often ran away. After being recaptured numerous times, Henson eventually was sold when his master feared that he would lose his money.[26]

In these circumstances very few slave husbands exhibited the valor it would have required to defend the integrity of their wives and families. Slave men lived in constant fear of their lives. One slave related his firsthand observations:

I done seen Mack Williams kill folks, and I done seen him have folks killed. One day he told me that if my wife had been good looking, I never would sleep with her again cause he'd kill me and take her and raise children offen her. They used to take women away from their husbands, and put with some other man to breed just like they would do cattle. They always kept a man penned up, and they used him like a stud hoss.[27]

The inability to protect their wives and children created such deep humiliation that many black men coped by acting as if they did not see the assaults on their wives.[28] Other black husbands laid down a line of tolerated behavior and did so at considerable personal risk. Sam Watkins, a Tennessee slave owner, was one of those who crossed that line once too often:

> He would ship their husbands [slaves] out of bed and get in with their wives. One man said he stood it as long as he could and one morning he just stood outside and when he got with his wife he just choked him to death. He said he knew it was death, but it was death anyhow, so he just killed him. They hanged him.[29]

Occasionally there was a riveting story of a love that was able to conquer slavery. One such story concerns François Tiocou, a free man of color who lived in Louisiana. His mate, Marie Aram, being a slave, was his wife in name only because she was a slave. François, a poor man, lived in fear that Marie would be seized from him and sold to the highest bidder. The couple dreamed of the day when they would be able to live as husband and wife. After reading the story of Jacob in the Old Testament, François decided to purchase Marie's freedom. Her owners agreed that François could buy Marie if he would work as a slave himself for seven years. François consented. After he worked as a voluntary slave for the designated number of years, Marie was granted her freedom and told that she could enjoy the "privileges of persons born free."[30]

The Roots of the Black Gender Conflict

As we have seen, slave couples often were denied the opportunity to live together as husband and wife in the same household with their biological children.[31] As a result, most slave families were matrifo-cal—that is, centered on and headed by the mother—even when the slave father lived on the same plantation or in the same locale.

Matrifocality in slave families was buttressed not only by the sep-aration of married couples but by colonial law as well. For example, in 1662 a colonial statute read as follows: "Be it therefore enacted and declared by the present grand assembly, that all children borne in this country shall be bound and or free according to the condition of the mother."[32] As the antebellum period advanced and interstate slave trade increased, more slave families and kin networks were de-stroyed as slaves were dispersed to various geographic areas.

The matrifocality of slave families elevated the black woman to a position of greater responsibility, influence, and power within the family than that enjoyed by black men. One example of the slave woman's superior jurisdiction over the family was that although the slave master had the authority to give permission for a female slave to marry, this authority fell to the bride's mother.[33] These gender patterns ran counter to those in the dominant culture as well as to the slaves' own traditional values. Thus it can be argued that the subsequent tension between black men and women can be directly linked to the man's quest to gain his "legitimate" place within his family and his community.

Planters' records suggest that as black males endeavored to gain their place of authority within the family, they sometimes engaged in abusive behavior. The owner of the Highland plantation, Benet Barrow, makes reference to a slave by the name of Hemps and his wife, Hetty. According to Barrow, "Hemps gave his wife Hetty a light cut or two and then locked her up to prevent her from going to the Frollick." On another occasion Barrow reported that his slave Jack had whipped his wife and then escaped to the woods.[34] Reported instances of domestic violence like these also revealed that black husbands' transgressions were generally excused on the grounds that they stemmed from the feelings of frustration and powerlessness caused by slavery.

Even though the slave family was matrifocal, male slaves had some advantages over female slaves in other areas. Male slaves had greater opportunity to hold supervisory positions such as foreman, overseer, and head craftsperson, and they were more likely to be skilled artisans.[35] Although females worked as domestics more often than males, males could earn more cash by hiring themselves out as manual laborers or artisans and to do various odd jobs. Men were also given more material provisions and food supplies than women, in spite of the fact that the women had to share their meager resources with their children. If a father could not always provide for his family as he wished, he could supplement their diets by hunting and fishing. After the field work was done it was the women, not surprisingly, who had to shoulder more of the burdens of childrearing and housework.

The White Mistress

One of the threads that runs through the story of gender conflict among African Americans is the complex and sometimes paradoxical relationship of black men and women to white women. Inasmuch as race and sex have always been the two key variables in any analysis of power, opportunity, and discrimination in American life, it would seem that women of all racial backgrounds would be able to make common cause around the issues and challenges they share as women. In fact, this has rarely occurred among black and white women. Moreover, white women have themselves been a source of conflict among blacks. Once again the roots of these developments can be traced to slavery.

White southern women had a social status that was one level higher than that of black slaves. White women, like blacks, had no legal rights; they could achieve social legitimization only through marriage. Although white mistresses were subjected to some of the same patriarchal abuses as the black female slaves, they were granted a degree of patriarchal protection in that they gave birth to white male progeny.[36]

Although the nineteenth century saw the beginnings of a woman's movement, the devalued status of white women in the South was not the basis of a coalition with black women. Not surprisingly, relationships between the two groups of women were strained. Antagonism existed for several reasons. First, white mistresses were dependent on the patriarchal system and consolidated their marginal social positions by denying the humanity of their female slaves. Second, if a white mistress suspected that a slave woman was sexually intimate with her husband, she could have her whipped, and many times there was no peace until the slave was sold. The mistress often wielded considerable influence over her husband, who made decisions that were usually not in the best interests of the slave woman and her family.[37] Finally, slave women were distressed by the special treatment that white women were given by white and black men alike. Slaveholding women could demand protection from their husbands and obedience, respect, and even veneration from slave men. Black women, meanwhile, could be sexually exploited with impunity by white masters, and it was the female slaves, not the masters, who were held accountable for violations of the conjugal sanctity of the white mistress.

White women may have been a subjugated class, but they saw no grounds for an alliance with black women on the basis of their gender. The white mistress "pitied herself as a martyr . . . and was incapable of feeling for the condition of shame and misery in which her unfortunate, helpless slave was placed."[38] In her book *Incidents in the Life of a Slave Girl*, Harriet Jacobs described the paradoxical characteristics of one of her white mistresses:

> Like many white southern women, [she] was totally deficient in energy. She had not strength to superintend her household affairs; but her nerves were so strong, that she could sit in her easy

chair and see a woman whipped, till the blood trickled from every stroke of her lash.[39]

As this example illustrates, white women exerted considerable power over black female slaves, and they wielded their power by punishing black women for what they perceived as their transgressions and those of their husbands. Historian Jacqueline Jones has noted that white mistresses were likely to attack with any weapon available—a fork, butcher knife, knitting needle, or pan of boiling water. Many of these attacks resulted in the mutilation and permanent scarring of female slaves.[40]

In oral testimony, one slave described her mother's attempt to defend herself against her white mistress:

My mother was the smartest black woman in Eden. She was quick as a flash of lightning, and whatever she did could not be done better. She could do anything. She cooked, washed, ironed, spun, nursed and labored in the field. She made as good a field hand as she did a cook. I have heard Master Jennings say to his wife, "Fannie has her faults, but she can outwork any nigger in the country. I'd bet my life on that."

My mother certainly had her faults as a slave. She was very different in nature from Aunt Caroline. Ma fussed, fought, and kicked all the time. . . . She said she wouldn't be whipped, and when she fussed all Eden must have known it. . . . With all her ability for work, she did not make a good slave. She was too high-spirited and independent. I tell you, she was a captain. . . .

One day my mother's temper ran wild. For some reason Mistress Jennings struck her with a stick. Ma struck back and a fight followed. . . . For half an hour they wrestled in the kitchen. Mistress, seeing that she could not get the better of ma, ran out on the road, with ma right on her heels. In the road, my mother flew into her again. The thought seemed to race across my mother's mind to tear mistress' clothing off her body. She suddenly began to tear Mistress Jennings' clothing off. She caught hold, pulled, ripped, and tore. Poor mistress was nearly naked when the storekeeper got to them and pulled ma off.

That evening Mistress Jennings came down to the cabin. "Well, Fannie," she said, "I'll have to send you away.... You can't take the baby, Fannie. Aunt Mary can keep it with the other children...."

"Fannie, leave the baby with Aunt Mary," said Mr. Jennings very quietly.

At this, ma took the baby by its feet, a foot in each hand, and with the baby's head swinging downward, she vowed to smash its brains out before she'd leave it. Tears were streaming down her face. It was seldom that ma cried, and everyone knew that she meant every word. Ma took her baby with her.[41]

Another slave by the name of Patsey likewise had an adversarial relationship with her white mistress:

Patsey was slim and straight.... There was an air of loftiness in her movement that neither labor, nor weariness, nor punishment could destroy.... She was a skillful teamster. She turned as true a furrow as the best, and at splitting rails there was none that could excel her.... Such lightning like motion was in her fingers ... that in cotton picking time, Patsey was queen of the field....

Her back bore the scars of a thousand stripes ... because it had fallen her lot to be the slave of a licentious master and a jealous mistress....

To be rid of Patsey—to place her beyond sight or reach, by sale, or death, or in any other manner of late years—seemed to be the ruling thought and passion of my mistress.

Finally, for a trifling offense, Patsey was given a savage whipping, while her mistress and the master's children watched with obvious satisfaction. She almost died.

From that time forward, she was not what she had been.... The bounding vigor, the sprightly ... spirit of her youth was gone.... She became more silent than she was, toiling all day in our midst, not uttering a word. A care-worn, pitiful expression settled on her face.... If ever there was a broken heart ... it was Patsey's.[42]

One emancipated slave, in the aftermath of slavery, was acquitted of assaulting a white woman. A black woman in Fredericksburg, Virginia, was accused of attacking a white woman for "stealing the affections" of her husband, prompting him to leave her. That was the only "justifiable" assault in the eyes of the white community that a black person could commit.[43]

Black men had a different relationship to the white mistress. To begin with, it is clear that white southern women did not view male slaves as harshly as they did female slaves. In return, male slaves were less derisive toward white slaveholding women than they were toward their male masters. White women often had a favorite male slave, usually a house servant, who was either very young or very old so as not to raise the ire of her husband. However, a white woman's ultimate act of rebellion against the dominance of white males was to have sexual relations with a black man. Indeed, there were cases in which white women not only became sexually intimate with slave men but fell in love with them. One slave man recalled that a man named Squire Green owned a slave and that the slave and his white mistress "knocked up a young one between them." There was "great talk about it," and the child was banished from the community. In the view of this slave, it was just as well that the child was sent away, since "a colored child wouldn't be treated any better from a white woman, than from a black woman by a white father."[44]

In simultaneously fostering matrifocal families and marginalizing black husbands and fathers, slavery itself was a major contributing factor to the strength and independence of slave women.

Conversely, the protection and safekeeping afforded to white women contributed to their being more fragile and helpless than black women. Not surprisingly, many slave men were drawn to the defenselessness and childlikeness—the "femininity"—they saw in white women. These attributes, coupled with the fact that during this period in American history the idealized white woman's beauty symbolized the highest standard of beauty, created a mystique that many slave men found irresistible and that lingers even today.[45]

Free at Last

The end of slavery brought dramatic changes to black family life in that it altered the economic, social, and legal arrangements that governed the family life of former slaves. Freed slaves immediately began creating communities, establishing a network of institutions, churches, schools, and mutual benefit societies. During slavery, blacks had also established networks of secret churches and families, and these institutions provided the basis for a new sense of community.

Of the social forces that were unleashed during this postbellum period, also known as Reconstruction, none was stronger than the former slaves' desperate efforts to find their lost families and to legalize the conjugal arrangements that they had established under slavery. Thousands of freed slaves set out across the South in search of loved ones, placing advertisements in the black press for lost family members. One such advertisement was published in *The Colored Tennessean* on August 5, 1865:

> Saml. Dove wishes to know of the whereabouts of his mother, Areno, his sisters Maria, Neziah, and Peggy, and his brother Edmond, who was owned by George Dove of Rockingham Co., Va. Sold in Richmond, after which Samuel and Edmond were taken to Nashville, Tenn., by Joe Mick; Areno was left at the Eagle Tavern, Richmond.[46]

John Dennett, a correspondent for *The Nation*, encountered a newly freed black man in September 1865. Weak from fatigue, his body hurting, this man said he had walked six hundred miles from a plantation in Georgia searching for his wife and children, who had been sold away from him.

Other black men were not as conscientious as this newly freed man in reuniting with their wives and children. Fanny Smart of Woodville, Mississippi, learned that her husband, Adam, who she thought was dead, was still alive. She was disappointed by his failure to contact her sooner and by his apparent indifference to the children he had fathered:

I received your letter yesterday. I am glad to hear from you. I heard that you were dead. I now think very strange, that you never wrote to me before. You could not think much of your children, as for me, I don't expect you to think much of as I have been confined, just got up, have a fine daughter. . . . I now have eight children, all dependent on me for support, only one large enough to work for herselfe, the rest I could not hire for their victuals and clothes. I think you might have sent the children something, or some money. Joe can walk and talk. Ned is a great big boy, bad as ever. My baby I call her Cassinda. The children all send howda to you they all want to see you.

The circumstances surrounding Adam and Fanny's separation may have accounted for Adam's failure to contact his wife sooner, and possibly even for the rumor that he had died. The postscript added to Fanny's letter by his former master suggests as much:

Adam you have acted the damn rascal with me in ever way you trid to make the Yanks distroy every thing I had I know worn you to neve put you foot on my place I think you a nary raskal after this yer you can send an git you your famley if they want to go with you.[47]

Many searches were complicated by new loyalties and emotional commitments that had been formed during the intervening years. One situation revealing this kind of emotional torment was that of the husband of Laura Spicer. Several years after their forced separation, he had remarried in the belief that his wife had died. When he learned that she was still alive, the news startled him, catalyzing the conflicting emotions of joy and remorse. "I read your letters over and over again," he wrote to her. "I keep them always in my pocket. If you are married I don't want to see you again." But in other letters he revised the hurried warning and urged her to remarry. "I would much rather you get married to some good man, for every time I gits a letter from you it tears me all to pieces. The reason why I have not written you before, in a long time, is because your letters disturbed me so very much." Even as he urged her to find another man, he declared his everlasting love for her.

> I would come and see you but I know that I could not bear it. I want to see you and I don't want to see you. I love you just as well as I did the last day I saw you, and it will not do for you and I to meet. I am married, and my wife have two children, and if you and I meets it would make a very dissatisfied family.[48]

Some reunions were bittersweet. Near Norfolk, Virginia, a long-separated couple found each other near the end of the war. In discussing this reunion the woman said afterward:

> Twas like a stroke of death to me. We threw ourselves into each others arms and cried. His wife looked on and was jealous, but she needn't have been. My husband is so kind, I shouldn't leave him even if he hadn't had another wife, and of course I shouldn't now. Yes, my husband is very kind, but I ain't happy.

The momentary reunion had been painful for both of them. Reflecting back on the days she had spent in her first marriage and the forced separation, she could only say, "White folk's got a heap to answer for the way they've done to colored folks! So much they won't never pray it away!"[49]

The Faustian Bargain

Slavery left the black family in a state of disarray. Apart from the heart-wrenching cases of family members who had been forcibly separated, former slaves were confronted with the daunting challenge of reinventing family life in the new conditions of freedom. Wives and husbands had to work out their roles and expectations of each other while at the same time find ways to provide themselves and their families with the necessities of life in an environment of widespread poverty and racial oppression. All of this would have been challenging enough, but the former slaves had the legacy of slavery to contend with as well. They could not begin the work of recreating family life with a clean slate. They brought with them the attitudes, values, and patterns of behavior that had been forged during slavery.

After years of laboring beside their husbands as slaves, black mothers were willing to give up wage labor in favor of devoting more time to their children and their household responsibilities. Sharecropping was the preferred method of employment for former slaves because it gave the recently reunited families more control over their lives.

When compared with slave families, sharecropping families had more authority in deciding when, where, and how much mothers would work. But there were some disadvantages to this system as well. The bigger the crop, the more favorable the economic outcome at the end of the year. To make the year successful, every able-bodied family member was needed. Black men's reliance on the labor of their wives and children placed them at a distinct disadvantage compared to even their poor white counterparts, who did not have a comparable dependence on their families. This represented a major setback for the newly freed black man, eager to assert himself as head of the household.

One way for black men to claim their "rightful" place at the head of their families was to domesticate their spouses. "When I married my wife," a Tennessee freedman told his employer in rejecting his request for her services, "I married her to wait on me, and she has all she can do right here for me, and the children." Laura Towne, a white teacher from the North, notes this attitude in the Sea Islands off the coast of North Carolina. In her view it was a natural response to the commanding role black women had assumed in the slave family. Towne observed the frequency with which black leaders urged black men to "rule their wives." According to Towne, the "notion of being bigger than women generally, is just now inflating the conceit of the males to an amazing degree."[50]

In spite of the attempts of black men to keep their wives in the home, black women still occupied a more important place in their community than their white counterparts did in theirs. For example, when there was a racial incident in Charleston and whites were threatening to regain power, black women were sighted "carrying axes or hatchets in their hands hanging down at their sides, their aprons or dresses half-concealing the weapons." Meanwhile, the black clergy were sending contradictory messages to the community. On the one hand, they exhorted black men to "get women into their proper place," yet on another occasion they warned a large white audience about "80,000 black men in the State who could use Winchesters and 200,000 women who can light a torch and use a knife."[51] If black men and women were not precisely equal in their relationships, they sometimes had a more equitable partnership thrust upon them by the common threat of racial hostility.

The dynamics of gender relations were complicated by the influence of the Freedmen's Bureau. The bureau was established by the Republican Congress in 1865, ostensibly to protect the rights of former slaves by providing them with education and medical care.

It was also the bureau's responsibility to monitor labor contracts and oversee the "problems" encountered by this new labor force. It soon became clear, however, that the primary aim of the bureau was to protect the interests of the planters, not the interests of black families and still less the interests of black women. Southern whites saw the aspiration of black women to attend to their own households and care for their own children as jeopardizing agricultural productivity.

Dismayed by the dramatic reduction in the black labor force with black women's (mostly mothers') withdrawal, planters appealed in writing to the Freedmen's Bureau for measures that would ensure their return to the fields. A letter from one planter linked two issues, control of family labor and labor discipline:

Dear sir— Allow me to call your attention to the fact that most of the Freedwomen who have husbands are not at work—never having made any contract at all— Their husbands are at work, while they are as nearly idle as it is possible for them to be, pretending to spin—knit or something that really amounts to nothing for their husbands have to buy them clothing I find from my own hands wishing to buy of me— Now these women have been used to working out & it would be far better for them to go to work for reasonable wages & their rations—both in regard to health & in furtherance of their family well being— Say their husbands get 10 to 12—or $13 per month and out of that feed their wives and from 1 to 3 or 4 children—& clothe the family—it is impossible for one man to do this and maintain his wife in idleness without stealing more or less of their support, whereas if their wives (where they are able) were at work for rations & fair wages—which they can all get; the family could live in some comfort & more happily—besides their labor is a very important percent of the entire labor of the South. . . . I have 4 or 5 good women hands now idle that ought to be at work because their families cannot really be supported honestly without it. This should not be so—& you will readily see how important it is to change it at once— I am respectfully

Your obt servant

M. C. Fulton[52]

Although both black women and their husbands may have preferred for them to wash, sew, cook, and care for their children, the economic inducements of the sharecropping system placed a heavier premium on their reproductive and agricultural labor. Black women were understandably deeply disappointed and embittered when the alternative of spending more time in their homes was denied.

Realizing that it had already placed itself in an adversarial relationship with black women by taking sides with the planters and mandating that black women return to the fields, the bureau set out to strengthen its relationship with black men. Black and white men alike understood that they had no authority if they could not tell women what to do. To ensure the cooperation of black men, the Freedmen's Bureau gave them authority over their wives.

The bureau designated the husband the head of the household, establishing his right to sign contracts for the labor of his entire family. To make matters worse, black women were paid a lower wage than black men for the same labor. (Although those white women who worked were paid less than white men, their labor was generally not as essential to their families' survival.) The bureau further demonstrated its commitment to the black man's leadership role in the family by allotting less land to families without a male head of household. Furthermore, black husbands were held accountable by bureau agents for their wives' work performance.[53]

The Faustian bargain struck by white and black men—designating the black man as head of household, allocating him higher wages, and giving him authority over black women in exchange for their labor in the fields—was the first signal after emancipation of the erosion of gender relations in the African-American community. The developments that followed this historic pact between black and white males were not surprising. Black women who had worked side by side with their husbands as equals had difficulty accepting their husbands' newly appointed role as patriarch and taskmaster. For their part, slave husbands often attempted to assert their authority in aggressive and sometimes violent ways.

The result was an alarming increase in family disputes and spousal abuse in the African-American community. The bureau reportedly received hundreds of complaints from black women of battery, adultery, and nonpayment of child support.[54] One such letter was received from a black woman by the name of Rosa Freeman, who had been married to David Freeman for about nine months:

> We lived at Fernandina Fla—about four months—during that time he beat and abused me. I reported it to the Officer in charge of the Freedmans Bureau; he had him arrested & he got out of the Guard House & left the place, remaining away until a new officer took charge—he (my husband) then came back and beat me again—I had him arrested—he knocked the officer down & ran away & came here to Savannah. Since that time he has abused me & refused to pay for the rent of my room & has not furnished me with any money, food, or clothing.

Other complaints received from working-class women are vivid indicators of how their relationships with their mates were faring after emancipation:

> My ole man got so trifling and mean that I quit him and work for myself.

> Dat was the meanest niggah dat ever lived. He would slip up behin' me when I was wukin' in the fiel' am beat me.

He got to runnin around with a ole 'oman. She got all his money. All I ever got was a beating and babies.

I got so I dreaded to see him coming, but I wuz nearly as big as him and I wasn't gonna stand no misabusin. I'd fights him back.

My ole man, he was a good field worker. He's a good man, but he's rough an' low down. I'm shore married to him though, and I got to make the bes' of a bad bargain.[55]

The Faustian bargain would have its greatest impact on working-class blacks, since the black elite generally did not work as share-croppers. Detailed ethnographic studies comparing working-class and middle-class blacks in a southern town during the 1930s suggest that the kinds of stipulations made by the Freedmen's Bureau may not have been necessary for middle-class families.[56] Even without the influence of the bureau, such families tended to approximate the patriarchal type characteristic of white families.

Black Women's "Catch-22"

Although all women in nineteenth-century America were obliged to defer to men, for black women this deference was further validated by the black community. For example, when a convention of black male leaders met in 1855 to "vindicate" black males' manhood, the attendees made it clear that black women were to assist in this effort:

We recommend to our mothers and our sisters to use every honorable means to secure for their sons and brothers places of profit and trust in stores and other places of business, such as will throw a halo around this proscribed people.[57]

The rationale for this deference to men was that slavery and racism sought to emasculate the black man and that it was the black woman's duty to counter these effects. Nothing was said about what slavery and racism sought to do to black women. Therefore, "good" black women supported and encouraged the manhood of black men even if on occasion it was to their own detriment to do so. For example, in the private sphere black women were admonished to learn how to tend to the needs of their men, care for their children, and perform their domestic duties and at the same time look "as pretty as possible."[58]

Black women were thus confronted with a catch-22: If they tried to safeguard their own self-interests at the expense of supporting and defending the "rights" of black men, they lost the support of their own community and so harmed themselves. Domestic violence is an excellent example of how women's interests often clashed with those of men and therefore with the "community." Forced to conceal their rage under an impassive or conciliatory mask in the presence of whites, black men found other ways to vent their frustrations. Planters' correspondence and journals during slavery frequently had mentioned violence perpetuated by slave men against their wives, and these patterns persisted after emancipation.

Autobiographies written by black men who grew up during this period chronicle their observations of their fathers' violent outbursts. Benjamin Mays, the eminent president of Morehouse College, remembered his father's hot temper and the number of times "we children had to hold him to keep him from hurting Mother." Benjamin felt that the arguments might have been fewer if his mother had endured these assaults in silence, "but Mother had to talk back. Our sympathy was with her."[59]

Similarly, in the biography *All God's Dangers*, Nate Shaw recalls looking on as his mother endured beatings from his father:

> If I had a twenty-dollar bill this mornin for every time I seed my daddy beat up my mother and beat up my stepmother I wouldn't be settin here this mornin because I'd have up in the

hundreds of dollars. Each one of them women—I didn't see no cause for it. I don't expect it ever come in my daddy's mind what his children thought about it or how they would remember him for it, but that was a poor example, to stamp and beat up children's mothers right before em.[60]

Many black wives were as reluctant to report a husband's abusive behavior to authorities as they had been during slavery. An article in the Mobile *Daily Register* noted that black women "usually begged the mayor to let their husbands off" when black men charged with spousal abuse were arrested.[61]

As opportunities for domestic service became more available in urban areas, many black women demonstrated their dissatisfaction with their husbands' abuse of power by moving to the cities. Census data during this period reflect the changing migration patterns and the higher proportion of single black mothers living in the urban areas.[62] What the changing migration suggests is that many black women were opting to stand up for themselves by moving to the city rather than staying in emotionally and physically abusive relationships.

Conclusion

For more than three centuries the system of slavery was the defining experience for African Americans. Slavery weakened the black family unit, disrupting and redefining family roles. It also inflicted profound indignities on the slaves, compelling them to respond and cope in ways that would deeply influence not only their views of gender roles but relationships with members of the opposite sex.

The tension that persists today in the relationships between black and white women likewise had its origins in slavery. Although all women in the nineteenth century were obliged to defer to men, for black women after emancipation this deference was further validated by the Freedmen's Bureau and by the black community itself. Little was said about what slavery and racism sought to do to black women. Black women were additionally isolated by the lack of an alliance with white women. Instead, the ambiguous figure of the white mistress became the source of division between black women and their men.

An analysis of the institution of slavery draws attention to the fact that gender relations in the African-American community are related to a distinctive set of experiences that blacks have had in this country. The conflicts between black men and women have been created as blacks have endeavored to cope with racism and oppression and simultaneously to maintain their dignity and self-respect. The challenge for African Americans is first to become cognizant of the continuity of these relational patterns and then to understand that conscious awareness is the initial step toward the process of change.

3

The Cult of True
Womanhood

O ye fairer sisters whose hands are never soiled, whose nerves
and muscles are never strained, go learn by experience. Had
we had the opportunity that you have had, to improve our
moral and mental faculties, what would have hindered our in-
tellects from being as bright, and our manners from being as
dignified as yours? Had it been our lot to have been nursed in
the lap of affluence and ease, and have basked beneath the
smiles and sunshine of fortune, should we not have naturally
supposed that we were never made to toil?

—MARIA MILLER STEWART

Some women are born free, and some amid insult and scarlet
letters achieve freedom, but our women in black had freedom
thrust contemptuously upon them. With that freedom they
are buying an untrammeled independence and dear as is
the price they pay for it, it will in the end be worth every
taunt and groan.

—W. E. B. DU BOIS

IN THE YEARS FOLLOWING
emancipation, African Americans
sought to reestablish family life. A number of social conditions
complicated their efforts, including the extreme poverty of most

black families, the collapse of Reconstruction with renewed repression in the South, cultural ideals that promoted the dominance of men and the submissiveness of women, and assaults on the morality of black women. Issues of race, class, and gender that were partially suppressed during slavery now emerged as potentially divisive influences in the black community. How black men and women responded to these challenges in this formative period would set the stage for the conflict in gender relations in the twentieth century. Black women formed an indispensable part of the labor force within the agricultural economy that dominated the South throughout the nineteenth and early twentieth centuries.

The Patriarchal Family Ethos

The period immediately after emancipation saw the emergence of a strong patriarchal ethos in the African-American family. As we saw in the last chapter, the "Faustian bargain" between the Freedmen's Bureau and sharecropping black men promoted patriarchal values among the poor black families in the South. It was in the growers' interests to strengthen the role of the black husband and father in return for the assurance of women's labor in the fields.

Even apart from the influence of the Freedmen's Bureau, black men, in effect, internalized the values of their white oppressors. The white society of the nineteenth century exemplified a set of social relations in which men dominate and often oppress women. These patriarchal values were clearly reflected in statements made by Martin R. Delaney in 1855. A leading black physician who had studied at Harvard Medical School, Delaney was one of two black commissioned officers in the 104th Regiment of the Union Army and a newspaper editor. Like many men during this period, Delaney objected to black women's working outside the home, especially "when it wasn't a question of dire necessity." He viewed working women as "undermining black manhood and the race as well."[1] These statements by Delaney, a northern black, suggest that patriarchal values were already in place among free black families in the North before emancipation. James O. Horton, a historian who has studied antebellum free blacks, described the gender conventions in this way:

> All women were expected to defer to men, but for black women deference was a racial imperative. Slavery and racism sought the emasculation of black men. Black people sought to counter such effects. Part of the responsibility of black men was to "act like a man," and part of the responsibility of black women was to encourage and support the manhood of our men ... never intimidate him with her knowledge or common sense, let him feel stable and dominant.[2]

The autobiographical narratives of African Americans reflect this patriarchal ethos. Nate Shaw, an illiterate tenant farmer, grew up in a society of former slaves and slaveholders and remembers his mother doing "anything my daddy told her to do."[3]

Benjamin Mays was the distinguished president of Morehouse College and the mentor of Martin Luther King, Jr. When writing about his parents' relationship, Dr. Mays recalled that his father was "mean to our mother." But he felt it was the "depth and sincerity" of his mother's religious faith that sustained her and had the "greatest influence" on him.[4]

Unlike the fathers of Shaw and Mays, Zora Neale Hurston's father was not a tenant farmer. John Hurston was an itinerant preacher and the mayor of the all-black town of Eatonville, Florida. Zora recalls her father boasting that he "never allowed his wife to go out and hit a lick of work for anybody a day in her life," but the expectations imposed on her mother in caring for eight children and performing many household tasks were arduous. Even though Zora's mother was "unhappy" at times, in looking back Zora felt that her parents were "really in love."[5]

How do we account for the proliferation of these patriarchal values in the black community? First, political developments brought new gender distinctions in the North and the South. After 1867, black men could hold office, serve on juries and as delegates to political conventions, vote, and take leadership positions in the Republican party; black women could not.

Second, the Christian religion played an important role. E. Franklin Frazier observed that the black church "sought to affirm the man's interest and authority in the black family."[6] Perhaps historian Orville Burton came closest to summarizing the church's influence when he wrote:

> The Bible delivered a powerful message to the agrarian former slave population. Old Testament theology, as preached and practiced, focused on a father figure and implanted patriarchal values. Preachers and deacons . . . were always men.[7]

One scholar who conducted detailed studies of southern middle-class black families found that "the family form tends to approximate the white patriarchal type."[8]

Women's Roles

The patriarchal family ethos worked hand in hand with images of women and their roles both in the family and in the community at large. Despite the emergence of a women's movement in the latter half of the nineteenth century, American society during this period largely relegated women to the "private" sphere of the home. The public sphere of work, business, and politics was reserved for men. White society could idealize the homebound woman as passive, virtuous, devoted to child rearing and homemaking, and unsullied by the world of work and public affairs. Black men might aspire to these values; like their white counterparts, they distinguished between "men's work" and "women's work." However, their situation was complicated by the need to have their wives contribute to the economic support of their families. For black women, the inevitable result was that they were compelled to do "double duty," fulfilling the prescribed role of mother and homemaker while also working in the fields or in wage labor. Moreover, even if they wanted to, black women could not generally aspire to the passive, protected status of white women.

Among black families in the South, the gender division of labor that was begun during slavery persisted once the slaves were emancipated. Gender roles are perhaps the most misunderstood aspect of African-American family life. Some evidence suggests that during slavery black men actively scorned women's work, especially cooking, sewing, housecleaning, laundering the clothes, and child care. Slave owners capitalized on black men's aversion to these tasks and devised forms of public humiliation. One Louisiana planter punished slave men by requiring them to wash clothes, and chronic offenders were compelled to wear women's clothing. One observer of the men who were embarrassed in this manner remarked, "So great was their shame before their fellows that many ran off and suffered the lash on their backs rather than submit to the discipline. Men clearly viewed certain chores as women's tasks, and female slaves largely respected the distinction."[9]

The gender division of labor would not become problematic until after emancipation. Then black families established their households within the context of kin networks and community with gender roles that conformed to the "traditional" family model. Although there was a marked withdrawal of black wives from wage labor during Reconstruction, as we have seen, the goal of black women to stay at home and care for their households proved to be illusory. A heavy premium was placed on the labor of black women both among tenant farmers and in the cities. In his 1899 survey of the black community in Philadelphia, W. E. B. Du Bois concluded that "the low wage of [black] men makes it necessary for mothers to work."[10]

By 1870 in the Cotton Belt, 98.4 percent of white women described their occupations as "keeping house." In contrast, four out of ten black wives listed their occupation as "field laborer."[11] Of course, although black women may have listed their occupation as "field laborer," they were also responsible for "keeping house."

What this meant for a black wife is that she had to get up at daybreak to prepare breakfast for her family and then join her husband and children in the field, plowing and hoeing the cotton. At midmorning she would have to return to the cabin to fix the noon meal before heading back to the field for more backbreaking labor until dusk. Furthermore, she somehow had to find the time to perform other household chores, and there were often cows to milk and chickens to feed as well.[12]

One black wife described her duties as follows: "I had my house work and de cookin' to do and to look after de chillun, but I'd go out and still pick my two hunnert pounds ob cotton a day."[13]

Nate Shaw remembers his mother and his two brothers doing practically all of the field work—"she'd plow, she'd hoe." While Nate's mother and brothers were working in the fields, his father would go hunting in the woods.[14] Benjamin Mays's mother likewise "hoed and picked cotton," although unlike Nate Shaw's father, Mays's father worked side by side with his wife.[15]

These conditions made marriage much less attractive to black women than it was to white women. Hortense Powdermaker, who conducted a cultural study in Cottonville, Mississippi, made the following observation regarding the disincentives for marriage in the African-American community: "In most cases it is assumed that a wife will have to continue working after marriage, and often to shoulder the greater or even the whole economic burden. . . . This means that need of support does not in itself compel women into marriage or cause them to dread separation."[16]

Changing Conceptions of Womanhood

While many former slaves labored as tenant farmers and field-workers in the South, the ascent of industrialism and the manufacturing economy, particularly in the northern United States, was having a major impact on social relations and on the family system in particular. In the predominantly agricultural economy before the industrial revolution, the family was the basic unit of economic production. Although wives were subordinate to their husbands and primarily responsible for the children, more value was placed on their productive labor as they worked side by side with their husbands. The new manufacturing economy transformed gender relations and roles in white households. Industrial capitalism is generally credited with separating household and market production by creating a new gender division of labor that assigned men to the market and women to the home. Changing market conditions further devalued women by clarifying their place as "in the home."[17]

These conceptions of womanhood were formalized and embodied in law. Justice Bradley's 1872 concurring opinion in *Bradwell v. Illinois* reflects the prevailing view of the roles of men and women:

> [T]he civil law, as well as nature herself, has always recognized a wide difference in the respective spheres and destinies of man and woman. Man is, or should be, woman's protector and defender. The natural and proper timidity and delicacy which belong to the female sex evidently unfits it for many of the occupations of civil life. The constitution of the family organization, which is founded in the divine ordinance, as well as the nature of things, indicates the domestic sphere as that which properly belongs to the domain and functions of womanhood.[18]

Barbara Welter, a feminist historian, has characterized the basic attributes of "true womanhood" as the cardinal virtues of piety, purity, submissiveness, and domesticity. The characteristic most valued in women was that of submissiveness—the women held in the highest regard were those who were subservient to their husbands.[19]

As industrial capitalism developed, the "nonproductive" woman also emerged as a symbol of bourgeois class hegemony. With the ascendancy of these values, three key factors further contributed to making marriage an attractive alternative to working for white women: low wages, impediments to achieving upward mobility, and poor working conditions. By eliminating wage-earning labor for upwardly mobile white women, industrialization contributed to the perception of these women as fragile, delicate, and economically dependent. A black woman, writing on labor issues during this period, took issue with these trends by asserting that "there was a great need for an occupation in which white women could support themselves."[20]

Industrial capitalism transformed mainstream America's views of domestic life in yet another way: It idealized the sphere of romantic love as the arena in which happiness was to be achieved for women. This notion completed the picture of the white woman as finding her "natural" fulfillment in love, marriage, homemaking, and subservience to her husband.

These cultural ideals would affect relations between black men and women as well, whether or not they fit the circumstances of the black family. The prevailing vision of "true womanhood" (and "true manhood") influenced the thinking of black men and women alike. Black men emerged from slavery eager to assert their dominance over their wives and households and to take their place as providers of the family's material needs. Black women generally were willing and even eager to take on the role of mothers and homemakers, but since they usually had to help support the family, they could not be isolated in the home and put on the same Victorian pedestal as their white counterparts. Moreover, black women were accustomed to playing a strong role in the family, working in partnership with their husbands when the men were present and holding the family together when they were not. Black families were thus caught in the crosscurrents of their history, their economic circumstances, and the cultural ideals that were being promulgated both in the larger society and in their own community.

The End of Reconstruction

By 1870 the Freedmen's Bureau had resettled more than thirty thousand ex-slaves who had been displaced during the war. According to an analysis of households selected from the 1870 federal population census, 80 percent of black households in the Cotton Belt included a husband and wife (a proportion identical to that of neighboring white populations). Although a surprisingly large number of black couples had worked side by side under oppressive conditions, they had achieved very little in economic terms. This is clearly evident in the fact that fewer than 8 percent of black families in the South owned their own farms.[21]

The bureau's greatest achievements were in education. Among the newly founded schools that received aid from the bureau were Howard University, Hampton Institute, Saint Augustine's College, Atlanta University, Fisk University, Storer College, and Biddle Memorial Institute (now Johnson C. Smith University). When the educational work of the bureau ended, it had spent more than $5 million in schooling ex-slaves, and there were 247,333 pupils in 4,329 schools.[22]

What is ironic about the bureau's achievements in education, however, is that the black children who were most in need of an education were the ones least likely to take advantage of these opportunities. Many of the children in sharecropper families were required to work in the fields instead of availing themselves of these educational opportunities. Consistent with the patriarchal family ethos, fathers generally had the last word in deciding which children went to the fields and for how long. Ann Matthews, a former slave, discussed her regrets about her own lack of schooling when she was interviewed by the Federal Writers Project: "I didn't go ter schul, mah daddy wouldn' let me. Said he needed me in de fiel wors den I needed schul."[23] In his autobiography, Benjamin Mays recalled that his greatest challenge in getting an education was to "overcome my father's immutable opposition." In Mays's view, his mother was the "sympathetic listener to my hopes and dreams."[24]

Mays defied the odds and managed to move beyond his humble beginnings and receive M.A. and Ph.D. degrees from the University of Chicago. Many black children from backgrounds similar to Mays's were not as fortunate. Because education was the insurance policy for the upward mobility of the race, educational inequality based on one's family of origin would contribute to the class cleavages that emerged later in the African-American community.

When Reconstruction collapsed in the 1870s, public education fell into the hands of southern whites who had no commitment to the intellectual development of black children. With the passage of legislation designed to deprive black men of voting rights, blacks had no voice in the allocation of education funds in southern states. This did not stop the newly disenfranchised blacks from making their voices heard, however. Blacks not only petitioned for adequate public school facilities but they also double-taxed themselves in order to raise funds for private schools. Not surprisingly, black women took the visionary leadership role in this endeavor, and it was the women who raised $14 million that was primarily used to educate more than twenty-five thousand black teachers.[25]

The creation of private educational institutions made secondary education available to southern blacks. The clearest indicator of the deficiency of public education in the South for blacks is reflected in the fact that as late as 1910, no southern community could claim a public school offering two years of high school.[26]

Another agency that offered both religious and material relief during Reconstruction was the black church. With southern laws to silence black ministers no longer in effect, black churches began to grow rapidly. By 1870 the Colored Methodist Episcopal Church had organized five conferences, and older black churches had likewise entered a new period of growth. For example, the African Methodist Episcopal Church had only 20,000 members in 1856; twenty years later its membership had expanded to 200,000. These dramatic increases in black church membership were due in part to the fact that as free people blacks were no longer forced to hear sermons on obedience to white masters. Reflecting on these sermons, a former slave ridiculed the repetitive theme: "The Lord say, don't you niggers steal chickens from your missus. Don't you steal your marster's hawgs."[27]

Reconstruction came to an end in the mid to late 1870s as the Radical Republican agenda began to fade, planters returned to power, and Democrats began to take over in the South. Just as northern whites were tiring of the crusade to protect the rights of blacks, black women once again began to challenge the tenets of white supremacy. Groups of women organized to participate in boycotts against the newly segregated public transit in twenty-five southern cities. Decades before Rosa Parks would take her historic stand in defiance of Jim Crow, black women refused to abide by southern customs and uphold the "deference ritual" imposed after slavery in the public arena. Complaints against young black women escalated when they were perceived as lacking the docility and deference of their slave mothers. One southern newspaper put black women on notice:

Negro girls are apt to be extremely insolent, not only to whites of their own age, but to ladies. . . . The negro girls who push white women and girls off the walks can be cured of that practice by the use of a horsewhip; and we advise white fathers and husbands to use the whip. It's a great corrective.[28]

The white backlash had begun.

Economic Disruption and Father "Absence"

The depressions of the 1870s inundated the credit system and triggered a catastrophic financial event. Ten thousand businesses failed, factories begin to lay off workers, and over half of the nation's railroads defaulted on their bonds. This cataclysm fueled race and class conflicts and shattered the public's faith in industrial capitalism and the inevitability of progress, especially in the South. With the economic downturn, recently emancipated black men were frantic to find work so that they could demonstrate to themselves and to those dependent on them that they could be self-supporting. One ex-slave asserted to his former white master, who doubted his ability to provide for his family, "I am going to feed and clothe them and I can do it on bare rock."[29]

In their search for economic opportunities, many black men traveled long distances. Their movement from region to region placed even more stress on black marriages already weakened by slavery and policies established by the Freedmen's Bureau.

Black men's travel during this period was motivated not only by their desire to find work but by the quest for freedom of movement. For men whose forefathers had excessive restrictions placed on their activities, the opportunity to move about freely was invigorating. The meaning of unrestricted movement for black men following emancipation was clearly articulated by the writer Ben Sidran:

> Freedom was equated with mobility, and thousands of Negroes took to the roads (establishing a pattern which was to become part of the black self-image in America).... Escape from the monotony and static hopelessness of black employment, combined with the potential for earning a living without having to rely on the white man—beating the white man at his own game...[30]

Black men's urge to travel was having an effect on their wives and lovers. Poor black women increasingly found themselves abandoned or left behind by their peripatetic men. For the lucky ones, these transitions were temporary, but for those not so lucky, the flight of husbands, lovers, and fathers was indefinite and sometimes permanent. Statistics on the rates of husband absence were not available until 1920. (See Figure 1 in Appendix.) Reflecting on his early years growing up in South Carolina, Dr. Benjamin Mays focused on the issue of indefinite absenteeism when remembering that black men rarely totally deserted their families.[31]

The dual responsibilities of child care and domestic work in the homes of white families placed restrictions on black women's freedom of movement. Their geographic confinement is reflected in the following lyrics:

> *When a woman gets the blues,*
> *She tucks her head and cries;*
> *When a man catches the blues,*
> *He catches a freight train and rides.*[32]

Chronic husband absence frustrates any wife's desire for companionship and emotional intimacy. For newly emancipated black women, the absence of their husbands coincided with the first time African Americans were in a position to freely select their sexual partners. Some of the unambiguous evidence as to how poor black women handled the extended absences of their husbands and lovers can be found in the popularity of particular blues lyrics:

UNIDENTIFIED MAN: Who's that knocking on that door?

"MA" RAINEY: It's me, baby.

MAN: Me who?

"MA" RAINEY: Don't you know I'm your wife?

MAN: What?! Wife?!

"MA" RAINEY: Yeah!

MAN: Ain't that awful? I don't let no woman quit me but one time.

"MA" RAINEY: But I just quit one li'l old time, just one time!

MAN: You left here with that other man, why didn't you stay?[33]

In reinterpreting the tradition and meaning of the blues, Hazel Carby has declared that they were a "privileged site" in which women were "free to assert themselves publicly as sexual beings."[34]

Retrogressionists: Black Women as Scapegoats

It was in the political and economic environment created by the Panic of 1873 that the "retrogressionist" ideology emerged. This term has been used by historians to describe a widespread belief among whites that blacks were regressing to a more "primitive" state. At the same time that resurgent white southerners were blaming economic and political problems in the South on the disempowerment of the white planter class, the retrogressionists focused attention on the family life and sexual behavior of African Americans. They postulated that the "loose" sexual practices of former slaves were rooted in their African heritage. The "restraining influence" of slavery had ended with emancipation, causing a moral and social "retrogression." According to this view, the newly freed slaves demonstrated an inability to "restrain" themselves and adapt responsibly to freedom and independence.

One of the first newspaper columnists to draw attention to the sexual practices allegedly found among freed people was Frank Wilkeson of the *New York Sun*. Reporting from St. Helena's Island in South Carolina in the early 1880s, he asserted that "almost without exception, the negro of these islands, who have negro blood in their veins, are prostitutes."[35] J. L. Tucker, a northerner by birth who later settled in the South after fighting in the Confederate Army, echoed Wilkeson's "retrogressionist" observations on blacks when he found that "whole neighborhoods" were without "a single legally married couple" and few married couples remained "faithful to each other beyond a few months . . . often a few weeks."[36]

It was the writings of Philip A. Bruce, a Harvard-trained attorney, that put the retrogressionist propaganda on a firmer foundation than any other book up to that time.[37] In his book *The Plantation Negro as a Freeman*, Bruce postulated that emancipation had created a severe deterioration in the social and moral condition of blacks by cutting them off from the "spirit of white society." In the chapters entitled "Parent and Child" and "Husband and Wife," Bruce averred that black parental authority could not replace "the discipline . . . enforced by the slaveholder" because black parents merely acted "upon the impulses of their nature." In Bruce's view, the average black parent was "morally obtuse and indifferent, and at times even openly and unreservedly licentious." In particular he charged black parents with not "fostering chastity" among their daughters. Bruce then asserted that black men found something "strangely alluring and seductive . . . in the appearance of white women" due to the "wantonness and sexual laxness" of black women. To remedy the problems blacks were experiencing, Bruce recommended that they be deported from the United States to prevent "anarchy and barbarism."[38]

White women echoed the views of Philip Bruce. For example, this description of black women appeared in a national magazine:

> They [black women] are evidently the chief instruments of the degradation of the men of their race. . . . I sometimes read of virtuous Negro women, hear of them, but the idea is absolutely inconceivable to me. . . . I cannot imagine such a creation as a virtuous black woman.[39]

In short, the racist discourse that was being written and published during this period depicted black women as licentious, immoral, and unworthy of male protection or respect.

Some black men also believed that it was difficult to find a black southern woman who was morally virtuous. A black minister charged activist Ida B. Wells, a champion of black men, with losing her teaching position in Memphis because of her involvement in some sexual impropriety.

Two black social scientists emerged during this period to analyze the problems of black women. In an 1883 essay entitled "The Black Woman in the South: Her Neglects and Her Needs," Alexander Crummell argued that in the life of the black woman there was "no sanctity of family, no binding tie of marriage, none of the fine felicities and the endearing affections of home."[40] In his 1896 Atlanta University study, Du Bois agreed with Crummell that these problems could be traced to slavery and the white man's exploitation of black women for both sex and labor. Whereas Crummell left the implications of this heritage to the reader's imagination, Du Bois did not. In one of his strongest indictments of black women Du Bois stated that their sexual immorality was the "greatest single plague spot" in the reputation of African Americans.[41]

The Club Women's Movement: "Lifting as We Climb"

The slanderous attacks on the black woman's sexual morality instigated a movement by affluent black women that came to be known as the club women's movement. The catalyst for this development was an 1894 letter written to a white male editor of a Missouri newspaper, John W. Jacks, who was also the president of the Missouri Press Association. The letter was forwarded to Josephine St. Pierre Ruffin, editor of *The Women's Era*, the first magazine in the United States owned and managed exclusively by black women.

The following passage provides some sense of the letter's tone and contents:

> Out of some 200 [Negroes] in this vicinity it is doubtful if there are a dozen virtuous women or that number who are not daily thieving from the white people. To illustrate how they regard virtue in a woman, one of them, a negro woman, was asked who a certain negro woman who had lately moved into the neighborhood was. She turned up her nose and said, "The negroes will have nothing to do with 'dat nigger,' she won't let any man except her husband sleep with her, and we don't 'sociate with her."[42]

Ruffin circulated the letter widely to prominent black women around the country, but it was thought to be too indecent for publication. Nevertheless, it was this letter that provoked the organization of the first national conference to discuss the social concerns of black women.

The following year, Ruffin, who was president of the Women's Club of Boston, called the first Conference of Negro Women to order. Meeting from July 29 to July 31, this conference launched the National Association of Colored Women (NACW) under the motto "Lifting as we climb." Imbued with the class values of Victorian America, the NACW set out to tackle the problems of poor black women by emphasizing respectable behavior and introducing alternate images of black women.

Although Ruffin stated that this first conference was not organized for "race work alone" but for "work along the lines that make for women's progress," she appealed for the support of black men. Ruffin saw it as "fitting" for the women of the race to take the lead in the movement, "but for all this we recognize the necessity of the sympathy of our husbands, brothers, and fathers." She went on to say that "our women's movement is a women's movement in that it is led and directed by women for the good of women and men, for the benefits of all humanity."[43]

Ruffin addressed the convention on July 29, 1895:

> We need to talk over those things that are of especial interest to us colored women, the training of our children, openings for our boys and girls, how they can be prepared for occupations and [what] occupations may be found or opened for them, what we can do especially in the moral education and physical development, the home training it is necessary to give our children in order to prepare them to meet the peculiar conditions in which they shall find themselves, how to make the most of our own, to some extent, limited opportunities.[44]

The NACW's decision to focus its attention on issues broader than gender was buttressed by two additional factors. First, Booker T. Washington, the powerful president of Tuskegee Institute who espoused a philosophy of racial advancement and self-help, had numerous representatives in attendance at the conference, including his wife, Margaret Murray Washington, who was influential in her own right.[45]

Second, the tensions between black and white women's groups escalated further when Ida B. Wells accused Frances Willard of condoning lynching. Willard had a reputation as a liberal and was president of the Women's Christian Temperance Union (WCTU), one of the most formidable organizations in the country. In addition, black women activists perceived white women reformers as focusing almost exclusively on the problems of immigrants and overlooking the unique challenges that were being faced by black women.[46]

Club women may not have passed a resolution to address issues of women's rights, but they did not refrain from addressing issues that would have a major impact on black women. For example, during an era when a woman's role was bound first and foremost by her responsibilities to her family and her value was determined by her status as a wife and mother, *The Women's Era* magazine stated that "not all women are intended for mothers. Some of us have not the temperament for family. . . . Clubs will make women think seriously of their future lives, and not make girls think their only alternative is to marry."[47] The feminist historian Linda Gordon has noted that those women who did marry, understood that "slavery had undermined the bases of maternalism—home and family ties, the sanctity of marriage, and the instincts of motherhood." These women viewed maternalistic reform as the highest priority, which included an emphasis on work with children.[48]

The club women were reformers and activists, but their values were decidedly those of Victorian and middle-class America. This newly anointed group of elite black women, with their class consciousness, set out to target those blacks who rejected the "womanly" values of hard work, piety, cleanliness, and sexual purity. Their primary goal was to plant middle-class values and behavioral patterns among the masses of urban blacks who retained rural folkways of speech, dress, and other distinct cultural patterns. The issue of sexual morality was so crucial from the perspective of black club women that one's status was based on "morals first, and then education, and finally means." This message had such universal appeal for black women that by the time of the Nashville Convention in 1897, the NACW had a membership of fifty thousand women.[49]

The club women's emphasis on "uplift" that targeted the sexual morals of poor women was not based on altruism so much as on their own self-interest. In their view, the "womanhood of our people" would be judged by the sexual conduct of the most impoverished women. In her 1904 NACW presidential address, Mary Church Terrell declared that black women "cannot escape altogether the consequences of the acts of their most depraved sisters. . . . Both policy and self-preservation demand that they go down among the lowly . . . to whom they are bound by ties of race and sex, and put forth every possible effort to reclaim them."[50]

Class Cleavages:
Training the Unskilled Masses

In addition to moral reform, the need to protect the virtue of black women from violation by white men provided the theme for many editorials, sermons, and speeches. Black parents were vigilant in their efforts to protect their daughters from being sexually assaulted by white men. One black domestic observed, "I believe nearly all white men take, and expect to take, undue liberties with their colored female servants, not only the fathers, but in many cases the sons also. Those servants who rebel against such familiarity must either leave or expect a mighty hard time if they stay." Another recalled, "The only thing that I can remember my parents talked about, when it came to race, is that they never wanted a girl of theirs to have to work in the home of a white person."[51]

Black club women with their emphasis on Victorian ideals felt the same way. What they overlooked, however, was that the majority of black women worked out of necessity and did not have the option of choosing teaching over domestic work. As noted earlier, Du Bois concluded from his survey of the black community in Philadelphia in 1899 that black women were forced to work because of the low wages earned by black men.

Recognizing this reality, reformer Nannie Burroughs promoted an alternative solution to the problem of "uplifting poor black women." Dubbed the "female Booker T. Washington" by her contemporaries, Burroughs set out to focus on the "hand training" of the masses rather than the "mind training" of black professionals.[52] She agreed with the club women that the training of black women was the "most essential factor" in "racial uplift." Unlike many club women, however, she focused her attention on the "great mass of laboring people."[53]

In October 1909 the National Training School for Women was officially opened in Washington, D.C., under the auspices of the Women's Convention, the auxiliary of the National Baptist Convention. The school was launched with Nannie Burroughs as its president. Its emphasis was preparing women for domestic service—and at the same time regulating the manners and morals of the students.[54]

In a letter written to Booker T. Washington in 1912, Nannie Burroughs pointed out that nine-tenths of the girls enrolled in her school would not have been admitted to Howard University, a liberal arts–oriented institution in the same city. Although Burroughs directed attention to educating black women who were being overlooked by the more elite educational institutions, there were mixed messages in the school's emphasis on the three B's—Bible, bath, and broom. Phyllis Palmer has pointed to the contradictory societal messages given to black and white women:

> The [white] wife's cleanliness was made possible by the domestic's dirtiness . . . and the work's distribution confirmed the dominant belief that class and race difference were due to the moral superiority of middle-class white women and the moral degradation of working-class and black women.[55]

Although the efforts of Burroughs and other black women reformers were well intended, the needs of black women compelled to work as domestics to support their families far exceeded the instruction being offered by the National Training School. Upon hearing that some whites proposed erecting statues in memory of the "Old Black Mammies," a Georgia woman ridiculed this narrow and distorted view of black womanhood when she declared:

> "What we need is present help, present sympathy, better wages, better hours, more protection, and a chance to breathe for once while alive as free women. . . . On the one hand, we are assailed by white men, and on the other hand, we are assailed by black men, who should be our natural protectors; and whether in the cook kitchen, at the washtub, over the sewing machine, behind the baby

carriage or at the ironing board, we are little more than pack horses, beasts of burden, slaves."[56]

A Women's Era

Despite the many challenges facing black women, the emergence of women leaders and the conscious efforts to improve the education and training of black women bore significant fruit around the turn of the century. Frances Harper, the novelist whose writings focused on the political struggles of African-American people, characterized this period as a "women's era." Although Chicago activist Fannie Barrier Williams declared "the colored woman and the colored man started even," the achievements of black women during this period eclipsed those of black men.[57]

From 1890 to 1910, for example, the number of professional black women increased by 219 percent, whereas that of black men increased by only 51 percent. In 1890 women were about 25 percent of all black professionals; by 1910 that number had risen to 43 percent. These patterns were reflected in the leading black high school in Washington, D.C. In the graduating class of Dunbar High School in 1910, the girl graduates outnumbered boys two to one.[58]

In her comprehensive study of black women's education, Jeanne Noble explained the higher educational achievements of black women compared to men in the following observations: "[The] social system of the Negro rewarded the enterprising, clever, ambitious woman. Later, when attitudes that challenged a woman's right to college education emerged, missionaries and earlier college founders were able to overcome these attitudes partly because of the need for teachers to educate the masses of ignorant Negroes."[59] The challenges that Noble made reference to were raised by black men. In spite of the dramatic gains in the educational achievements of black women, club woman Anna J. Cooper feared that the "majority of colored men do not yet think it worth-while that women aspire to a higher education."[60]

A further explanation for the disparities between male and fe-male academic achievement can be found in the perceived limita-tions in job opportunities for black men. The strongest opposition to Benjamin Mays's getting an education came from his father, who believed that the only honest occupations for black men were preaching and farming.[61]

Another indicator of the growth of black women's quest for ed-ucation during this period is the enrollment trends in the Baptist Home Mission schools. In 1880 the male enrollment in these schools was twice as high as the female enrollment. By 1892, of 202 teachers in thirteen Baptist schools of higher education, 120 were women, and female students outnumbered males 2,948 to 2,219. The preponderance of these female students specialized in teacher training. Even in the Baptist schools, teacher training had sur-passed ministerial training, with 1,829 female teacher trainees in attendance, compared to 458 male ministerial students.[62]

These trends were fueled by club women like Anna J. Cooper, who believed that "well-trained" black women were more impor-tant and necessary than black ministers.[63] Addie Hunton, an NACW organizer during this period, went even further than Cooper with her observation that "the Negro woman has been the motive power in whatever has been accomplished by the race."[64]

Black women not only were going to school in increasing num-bers but also were providing leadership by establishing new schools to train black women. Lucy C. Laney, Nannie Helen Bur-roughs, Charlotte Hawkins Brown, and Mary McLeod Bethune all founded training institutions with curricula that included aca-demic subjects as well as industrial arts courses, with an emphasis on thrift and morality.

In addition to accepting the mantle of leadership, black women challenged the authority of black men. Charlotte Hawkins Brown, for example, declared that her own work and thoughts were just as important as those of Booker T. Washington.[65] Nannie Burroughs defied the male-dominated Baptist leadership so forcibly that the church almost cut off financial support for the National Training School for Women. Burroughs also canceled a speaking engagement before the National Christian Mission because bureaucratic administrators insisted on censoring her speech.[66]

The educational achievements of black women were escalating, and their organizational, entrepreneurial, and management efforts were gaining momentum as well. When Booker T. Washington founded the National Negro Business League in 1900 to provide a forum for black businesspersons, some of the chief beneficiaries of this organization were black women. According to the National Negro Business League's Annual Report, by the turn of the century black women had made unprecedented entry into many professions. There were 160 black women physicians, 7 dentists, 10 lawyers, 164 ministers, 1,185 music instructors, and 13,525 elementary school teachers.[67] By 1916, the Household of Ruth, the female affiliate of the Black Odd Fellows, had 197,000 members in five thousand lodges, two-thirds the male membership.[68]

The Commitment to Marriage

The arduous tasks black wives had to undertake, whether on the farm or in the city, did not seem to dampen black women's enthusiasm for marriage. In her cultural study in 1939, Hortense Powdermaker compared the marriage patterns of blacks and whites and found "marriage expectations and mating [among black women] continue longer than among the white women in the community."[69] The contrast between female activists was especially striking. A comparison of black and white women reformers showed that 85 percent of the black women were married, compared to only 34 percent of the white.[70] White women activists evidently saw marriage responsibilities as an impediment to their work, whereas black female activists elected to shoulder both their public and private responsibilities. Similarly, when historian Stephanie J. Shaw examined the lives of forty-six professional black women from the 1870s through the 1950s, she found that thirty-four (74 percent) were married at least once in their lifetime. Shaw explained this phenomenon in this way: "Black women who were able to succeed in both private and public endeavors represented a community ideal."[71]

Another important difference between white and black women concerned their social class of origin and the upward mobility of black women. About 90 percent of the black women who were classified as middle to upper class had been born into working-class families, compared to 35 percent of white women. Surveys conducted during this period found that black women were going to college for two primary reasons: to prepare for a vocation and to prepare for marriage and family life.

Among the more affluent black women who emerged as leaders, marriage to prominent men often gave them a distinct advantage in their leadership positions. Not only were the black activists more likely than their white counterparts to be married but 51 percent of them had professional husbands.[72]

There were a number of alliances between prominent black women and professional-class black men. Ida Wells Barnett's husband, Ferdinand Barnett, published Chicago's leading newspaper. Fannie Barrier Williams, a correspondent for *The Women's Era,* was married to S. Laing Williams, a former law partner of Ferdinand Barnett. Margaret Murray Washington, president of the National Federation of Afro-American Women, was the wife of Booker T. Washington, the president of Tuskegee Institute. Lavinia Sneed of Kentucky was married to a state university professor. Lugenia Burns Hope was married to the first black president of Atlanta University, John Hope. Mrs. John Langston was the wife of a congressman. Josephine St. Pierre Ruffin's husband, George L. Ruffin, was a member of the Boston City Council and Boston's first black judge. Irene McCoy Gaines, a civil rights and welfare activist, was married to an Illinois state legislator. Josephine Bruce, a club woman and author, was the wife of Blanche K. Bruce, a Reconstruction-era U.S. Senator from Mississippi. Marie Steward taught at Kentucky State University and was married to a newspaper editor. Madam C. J. Walker, the beauty culturalist, was married to newspaperman Charles J. Walker. Elizabeth Ross Haynes, a pioneer social worker, was the wife of George Edmund Haynes, cofounder of the National Urban League.

Black men were also enthusiastic about the institution of marriage. When Lugenia Burns declined John Hope's first proposal of marriage, he was not deterred. During the period that she was trying to make a decision whether to marry John, Lugenia had four other men vying for her hand.[73]

Marriage may not have held these prominent women back, but many of them had to make compromises and sacrifices that their husbands were not asked to make in order to devote the time they wanted to their professional endeavors. Although these couples were attempting to form partnerships, ideals of equality vied with the prevailing attitudes about men's and women's roles. One example was the marriage of John and Lugenia Hope. During their dating and courtship, when they were both students at the University of Chicago, John expressed his desire for equality in a marriage. Lugenia received her master's degree and was looking forward to building a career based on a life of service. In a letter John wrote before their marriage, he asserted, "Neither of us is to be the servant, yet both of us gladly serve each other in love and patience." Once they were married, however, he expected his wife to give up her ambitions and make a career out of supporting his wants and needs. In a letter written after they married, he put it this way: "This is what you were born to do."[74]

Like their white counterparts, many black males exercised their male prerogative to usurp their wife's decision to work, especially if they made enough money to support the family. When the Black

Women's Oral History Project interviewed black women about work and marriage, many of the married activists indicated they were not successful in convincing their husbands of the importance of their work. As a result, they either did not enter the workplace or did so for only a short period of time. When Ardie Clark Halyard was asked how her husband felt about her working, she replied, "At first he thought it was very necessary. But afterwards, when he became able to support us, he would ask, 'When are you going to quit?'" Martha Harrison recalled, "My husband never did like for me to work," and he would ask her why she continued to work when he was doing everything in his power to provide for her needs. "Looks like you don't appreciate what I'm trying to do for you," he would say. "Yes, I do, honey," she would reply, "[I] jest help you 'cause I don't want you to break down. If you put a load on one horse it will pull him down, but two horses can pull it jest as easy."[75]

In spite of many black husbands' ambivalence regarding their wives' work, Marion Culbert described these marriages as a "deference of comradeship" on the part of men to their wives because these women "set forth with them daily to earn bread for their children."[76] Josephine Turpin Washington, a Richmond educator, agreed with Culbert that these husbands and wives were "companions, co-workers, helpmates, and equals."[77] Victoria Earle Matthews, an author and activist, likewise reiterated this point in her address to the Annual Convention of the Society of Christian Endeavor in 1897 when she characterized black women as "co-breadwinners" in their families who raised their daughters to be the "arch" of the black church.[78]

Black women activists exemplified the willingness of African-American women to juggle family and work responsibilities. Ida B. Wells Barnett is a case in point. She was thirty-three years old and her antilynching crusade was already in full swing when she married Ferdinand Lee Barnett and relocated to Chicago. Barnett was a lawyer and the founder of the *Conservator*, the first black newspaper in Chicago. He was also a widower and the father of two young sons. He and Ida added four children of their own to the family. Although she accepted speaking engagements, Ida B. Wells-Barnett did not take paid work outside the home until the youngest child was eight years old and enrolled in school. When discussing her attempts to balance her parenting responsibilities with her travels, she once said, "I honestly believe that I am the only woman in the United States who ever traveled throughout the country with a nursing baby to make a speech."[79]

The marriage of Ida B. Wells and Ferdinand Barnett was unique in many ways. After their marriage, Barnett never expected Wells to stay at home and be a housewife. He employed household help and he did most of the cooking for the family. In fact, he not only loved to cook but had better culinary skills than his wife. In temperament, Barnett and Wells also complemented each other. In reminiscing about her parents, Alfreda Duster remembered that her "father was a very mild mannered man, he was not aggressive ... or outspoken like my mother."[80]

Once again the contrast between black and white women reformers is instructive. Differences in the attitudes of these women toward finding balance in their family and professional responsibilities is reflected in Susan B. Anthony's correspondence with Ida B. Wells-Barnett. Anthony, a never-married women's rights activist, developed a friendship with Wells over the years. In one of her letters she admonished Wells about the formidable tasks in "divided duty":

Women like you who have a special call for work [should never marry]. I know of no one in all this country better fitted to do the work you had in hand. Since you've gotten married, agitation seems practically to have ceased. Besides, you're trying to help in the formation of this league and your baby needs your attention at home. You're distracted over the thought that he's not being looked after as he would be if you were there, and that makes for divided duty.[81]

One of the more interesting compromises was the one made by Fostine Riddick, a nurse anesthetist. When she married Henry Riddick, a postal worker, he did not want her to work outside the home. What is interesting about the Riddick marriage is that he was not a professional and they had no children. After the wedding, Fostine gave up her professional duties and learned to cook and give parties. After two years of "complete housewifery," Riddick became so bored that she found part-time employment in a nearby hospital. She worked at the hospital for ten years without her husband's knowledge. As far as he knew, she confined her work to unpaid church and community projects and occasional private-duty nursing.[82]

Black Women's Discontent

The idea that gender relations were more egalitarian for blacks than whites during the late nineteenth and early twentieth centuries is reflected in a resolution passed by the National Federation of Afro-American Women in 1895. This "social purity" resolution stated that "we require the same standard of morality for men as women, and that the mothers teach their sons social purity as well as their daughters."[83] When black women reformers sensed that sexual double standards existed, they spoke out against them. For example, Lucy Laney, the founder of the Haines Institute, a training school for black women, charged, "Too often the mother is careful of her daughter's environment and character . . . [and] is negligent as to her son's."[84] Mary Terrell criticized values that "turn[ed] the cold shoulder upon a fallen sister, but greet[ed] her destroyer with open arms."[85]

Compare the wording of the "sexual purity" resolution to the double standards operating among whites. Many of the white men who venerated white women as paragons of virtue and purity were having illicit sex with black women. Much of the sex between white men and black women was in the form of either rape or sexual abuse that was justified by the myths that black women were sexually promiscuous. Apart from the double standard for men and women, there was also a double standard for the two races. The same set of assumptions that denied that any black woman could not be raped asserted that no white woman would voluntarily consent to sex with a black man. Consequently, any white woman who had sexual intercourse with a black man had to be a victim of rape.

Black women were becoming impatient with sexual mistreatment at the hands of white men, and many learned how to protect themselves. A South Carolina woman recalled how she and her sister armed themselves with a two-by-four when they needed to obtain water at a neighborhood well. "We slashed fellows' shoulders several times when they tried to attack us. They were never successful. My sister shot a white guy once when he broke into our house and tried to rape her."[86] If black males had treated white women in a comparable fashion, they would no doubt have provoked an even more violent response.

For both races the societal conception of manhood included being the "protector and defender" of women. As black women continued to suffer sexual insults from white men, they began to express publicly their dissatisfaction with black men for not giving them the protection they felt they deserved. Fannie Barrier Williams pointed out there was "no protection against the libelous attacks on their characters, and no chivalry generous enough to guarantee their safety against man's inhumanity to women." Williams then exhorted black men "brave enough to stand out and say to all the world, 'This far and no farther in your attempt to insult or degrade our women.'"[87] Nannie Helen Burroughs echoed Williams's views and angrily declared, "White men offer more protection to their prostitutes than many black men offer to their best women."[88]

In an effort to build bridges with black men, the Atlanta club women invited John Hope, an ally of W. E. B. Du Bois and the first black president of Atlanta Baptist College, to speak to their club. The Atlanta women must have been ecstatic when he accepted the invitation. In Hope's opening statement, however, he referred to the "caustic remarks" club women had made about men and berated them for their "brow-beating spirit." He further asserted that black people "are in need of men" and felt it was a "great calamity for our women to act as substitutes." He admonished the club women that "the surest way for our men to become manly is for our women to become more womanly."[89] Hope's speech was one of the early indicators that tensions were beginning to escalate between black men and women—tensions that would proliferate in the years ahead.

Conclusion

After emancipation, a strong patriarchal ethos took hold in black families. However, at a time when white women were firmly placed on pedestals and ensconced in paternal concern and protection, the majority of their black counterparts were thrust into the workplace with low wages and poor working conditions. And whereas white women were perceived as submissive, vulnerable, and the weaker sex, black women from all class strata were becoming more autonomous and self-reliant. The spirit of independence that was emerging as one of the salient characteristics of black women would later be pejoratively characterized by E. Franklin Frazier as lacking a "spirit of subordination to masculine authority."[90]

Although many black couples were able to sustain lasting marriages, quarreling, infidelity, spousal abuse, and the search for employment were all contributing to the increasing absence of black husbands among working-class black families. These conflicts were exacerbated by the fact that many black families were forced to reside in cramped living quarters as they struggled to eke out an existence for themselves. Furthermore, the daily humiliations of life in the Jim Crow era reflected a callous disregard for the sanctity of the black family.

As retrogressionists and others assaulted black women for their alleged lack of sexual morality, black women responded with the club women's movement and Nannie Burroughs's efforts to train lower-class black women. During the latter part of the nineteenth century, black women made their mark as leaders, professionals, teachers, and businesspeople. Unlike many white women activists, middle-class black reformers tried to balance the responsibilities of marriage and public life, while the masses of black wives continued to do double duty as homemakers and wage earners, including being farm laborers.

In many respects black marriages during this period were more egalitarian than those of whites, but this greater equality was a matter of necessity rather than choice, and it depended on black women's willingness to do "double duty." Black husbands continued to reflect the patriarchal attitudes of the dominant society, resisting their wives' independence and frequently objecting to their working outside the home when it was absolutely necessary for them to do so. The very success of black women in education, the professions, and business would become a source of further tensions with black men. For their part, black women openly expressed their unhappiness over black men's failure to fill their roles as providers and protectors. Instead of uniting against a common oppressor and forging more constructive partnerships, black men and women began to blame each other for the formidable challenges they continued to face in the years ahead.

4

A Shifting Landscape: The "New Manhood" Movement

Let us go back to the days of true manhood when women . . . truly reverenced us . . . let us again place our women upon the pedestal whence they have been forced into the vortex of the seething world of business.

—MARCUS GARVEY

Be not discouraged black women of the world, but push forward, regardless of the lack of appreciation shown you. A race must be saved, a country must be redeemed, and unless you strengthen the leadership of vacillating Negro men, we will remain marking time. . . . Mr. Black Man, watch your step! Ethiopia's queens will reign again, and her Amazons protect her shores and people. Strengthen your shaking knees, and move forward or we will displace you and lead on to victory and to glory.

—AMY JACQUES GARVEY

MARY ANN SHADD CARY was born to abolitionist parents in 1823 in Delaware. A graduate of Howard University Law School, she became the first black woman lawyer in the United States. She also became the first black woman newspaper editor in North America. In 1880 she founded the Colored Women's Progressive Franchise Association in Washington, D.C., one of the earliest black women's organizations established exclusively for women's rights. Cary's goal was to assert equal rights for women and to take "an aggressive stand against the assumption that men only begin and conduct industrial and other things." The organization's twenty-point agenda included broadening job opportunities for black women, and a newspaper published by the association asserted that women "must be the controlling official power."[1]

Seven years after Cary established her women-only fraternity, a group of black men came together to found the American Negro Academy. Its purpose was ostensibly to bring together some of the leading intellectuals, including Reverend Alexander Crummell, Reverend Francis Grimke, W. E. B. Du Bois—graduates of Princeton, Cambridge, and Harvard respectively. This academy was one of the first African-American organizations whose bylaws stipulated that only men of African descent could become members.

The stipulations regarding gender found in the establishment of these two organizations were among the first indicators that the achievements of black women were creating conflicts in gender relations in the African-American community.[2] In this chapter we will see how black women retreated as men came to the forefront and resistance to white oppression became simultaneously a racial movement and a men's movement. These developments took place even as a beauty industry evolved that heaped more contradictions onto the plight of black women, creating a financial empire for a few black women while resting on the disempowering premise that African-American women should emulate a white ideal.

Black Women and the Entrepreneurial Spirit

As black women became more adept at juggling the responsibilities of work and home, they began to capture the entrepreneurial spirit. The fervor of black women was captured in a prediction advanced by Sadie T. M. Alexander in 1930. The first black woman to receive a doctorate in economics from the University of Pennsylvania, Alexander had found it difficult because of racism and sexism to secure a suitable job upon graduation. In 1927 she earned a second degree, this time from the University of Pennsylvania Law School. Joining a law firm that same year, she became the first black woman to practice law in Pennsylvania. Alexander knew that the work of the housewife would be increasingly viewed as a "valueless consumption" and that women should become involved in work that "resulted in the production of goods that have a price value."[3]

One of the clearest examples of the resourcefulness and economic independence of leading black women was the life of Maggie L. Walker. The daughter of a washerwoman, Walker began her career at the age of fourteen in the Independent Order of St. Luke, a mutual benefit society that provided illness and burial insurance for blacks. In 1903 she founded the St. Luke Penny Saving Bank, becoming the first woman bank president in the United States. She also opened a black-owned department store in Richmond, Virginia, and her enterprises stimulated black ownership and employment.[4]

The popularity of commercialized beauty products also unleashed tremendous entrepreneurial energy among black women in the early years of the twentieth century. Across the backwoods of the rural South and in hamlets throughout the urban North, black women were making a transition to new beauty rituals. Whether they were working poor or members of more affluent classes, black women were taking part in this new consumer culture. In the process they were creating a new industry and higher-paying jobs for many black women.

Madam C. J. Walker (the former Sarah Breedlove) emerged as the first self-made American woman millionaire. She developed the "hot-iron" process for straightening hair as well as other hair care products. By 1910, Walker achieved annual gross sales of $275,000, an unparalleled success, and employed five thousand black female agents working seven days a week. One of Walker's agents asserted that she had enabled "hundreds of colored women to make an honest and profitable living where they make as much in one week as a month's salary would bring from any other position."

Madam Walker identified closely with poor black women, whose life experiences she shared even as she sought entry into the ranks of the black economic elite. Walker secured what she wanted by aggressively pursuing her goals. For example, Booker T. Washington openly discouraged Walker from attending the annual meeting of the National Negro Business League because of his skepticism of female entrepreneurs. When she attended the annual meeting in 1912 and attempted to address the detegates, he repeatedly refused to recognize her. Finally, she rushed up to the podium and captured the audience's attention when she blurted out, "I am a woman that came from the cotton fields of the South; I was promoted from there to the washtub . . . and from there I was promoted to the cook kitchen and from there I promoted myself into the business of manufacturing hair goods and preparations."[5] After her remarks, Washington told those convened, "We thank her for her excellent address and for our race. You talk about what the men are doing in a business way. Why if we don't watch out, the women will excel us." The following year Washington invited her back as one of the featured speakers.[6]

Another pioneer in the direct sales methods in the beauty trade was Annie Turnbo. In the 1890s she began experimenting with preparations to help black women care for their hair and scalp. She produced a hair treatment containing sage and egg rinses, common substances in the "folk" cosmetic tradition, and manufactured a product called Wonderful Hair Grower. Demand quickly outstripped her ability to produce the hair grower, and Turnbo hired three young women as assistants. In 1906, as competitors began to imitate her product, she registered the trade name "Poro."

In 1914, Turnbo married Aaron Malone. He became her business partner, and together they built Poro College, a training institute for saleswomen. Annie envisioned this college as "more than a mere business enterprise" and nothing less than an institution "consecrated to the uplift of humanity—race women in particular." Opened in 1918, it not only housed Poro's factory and offices but offered theater, music, athletics, art murals, and a chapel. Malone also reached out to young black women in need of jobs and training and stressed that "every Poro agent should be an active force for good."[7]

Black women's hair care businesses were successful in part because they utilized the black women's professional network. Black beauty culturists addressed audiences at women's clubs, Baptist and Methodist churches, and historically black colleges. Two hundred Walker agents attended their first national convention in 1917 and heard Walker speak on "Women's Duty to Women." Walker took an active part in the National Association of Colored Women and appealed to the class-conscious club women "to get closer in touch with women in the factory."[8]

The hair care business was so profitable that even educated and professional black women seized the chance to augment their income. A black teacher in Portsmouth, Virginia, started out selling Walker products to increase her meager income but soon gave up teaching and expanded her sales efforts into full-time work.[9] She also began to train women to become hairdressers and ultimately became a manager of a distribution depot. Another college-educated woman, Ezella Mathis Carter, a Spelman alumna, left her job as a teacher and a principal in rural Georgia to enter the hair care industry. Sarah Spencer Washington's family urged her to remain in the teaching profession, but she chose instead to start the

Apex Hair and News Company. This company became one of the largest black-owned businesses in the 1920s and 1930s.[10]

The dramatic achievements of black women professionals and entrepreneurs did not mean that there was economic, social, and political parity between black men and women. As we have seen, almost immediately after emancipation "there was a new determination for [black] men to reassert their position as head of the family."[11] Despite notable attempts at partnership, many black husbands of enterprising women continued to be uneasy with their wives' activities outside the home. Moreover, the success of such high-profile black women as Madam C. J. Walker, Annie Turnbo Malone, Maggie L. Walker, and Sarah Spencer Washington was not typical of black women. Most black women entrepreneurs ran small businesses out of their own homes, working mostly as seamstresses or hairdressers. Men invariably headed black-owned businesses such as banks, insurance companies, funeral parlors, and newspapers, with women making the primary contribution as "sacrificing wives." And as we shall see, the success of the beauty industry entrepreneurs would lead to mixed results for black women.

The "New Manhood" Movement

A new militancy emerged among African Americans after World War I. In part the "new manhood" movement grew out of a period of increased restiveness that began with the postslavery generation ("the new Negro") and the corresponding increase in vicious repression in the South. The experience of World War I itself contributed to the new militancy as black men fought and died "to make the world safe for democracy." Meanwhile, the migration of millions of southern blacks to the North created large bodies of urban blacks.

While the new manhood movement was a racial movement, it was also a man's movement in which the black man emerged as leader and primary beneficiary. Black women, who had become visible leaders in the postslavery years, became eclipsed as the men moved to the forefront. In short, the same movement that promoted blacks' self-respect and militancy also promoted men's dominance in the community.

By the end of the war in 1919 the more progressive African Americans were already serving notice that the blacks of postwar America were going to be much more militant than the prewar prototype. The *Messenger* declared that the "new style" Negro would not ignore grievances even in the interests of national security. The "New Negro" would no longer "turn the other cheek," be humble and retiring. It was Marcus Garvey who best articulated the new mood of assertiveness when he declared that men who were members of his Universal Negro Improvement Association (UNIA) symbolized the "new manhood of the Negro."[12]

The Jamaican-born Garvey had come to New York in 1916. The primary purpose of his organizational efforts was to empower blacks economically by creating black enterprises. According to historian John Hope Franklin, Garvey's appeal was to "race pride at a time when African-Americans generally had so little of which to be proud."[13] He captured the imaginations of African Americans, particularly working-class blacks, more than any other leader of this period. During World War I and the 1920s, UNIA was the largest black secular organization in African-American history. Possibly a million men and women from the United States, the Caribbean, and Africa joined the organization. One example of Garvey's ability to seize the black community's attention—men and women alike—can be found in the grandeur and splendor of a UNIA parade. On August 2, 1920, residents of Harlem lined the streets of Lenox Avenue to view the spectacular procession. The marchers at the head of the ladies' auxiliary carried a banner that read GOD GIVE US REAL MEN.[14]

More than other black leaders, Garvey promised to give black women what they had been wanting and needing from black men. UNIA women also used the term "new manhood"; to them it meant men who were responsible providers and respectful fathers and husbands. In an article in Garvey's newspaper, *Negro World,* he was quoted as promising to liberate black women from the world of work and declared:

> Let us go back to the days of true manhood when women . . . truly reverenced us . . . let us again place our women upon the pedestal whence they have been forced into the vortex of the seething world of business.[15]

According to historian Barbara Bair, Garvey's movement was the personification of independent manhood and symbolized the ideas of force and dominance. Although women were technically granted an equal share of power, the organizational structure of the UNIA was not "separate and equal" but "separate and hierarchical." Garvey targeted his message to black women who valued "marriage, motherhood, and a single-income family."[16] As one Garveyite official wrote, "If you find any women—especially a black woman—who does not want to be a mother, you may rest assured she is not a true woman."[17]

According to articles in the *Negro World,* men in UNIA were to uplift the race through their engagement in business and commerce, whereas women were to produce a "better and stronger race." According to columnists in the *Negro World* for women this was the "greatest privilege that can come to any woman in this age, and to the negro woman in particular."[18]

In an effort to obliterate the images of black men as powerless and black women as Amazons, the UNIA sanctioned separate spheres of influence along traditional gender lines. Men were dominant in the public sphere, and their roles were associated with authority, control, and power. Women were assigned to roles in the private sphere that were associated with nurturing and cooperation. In addition, women were glorified for having the "power to win and conquer the beastly side of a man."[19]

The distinct spheres found in UNIA are best illustrated in the women and men's auxiliaries—the Black Cross Nurses and the Universal African Legions. Patterned after Red Cross workers, the Black Cross Nurses provided primary public health services to black communities that were not receiving them from government agencies. They performed duties such as visiting the sick and dispensing food and clothing to the poor. These women were also important as role models and were helpful in enrolling young women into the UNIA. In contrast, the Universal African Legions were modeled after the U.S. infantry and symbolized the power and force necessary for blacks to achieve nationhood. Their function was primarily ceremonial in that they marched in parades and provided security services at massive gatherings. Barbara Bair has characterized the differences in the dress codes of Garveyite men and women in this way: Male members of the Universal African Legions wore elaborate military-style costumes, while the Black Cross nurses wore loose dresses and capes suggestive of self-sacrificing nuns and nurses.[20]

Many women within UNIA felt restricted in their gender roles. At the 1922 UNIA convention they expressed a need for greater independence. A delegate from St. Louis, Victoria Turner, approached the platform when Garvey was out of the room and presented a set of five resolutions that had been ratified by a majority of the women. This petition was an attempt by the women to gain more autonomy in order to "function without restriction from the men." Clara Morgan, a Black Cross nurse, declared that "she was not in favor of the women standing behind and pushing the men." Mrs. Dora Scott, a delegate from Detroit, expressed concern that "whenever women begin to function in the organization the men presumed to dictate to them."[21]

Two years following this conference a high-ranking UNIA member, Maymie Leona Turpeau De Mena, published a paper complaining that although women formed "the backbone and sinew" of the organization, they were given to understand "they must remain in their place."[22]

Garvey ran afoul of club women when he took a stand against miscegenation and association with the "hybrids of the race."[23] Because most of the club women in leadership positions had fair complexions—many could pass for white—his public pronouncements put him at odds with them. During a period when light-skinned black women were perceived as paragons of beauty, Garvey advocated replacing white standards of beauty with black ones. He declared his admiration for dark-skinned women in the following poem:

> Black Queen of beauty, thou hast given colour to the world!
> Among other women thou art royal and the fairest!
> Like the highest of jewels in the regal diadem,
> Shin'st thou, Goddess of Africa, Nature's purest emblem!
> Black men worship the virginal shrine in truest Love,
> Because in thine eyes are virtue's steady and holy mark,
> As we see in no other, clothed in silk or fine linen,
> From ancient Venus, the Goddess to mythical Helen,
> Superior Angels look like you in heaven above,
> For thou art fairest, queen of the seasons, queen of our love: No
>   Condition shall make us ever in life desert thee,
> Sweet Goddess of the ever green land and placid blue sea.[24]

Ironically, when Garvey was convicted of mail fraud and jailed from 1925 to 1927, his second wife, Amy Jacques Garvey, a feminist, became his representative and spokesperson. Sounding like some of the club women's leaders, she declared, "We serve notice on our men that Negro women will demand equal opportunity to fill any position in the UNIA." She went even further than the club women when she added, "We not only make the demand but we intend to enforce it."[25] Amy Jacques Garvey differed from the club women in that she opposed the goal of integration for the purposes of achieving equality with white Americans. In contrast, she advocated a black nationalistic platform.

Amy Jacques Garvey fulfilled the multiple roles of wife, legal adviser, fund-raiser, secretary, and writer/propagandist until the birth of her children in 1930 and 1933. The children were born during a period when she received little if any support from Garvey because of his extensive travel schedule and financial difficulties. When Jacques Garvey would later review her life with Garvey she bitterly noted, "What did he ever give in return? The value of a wife to him was like a gold coin—expendable to get what he wanted, and hard enough to withstand rough usage in the process."[26]

According to the Department of Justice, the mail fraud charges brought against Marcus Garvey were initiated by J. Edgar Hoover's Federal Bureau of Investigation, fueling widespread belief in the black community that he had been framed. He entered the Atlanta penitentiary to serve a five-year term and in one of his letters shared his optimism regarding the eventual liberation of black people:

> My months of forcible removal from among you, being imprisoned as a punishment for advocating the cause of our real emancipation, have not left me hopeless or despondent; but to the contrary, I see a great ray of light and the bursting of a mighty political cloud which will bring you complete freedom. . . .
>
> We have gradually won our way back into the confidence of the God of Africa, and He shall speak with a voice of thunder, that shall shake the pillars of a corrupt and unjust world, and once more restore Ethiopia to her ancient glory.
>
> Hold fast to the Faith. Desert not the ranks, but as brave soldiers march on to victory. I am happy, and shall remain so, as long as you keep the flag flying.[27]

Garvey remained in prison until President Coolidge pardoned him in 1927; he was then deported to Jamaica. His departure was effectively the end of the UNIA. Unable to resurrect the UNIA, Garvey moved to London, where he died in 1940. In spite of the political activism and defiant leadership provided by Amy Jacques Garvey, black women did not succeed in appropriating power from black men. Garvey's enduring legacy to the African-American community was that the pattern established by the UNIA would continue in the black nationalist and civil rights movements.

The Displacement of Female Leadership

As the example of Garvey's UNIA suggests, the new militancy of African Americans was simultaneously a movement that promoted male dominance. In the process, female leaders began to be displaced. With black women having such phenomenal success as entrepreneurs in the beauty culture industry, for example, it was inevitable that black businessmen would launch businesses in this industry as well. One of the first black males to enter the field was Anthony Overton. Trained as a lawyer, Overton had worked as a judge, Pullman porter, and general store proprietor. In 1898 he founded the Overton Hygienic Company to manufacture baking powder. He soon realized that women used "face powder more than baking powder." Like Madam Walker and Annie Malone, he used door-to-door agents to sell products and hired only black sales agents and office clerks.[28]

In 1918 a group of black male investors launched the Nile Cosmetics company. The following year Walker introduced her line of face powders and skin care cosmetics, and in 1922 Malone followed suit. Walker and Malone thus placed their companies in direct competition with the black businessmen. Although Overton was the self-proclaimed "largest Negro manufacturing enterprise in the United States," he never achieved the financial success of either Walker or Malone in the beauty industry.[29]

One of the clearest examples of the inordinate tensions in the marriages of high-profile businesswomen and their husbands can be found in the dissolution of the marriages of Walker and Malone. Like Annie Malone, Madam C. J. Walker achieved considerable success in her business prior to her marriage to newspaperman Charles J. Walker, who became her business partner and helped her with her advertising campaign and the mail order business. (Her first marriage, to Moses McWilliams, a laborer, ended with the death of McWilliams.)

Annie Malone's business experienced a major setback in 1927, the same year she divorced. Even though Annie's company was firmly established and prosperous when she married Aaron, he fought her for control of the company. When the marriage ended, a St. Louis court put "Poro" into receivership and a white man in charge. The black community rallied to Annie's defense. "Madam Malone's fight becomes the Race's fight," said one newspaper. Annie Malone eventually won, but at a tremendous cost and with her company in ruins.[30]

Another indicator of the tensions surfacing between African-American men and women can be found in black men's attacks on Ida B. Wells-Barnett. Wells-Barnett, a journalist and advocate for racial justice and woman suffrage, had begun campaigning against the lynching of black men as early as 1891 when she cofounded the militant newspaper *Free Speech* in Memphis. She had survived death threats and the burning of her press by a white mob to launch an international crusade against lynching. Ironically, black men—the prime beneficiaries of her antilynching campaign— grew increasingly resentful of her leadership role. Evidence of this displeasure was found in an editorial in the *Colored American* newspaper in response to her election as the financial secretary of the Afro-American Council. The newspaper commentary asserted that the financial secretary of the council should be a man and recommended Wells-Barnett for the leader of a women's auxiliary. In a similar vein, black men accused Wells of "jumping ahead of them" and even discouraged the foremost antilynching crusader from going to the scene of a lynching in 1909.[31]

During this period we see the proliferation of black men's public expression of their discontent with the perceived progress of black women. T. Thomas Fortune, editor of *New York Age*, deviated from other black men when he came to the defense of black women, declaring, "The race could not succeed nor build strong citizens until we have a race of women competent to do more than hear a brood of negative men."[32] Nevertheless, the prevailing view was that black women's progress was eclipsing that of black men and the retreat of black women would facilitate the advancement of black men.

The Politics of "Beauty"

As tensions between black men and women escalated, another divisive issue surfaced. The entrepreneurial success of black women in the hair care business brought commercialized beauty—and the new aesthetic these products were promoting—to the forefront. Skin color, hair texture, and the utilization of hair care products to transform them became a political issue in the black community even more than an aesthetic one.

These debates were fueled by the emergence of the Harlem Renaissance and the self-proclaimed "New Negro" movements in the 1910s and 1920s. In 1917, A. Philip Randolph and Chandler Owens, two radical intellectuals, founded the *Messenger,* which claimed to be "the only radical Negro magazine in America." In rejecting the emulation of a white standard of beauty, Owens's editorial in the *Messenger* articulated the issue this way: "If people of color ruled the world, white people would curl their hair and darken their skin."[33]

The UNIA under the auspices of Marcus Garvey not only affirmed a new political destiny for the masses of dark-skinned African Americans but also espoused a new and different aesthetic. The more progressive journals like the *Crusader* and *Negro World* affirmed this aesthetic by featuring dark-skinned women wearing their hair in more "natural" hair arrangements. A poem in the *Mes-*

senger exalted the black woman who used a more "natural" approach to beauty as the truest representation of the race:

> *No vulgar grease or hated iron ever touched*
> *Your tangled hair;*
> *No rouge your full red lips, no powder*
> *Ever streaked the midnight blackness of your skin.*[34]

African-American writers, reformers, and educators denounced the cosmetics industry for imposing white standards of beauty on unsophisticated black consumers. In the view of these critics, the irony was that the icons of black economic development exploited black women's desire to look like white women. When the black newspaper *New York Age* accepted an advertisement for a skin-bleaching product with the trade name "Black No More," the politics of the debate escalated.

During this period, ads from the cosmetics industry accounted for 30 to 40 percent of the advertising in black newspapers, and in some cases up to 50 percent. George Schuyler, a columnist for the *Messenger,* declared war on the skin-bleaching industry. He used his column to attack black newspapers and magazines that advertised skin lighteners. To Schuyler and other critics, the contradiction was palpable: How could newspapers that espoused black advancement run hair straightener and skin bleach advertisements? One of Schuyler's strongest invectives was directed at an ad for skin bleaching taken out in Garvey's *Negro World.* The columnist observed sarcastically, "Evidently brother Marcus has a new plan for solving the race problem."[35]

Schuyler's opposition to skin bleaching also mobilized him to write a satiric novel entitled *Black No More.* The novel's protagonist is an inventor who produces a device that turns African Americans white, thereby creating a crisis for black leaders and the Ku Klux Klan.[36]

Despite the fact that women had pioneered the black cosmetics industry, it was black men who came under attack for upholding the white standard of beauty. Some of the strongest indictments came from club women such as Anna Julia Cooper and Fannie Barrier Williams. Cooper asserted that all black men wanted in women were the "three R's, a little music and a good deal of dancing, a first-rate dress-maker and a bottle of magnolia balm [a skin whitener]."[37] Williams declared that black women have a right "to demand from our best men . . . that they cease to imitate the artificial standards of other people and create a race standard of their own."[38] It was T. Thomas Fortune, the *New York Age* editor, who pointed out the contradiction that the black leaders who "clamor most loudly and persistently for the purity of Negro blood have taken themselves mulatto wives."[39]

In her oft-quoted essay "Not Color but Character," Nannie Burroughs shifted the condemnation from black men to the black women who purchased the products. What every woman who "bleached and straightened" her hair needed was not her "appearance changed" but "her mind." In Burroughs's view these women had a "false notion as to the value of color and hair in solving the problems of her life." Many blacks, she asserted, "have colorphobia as badly as white folks have Negrophobia." She traced the history of the "color" problem within the black community to slavery, arguing that more advantages had accrued to those lighter-skinned blacks who were the progeny of the slave owners. These advantages persisted after emancipation, and by the 1890s the "mulatto elite" had a distinctive advantage over other blacks.[40]

Perhaps criticisms were directed at black men during this period rather than the black women entrepreneurs in the cosmetics industry because businesswomen like Walker and Malone worked tirelessly to counter them. These women stressed racial pride, refusing to sell skin bleach and emphasizing hair care rather than straightening. They also neutralized their critics by their energetic and influential involvement in political and social activism.

Madam C. J. Walker, in particular, utilized innovative approaches to obtain the support of her opposition. One example is the contest run by the Walker Company to reward a "race leader" with a trip to the Holy Land. Even George Schuyler, one of the strongest critics of the black cosmetics industry, commended her meritorious leadership and designated her a "Race Wonder Woman." Upon the death of Madam C. J. Walker, however, the Negro Universal Protective Association denounced her for having promoted white emulation.[41]

The evolution of the beauty industry heaped more contradictions onto the plight of black women, which had always been replete with irony. The success of the black women entrepreneurs was initially empowering, setting an example of successful independent achievement by enterprising women. Because of its very success, however, the industry was partly coopted by men. Moreover, much of the industry rested on the premise that black women consumers should emulate a white ideal. As Jim Crow tightened its grip on black southerners, caricatures of unruly hair and oily skin proliferated, and new cosmetic preparations promised relief from these stereotypical images.

Nor was this all. As the white standard underlying products like skin bleachers and hair straighteners came under fire, many advocated a black standard of beauty. While such a standard might have been an advance in terms of racial pride and identity, it hardly represented progress for women. Either standard only served to elevate beauty—outward appearance—over women's authentic qualities and achievements. As so often in the history of black Americans, what was "good" for the race was disastrous for women.

Commercialized "Beauty" and Black Womanhood

At the same time that the "New Negro" movement transformed the image of the African-American male into a militant and aggressive figure, attention was being focused on the outward appearance of black women. In a 1904 issue of the magazine *Voice of the Negro,* John H. Adams, Jr., sketched the "New Negro" woman and described her as possessing "the sober consciousness of true womanhood the same as her white or red or olive sisters." Adams envisioned her countenance, mannerisms, and facial features in the likeness of white Victorian womanhood.[42] The black press had always documented women's work and influence in clubs, churches, and civic organizations, but now attention shifted to women's grooming and beauty. Photographs of beautiful black women—usually with light skin and anglicized features—ran in black newspapers and magazines as representing icons of racial pride.

One of the most demeaning examples of this double standard was found in the *Pittsburgh Courier.* On the front page of the April 7, 1923, issue there was a photograph of a beautiful African-American woman with the caption "Must the Flapper go? We hope not."[43] A scarcely more subtle example appeared in an editorial entitled "The 'New Negro'" in the *Messenger,* the self-proclaimed only "radical" magazine. Whereas the editorial described the "New Negro" man as demanding political and economic equality, it portrayed the "New Negro" woman as "beautiful and intelligent."[44]

Capitalizing on the status hierarchy based on skin color and hair texture and the boom in commercialized beauty, Claude Barnett designed a captivating advertising campaign with visual innovation and sophisticated copy targeted at a more urbane and sophisticated black consumer.[45] What was especially new and different about Barnett's approach to advertising, however, is that it appealed to "modernity, beauty, and romance." In particular, whereas the ads of Walker and Malone focused on hair growth, scalp disease, and poorly attended-to skin, Barnett's ads linked women's beauty to courtship and marriage. The subliminal message was that the consumer of his cosmetic products would soon be headed for the bridal altar. One ad guaranteed that if the product was used properly, the consumer would get what "every" woman wanted—"masculine admiration and matrimony." An ad for Kashmir, a hair product, featured a black soldier being reunited with his beloved. The caption read, "Those French Mam'selles haven't a thing on my Kashmir Girl."[46]

At the same time that Barnett was showcasing his innovative approach to advertising, beauty culturalists such as Walker and Malone marketed their products in churches, club women's meetings, and black colleges, using a combination of conventional advertising and word of mouth. In contrast, Barnett utilized attractive black models with images that were interchangeable with those found in white women's magazines, with the exception that black models generally had long hair whereas white models wore the flapper's bob. His approach was so successful that Walker and Malone adopted it.

While other black men entered the commercialized beauty industry, Claude Barnett was more successful than his male predecessors. He not only built a financially lucrative business but is generally credited with teaching Walker and Malone how to market their products more successfully. Although Nannie Burroughs predicted that black women wouldn't "give a cent for a changed appearance of this sort—a superficial nothing," Barnett discovered that black women from all walks of life were willing to pay substantial sums of money. He understood that the romantic attraction between black men and women was based on external characteristics that emulated a white standard of beauty. In addition, he grasped black women's desire for romance and marriage and developed a marketing strategy that assured them of tangible results.[47]

Despite the seeming growth in political and social consciousness in the African-American community, advertisers found that visual images based on the consumer's African heritage generally did not produce profits. Over time, the issue of an appropriate standard of beauty was depoliticized. While the controversy faded, what remained was the emphasis on external beauty as a defining ideal for black women.

When marriage rates for black men and white men were compared for the first time in 1939, there were some surprisingly dramatic differences. Whereas 72 per 1,000 white males married that year, 99 per 1,000 of the black males married. This gap in men's marriage rates remained constant until 1950 when white men finally caught up with black men.[48] (See Figure 2 in Appendix.) Although there are no data on whether marriage rates for black women increased simultaneously with their newly acquired ability to emulate white beauty standards, the commercialized beauty industry can probably take some of the credit for the marital achievements of black women during this period. What also seems clear is that this emphasis on beauty and romance was consistent with other efforts to disparage black women's leadership and propel them back into their "rightful" place in the home. The fact that these marriages were built on such a dubious foundation may also explain in part why eventually they would be in a state of jeopardy.

The Declining Influence of the Club Women

The end of World War I, coupled with the passage of the woman suffrage amendment in 1920, ushered in the era of the "New Negro" and the "New Woman." The New Woman movement represented middle-class and upper-class white women's foray into the partisan political arena. The term came into vogue in 1890 and signaled the expansion of women's opportunities and roles. As both movements gained support, there was a decline in the appeal of the "women's era" philosophy espoused by the black club women. What is more interesting about these parallel developments is that as white women were coming off the pedestal and being given a voice in the public sphere, the leadership role that women had historically occupied in the black community was being diminished. The most shattering blows to black club women came from a shift in the attitudes toward sexuality.

The club women's movement had its roots in a middle-class,

Victorian morality. During the 1920s, however, both black and white women moved toward a set of beliefs that affirmed sexual pleasure as a value in itself. For white women this period represented not only the ability to vote but the ability to give expression to the modern sexual freedom represented by the flapper. For poor and working-class black women, the blues culture emerged to provide an antidote to their life of never-ending work. This culture conveyed black women's desire to give expression to their sensual side—to enjoy sex for both emotional and financial gain.[49] This shift in values contributed to the erosion of the popularity of the club women's message of sexual purity and chastity.

There were some clear differences in the messages transmitted by the white flappers and the black blues singers. Although both groups were asserting their autonomy and independence, the flapper was puerile and feminine, whereas the blues singer was erotic and lascivious.[50]

Blues singers and their listeners were part of a sexual liberation development that was alarming to the club women. They had worked hard to instill the values of moral purity and chastity into their poorer counterparts, and they viewed these changes in sexual mores as an affront to all their burdensome labor.

As the decade of the 1920s progressed, club women were vociferous in their repudiation of black women's public expression of their sexuality. The views of club women on this issue were discussed in a symposium convened in 1927 titled "Negro Woman's Greatest Needs." Mrs. Joe Brown, one of the presenters at the assembly of black club women, echoed the views of women in attendance that black women could not afford to "imitate" those white women who adopted the new sexuality. She further asserted that the "greatest need of the Negro woman is to set up a standard of her own."[51] The club women's protest went unheeded.

Another major contributing factor in the decline of the club women's influence was the impetus of the "New Negro" movement in the 1920s with its emphasis on black male leadership and authority.[52] The tide turned for black men during this new era. Club women receded from visible leadership, and black women generally were eclipsed by black men. Gloria Hull, who has written extensively about the Harlem Renaissance, observed that "men were in vogue."[53] During this period the groundwork was laid for black males to emerge as spokespersons on matters of importance to the African-American community and to be selected as advisers when policies were developed that would affect the black community. When Franklin Delano Roosevelt drafted his New Deal policies in the 1930s, his "Black Cabinet" included Robert L. Vann, William H. Hastie, Robert C. Weaver, Eugene Kinckle Jones, and Lawrence A. Oxley.

The only African-American woman included as an adviser to FDR was Mary McLeod Bethune, founder-president of the Bethune-Cookman College and the director of the Division of Negro Affairs of the National Youth Administration (NYA).[54] The insight she gleaned from her position at the NYA set the ideological foundation for the National Council of Negro Women (NCNW). Her conception was that the council would be a voice for Negro womanhood in all agencies of the Roosevelt administration. The council was the most influential of all the national black women's organizations to emerge during this period, and the longest lived. Given that there was so little input from black women, it is not surprising that FDR left an ambiguous legacy for African Americans, especially policies that would affect black single mothers and their children living in poverty.[55]

In the 1960s when President Lyndon B. Johnson, FDR's spiritual heir, wanted to tap black advisers on a speech he was planning to deliver at the Howard University commencement, three black men consulted with him—Martin Luther King, Jr., Roy Wilkins, and Whitney Young—and other male representatives from their respective organizations.[56] In this speech Johnson was planning to discuss what he thought could be a controversial topic: the problems with the black family structure and some statistics included in a report by one of his aides, Daniel Patrick Moynihan. The Moynihan Report, as it came to be known, presented a condensation of over three decades of social science research on the marriage and family patterns of black Americans, characterizing them as a "tangle of pathology." The report's contents created a controversy that would reverberate for years throughout a nation already beleaguered by some of the most menacing racial turmoil in its history. Without including black women in the decision-making process, these leaders expressed approval of the speech. Robert Carter, the general counsel for the NAACP, commended the president for having an amazing comprehension of the "debilitation that results from slum living." A spokesman for the National Urban League commented that many of the ideas in the speech seemed to come from Whitney Young's book *To Be Equal.* Martin Luther King stressed that public awareness of the problems experienced by the black family would offer the opportunity to "deal fully rather than haphazardly with the problem as a whole."[57]

Like her mentor and predecessor in the NCNW, Mary McLeod Bethune, Dorothy Height was generally the only black woman invited to meetings that brought major civil rights leaders together. For example, when there was an organizing session for the March on Washington in 1963, where King delivered his celebrated "I Have a Dream" speech, she was the only woman invited to attend. The fact that Height was the only woman in attendance probably explains why women were not included as speakers on the original program.[58] Attention to these patterns of male dominance and leadership in the African-American community were eclipsed in part by the Moynihan Report when it focused attention on the "matriarchal" black family.

Conclusion

The first few decades of the twentieth century brought striking changes in the relations of black women and their men. While black women entrepreneurs in the beauty industry continued the tradition of women's enterprise and leadership that had begun after Reconstruction, black businessmen soon entered into competition with them. Moreover, the beauty culturalists left an ambiguous legacy for black women whether they fostered emulation of a white standard of beauty or simply emphasized women's external characteristics over substantial attributes and achievements.

Meanwhile, the new militancy among African Americans that developed during and after World War I was entwined with a philosophy of male dominance. Progressive opposition to racism took the form of a "new manhood" exemplified by Marcus Garvey's Universal Negro Improvement Association. The new manhood movement simultaneously promoted the interests of blacks and reinforced the submission of black women, creating a legacy that would reappear in the civil rights movement of the 1960s.

By the 1920s the heyday of the black club women was passing under the twin assaults of the new manhood movement and a post-Victorian sexual morality. The demise of the club women's movement symbolized the more general eclipse of black women as leaders. Black men came to the forefront as the primary victims of racism and spokespersons for race. The two exceptions were Mary McLeod Bethune and her successor, Dorothy Height. As we will see in the next chapter, these dynamics would only be heightened by the phenomenon of lynching and the symbolic meaning it acquired in the minds of blacks and whites alike.

5

The Allure of
Miss Anne

By loving me she [the white woman] proves I am
worthy of white love. I am loved like a white man. I
am a white man. Her love takes me onto the noble
road that leads to total realization. I marry white culture, white beauty, white whiteness.

— FRANTZ FANON, *Black Skin, White Masks*

The myth of the sanctity of "white womanhood"
is nothing more than a myth, but because this
myth is acted upon as if it were real both by blacks
and whites alike, then it becomes real as far
as the behavior and sensitivities of those who
encounter it are concerned.

— CALVIN C. HERNTON, *Sex and Racism in America*

AMONG THE MANY TENSIONS
and stresses operating in rela-
tionships between black women and their men, perhaps none is
more emotionally volatile than the issue of sexual liaisons between
black men and white women. This issue entered into popular culture in 1967 when Sidney Poitier starred as a young white woman's
fiancé in Stanley Kramer's film *Guess Who's Coming to Dinner*. A

generation later, Spike Lee captured the black community's attention with his 1991 film *Jungle Fever*. In Lee's film a dark-skinned black man named Flipper (played by Wesley Snipes) is married to a fair-skinned woman, Drew (Lonette McKee). They live in what appears to be wedded bliss until Flipper becomes romantically involved with his white secretary, Angie (Annabella Sciorra). When Drew discovers they are having an affair, she is predictably incensed, but it is not so much because Flipper has been unfaithful as it is that the vixen is a white woman.

A number of historical and social influences have interacted to make the issue of relationships between black men and white women both potent and symbolic. To understand the allure of Miss Anne is to understand some of the most profound factors at work in the relationships of black women and their men.[1]

The Threat of the "New Negro"

In the decades following the collapse of Reconstruction in the South, the "slavery problem" that had ripped the country apart in the 1860s was transmuted into the "race problem." For white southerners the issue was not how the races could live peaceably, let alone in harmony, but how to keep the millions of blacks "in their place" as a source of cheap labor and domestic help while ensuring the survival of whites' social, political, and economic dominance. In short, the "race problem" reduced to a question of social control. Any signs that white control was threatened provoked deep fear and violent repression.

The obsession with control of blacks, particularly black men, was nowhere more obvious than in matters related to sex. Both as an issue in its own right and as symbolic expression of the larger issue of social control, sex was never far from the surface of white southerners' view of the race problem. Not only did whites' racial ideology call for safeguarding the "purity" of the white race but nothing was more symbolically threatening to the established social order than the prospect of black men having sexual relations with white women. This idea was so abhorrent to white men that they could never consciously acknowledge the reality of white women freely engaging in sexual relations with a black man. The only way they could conceive of these liaisons was with the black man assaulting the white woman. As for relations between white men and black women, the same double standard persisted that had prevailed during slavery: Whereas white women would never willingly have relations with black men, it was impossible for black women, who were "naturally lascivious," to be raped.

The imagery of sexual assault frequently dominated white southerners' depictions of the "New Negro" who had grown up in freedom and failed to show the submissiveness whites increasingly associated with the "Old Negro" of antebellum times. The "New Negro" was said to be prone to criminal behavior, and the exemplar of such behavior was the crime of sexual assault. At a conference convened in 1900, ostensibly to examine deteriorating race relations, a prominent psychologist told those in attendance that "the crime of assault is the crime of the 'New Negro'—not of the slave nor the ex-slave." This psychologist was not saying anything new but was simply repeating arguments being verbalized throughout the country. At the same conference, Alexander C. King, an eminent lawyer, asserted that black men were demonstrating their "power for revenge" by assaulting white women.[2] A Harvard-trained attorney and historian of the New South, Philip A. Bruce likewise lamented the passing of the "Old Negro" and charged black men with committing "beastly and loathsome" sexual attacks on white women. He went further than any of the others, however, when he stated that these attacks were unique even in the "natural history of the most bestial and ferocious animals."[3]

Some of the clearest messages during this period were delivered by white elected officials. For example, Ben "Pitchfork" Tillman, who served as governor of South Carolina and was later in the U.S.

Senate, was often quoted as saying one of his greatest fears was that one of his daughters would be "robbed" of the "purity" of her "maidenhood" by a "black fiend."[4]

Leon Litwack has suggested that, in part at least, the white community's obsession with protecting the chastity of white women betrayed whites' awareness of their double standard: "Concern over black rapists ... sometimes masked the fear that the sexual aggression by whites on black women would stimulate in black men the desire for revenge on white women."[5] It was Rebecca Felton, an ardent Georgia crusader, who accepted the challenge of raising the public's awareness concerning the dangers the "New Negro" posed to white womanhood. She applauded "old-time" Negroes for their "loyalty and fidelity" and described younger blacks as "half-civilized gorillas." To protect against criminal assaults by black men, Felton advocated around-the-clock male protection for white women. The governor of Georgia, William J. Northern, echoed Felton's concerns and recommended that whites' homes be turned into "miniature arsenals" and that women be taught the use and handling of firearms and be allowed to carry them.[6]

James K. Vardaman, a Mississippi politician, simultaneously praised the "good Negroes" of the South and defended whites' right to slaughter "every Ethiopian on the earth to preserve unsullied the honor of one Caucasian home." Vardaman acknowledged that "good Negroes" might occasionally be victimized but rationalized that "the good are few, the bad are many." He concluded with a Machiavellian caveat: Racial self-preservation took precedence over legal and moral niceties.[7]

As white fear continued to escalate, some blacks in leadership positions placed the blame for rousing whites to violence on the "criminal" class of young blacks. In an 1899 article entitled "Possible Remedies for Lynching," Kelly Miller, a black college professor, cautioned that there were blacks who "were giving the whole race an evil reputation." According to Miller, black women likewise needed protection from these "black ruffians."[8] Ten years later Sutton Griggs, a black author and Baptist minister, echoed Miller's concerns. Although Griggs used fictional characters to invoke racial pride, his heroes eschewed the use of violence to redress racial wrongs. In contrast, Griggs lamented the appearance of the "bad Negro" and his "demoralizing influence" on the black community.[9]

As a child growing up in Mississippi, novelist Richard Wright remembered black men in his community who had disdain for customs and taboos, violated the laws, and were gratified only when they outsmarted whites. Wright admitted that these men left a "marked impression" on him and that he wanted to emulate some of them. As he matured, he realized that they paid an incredibly high price in that they were "shot, hanged, maimed, or lynched" until they were dead or their spirits were broken.[10] The message to black men was abundantly clear: Defy any of the taboos defined by whites and you will pay, very likely with your life.

The Legacy of Jack Johnson

One of the black men who left a "marked impression" on Richard Wright was Jack Johnson. Born in Galveston, Texas, in 1878, Johnson shocked the country in 1908 when he defeated Tommy Burns, a white man, in a championship boxing match. Johnson not only outfought Burns but taunted, ridiculed, and humiliated him in the ring. The outcome of the fight electrified the black community. The headline in a black newspaper in Richmond, Virginia, proudly proclaimed, "A Southern Negro Is Heavyweight Champion of the World." The newspaper report went on to say that "no event in forty years has given more genuine satisfaction to the colored people of this country."[11]

After Johnson defeated Burns, Jim Jeffries, a previously unbeaten champion, was persuaded to come out of retirement even

117

though he had publicly stated that he would never step into the ring with a black man. The Jeffries-Johnson bout was billed as the "fight of the century," and blacks and whites alike accorded it enormous symbolic importance. When Johnson entered the ring, the band tunefully expressed the attitudes of white spectators by playing "All Coons Look Alike to Me." Jeffries, however, was no match for Johnson and suffered a humiliating beating.

For the black community, Johnson's victory was an extraordinary triumph in an era of bewildering setbacks. By the same token, southern whites responded with anger and stepped up their violent repression of black men. In the racially tense postfight atmosphere, an Alabama judge admonished friends of a recently released black assailant:

> You niggers are getting beside yourselves since Jack Johnson won a fight from a white man. I want you to mind what you do in this town. Remember, you are in the South, and remember further that when you speak to white gentlemen you should speak in a way that is best becoming a Nigger.[12]

Benjamin Mays was fourteen at the time of the bout and remembers that blacks could not discuss the outcome of the fight in the presence of whites. Riots broke out in a number of places, and many blacks were killed. In Mays's view, Jack Johnson committed two grave blunders as far as whites were concerned: "He beat up a white man and he was socializing with a white woman—both deadly sins in 1908."[13]

Among black men, especially working-class blacks in desperate need of a hero, Johnson commanded enormous admiration. At a time when southern blacks were assaulted or killed for no better reason than that they had begun to achieve some material success, Johnson brandished his fashionable clothes, high-priced jewelry, and expensive automobiles. Whereas the majority of black men felt compelled to wear a mask of submissiveness, Johnson made no attempt to conceal his feelings toward whites and brazenly violated nearly every custom and social taboo. Most strikingly of all, he not only consorted with white women but married three of them.

Reports of Johnson's prowess and wit were disseminated throughout the black community. The accuracy of the folkloric tales made little difference:

It was a hot day in Georgia when Jack Johnson drove into town. He was really flying. Zoooom! Behind his fine car was a cloud of red Georgia dust as far as the eye could see. The sheriff flagged him down and said, "Where do you think you are going, boy, speeding like that? That'll cost you $50.00!" Jack Johnson never looked up; he just reached in his pocket and handed the sheriff a $100.00 bill and started to gun the motor; ruuummm, ruu-ummm. Just before Jack pulled off the sheriff shouted, " Don't you want your change?" And Jack replied, "Keep it, 'cause I'm coming back the same way I'm going!" Zooooooom.[14]

While many poor and working-class blacks celebrated John-son's exploits, black leaders, more concerned with accommoda-tion than defiance, did not embrace Johnson and viewed his victory as a major setback for race relations. Middle-class blacks, in general, did not view Johnson's image as having a positive effect on either the black community or relations with whites. Through an intermediary, Emmett J. Scott, the personal secretary to Booker T. Washington, endeavored to persuade Johnson to modify his behavior. Scott recommended that Johnson retain a strong manager to subdue his approach. He justified his actions by saying, "I don't like white men to feel that Negroes cannot stand large prosperity."[15]

When D. W. Griffith's racist motion picture *Birth of a Nation* was released to rave reviews in 1915, attention was focused on the black villain, Silas Lynch (the pun was intentional). In the mind of whites, Lynch represented the kind of black male who, much like

Jack Johnson, was insolent and brazen, and lusted after white women. In the aftermath of Johnson's victory, legislation was passed in more than thirty states prohibiting the marriage of blacks and whites. It was not until 1967 that the U.S. Supreme Court struck down the last such law in *Loving v. Virginia.*

Despite the concerns of more conservative black leaders, for many black men Johnson represented the idea of asserting oneself and achieving victory over white men. The tales about him emphasized his bold "impudence," his victories over whites not only in courage and strength but in cunning, and his enjoyment of success and material pleasures—the very things southern black men could not openly achieve or display. But a crucial part of his story was his appropriation of white women. Johnson's sexual adventures represented the smashing of a taboo and a triumph over white men in the most fearfully guarded aspect of their lives. More than that, they represented a validation of his manhood. Johnson had seized the forbidden fruit. In the perverse environment created by racial oppression, conquests of white women counted for more than gaining the respect and affection of black women. Whites saw the same image in reverse: For them, Jack Johnson represented more than an aggressive "New Negro"; he raised the terrifying specter of sexually empowered black men assaulting (or stealing) their women. Southern whites had any number of reasons, acknowledged and otherwise, for maintaining an oppressive control over blacks—but fear of the phallus was never the least of them.

A Reign of Terror

In response to the threat of the "New Negro," lynching, a barbaric form of social control, began to escalate in the post-Reconstruction period. The issue of sex symbolized the threat to the social order that whites perceived. Regardless of all the reasons given by whites for the lynchings of blacks, the number one reason was sexual fear on the part of white men. The situation was exacerbated by Jack

Johnson's ostentatious exhibition of his relationships with white women.

Charges of sexual assault on white women were leveled so systematically against black men that many liberal reformers believed there must be some validity to them. Even Frederick Douglass thought there was "an increasing lasciviousness on the part of Negroes." Although Jane Addams, an advocate for the poor and founder of Hull House, opposed lynchings, she believed that black men had a proclivity for rape. When Ida B. Wells first read about lynching, she likewise questioned whether "perhaps the brute deserved death anyhow and the mob was justified in taking his life."[16]

Wells, however, soon recognized the true nature of lynchings and became a fervent antilynching crusader. Frederick Douglass invited her to Washington, D.C., to speak before a group of black club women, including Anna Julia Cooper and Mary Church Terrell. Wells raised $200 for the antilynching cause, and the meeting concluded in a "blaze of glory." When she opened the newspaper the following morning, she became visibly distraught as she read about one of the most ghastly lynchings to occur during this period. Henry Smith, a black man charged with raping a five-year-old white girl, was tortured with red-hot irons and then burned alive. Schoolchildren were let out of school so they could witness the burning. What was most unsettling for Wells was that after Smith was burned, a mob fought over his remains so they could preserve them for souvenirs.

Horrified by this incident, Wells used the money collected the previous evening to hire a detective to investigate the facts in the case.[17] When the facts were gathered, the story was picked up by periodicals both domestic and abroad. One of the publications to give the issue attention was *The Women's Era,* which scathingly attacked southern white men:

Up to their ears in guilt against Negro women, they offer as their excuse for murdering Negro men, Negro women, and Negro children, that white women are not safe from the Negro rapist. . . . Why did not the slaves, when their masters were away trying to shoot the Union to death and keep them forever slaves, out-rage the wives and daughters of these traitors confided to their care?[18]

Wells, a militant journalist, emerged as the leader of the anti-lynching crusade at the turn of the century. She informed the nation and the world about the powerful connection between lynching, racism, and the cultural notions of white womanhood and black sexuality. Her impassioned editorial in the May 21, 1892, issue of *Free Speech,* which suggested that white women voluntarily engaged in sexual liaisons with black men, aroused hostility and rage among southern white men.

Whatever the reason given for particular lynchings, in reality they were perpetrated to keep blacks in their place, men and women alike. The violation of white women's virtue was the crime that "justified," more than any other, a violent reprisal. So, while lynchings were occasioned by many things and were done to terrorize blacks, they were justified on the basis of sexual "crimes" and never lost their symbolic connection to the sexual issue.

The goal of social control was achieved primarily by exerting every effort to make a public example of the victim. In many instances lynchings were publicized in advance and reported in the newspapers afterward. Many "upstanding" citizens willingly attended the grisly spectacles. Often, the remains of a lynching victim were preserved and sold as souvenirs. On those few occasions when an official inquiry was made into a particular lynching, the typical verdict was that the acts were performed by "persons unknown."

Speculation that a white woman had been sexually assaulted had the effect of justifying almost any kind of action against the alleged black rapist. In Rocky Ford, Mississippi, a white woman reported that she had been raped by a black field hand. When a young black man, J. P. Ivey, was brought in for identification, the rape victim's reaction was that she "thought" he looked like the one who attacked her, but she was not sure. In spite of this inconclusive evidence, an angry mob restrained Ivey and poured gasoline over his body. A crowd of about six hundred spectators watched the flames envelop him as he cried out, "Have mercy, I didn't do it, I didn't do it."[19] In their anxiety to deter sexual assault, lynch mobs did not always pause to ascertain whether the accused was actually guilty. Lynching served its purpose of deterrence and terror regardless.

Most blacks understood that whites' obsession with black men raping white women was not what it seemed. James H. Robinson, a celebrated preacher in the first half of the century, remembered hearing discussions when he was growing up about white women's attraction to black men. It was said that when white men butchered blacks, they were acting out their sexual insecurities. "Negroes were lynched," Robinson heard, "not because they committed crimes but because white men wanted to put fear in their hearts and keep it there."[20] Ida B. Wells captured the prevailing outlook among African-Americans when she wrote: "White men lynch the offending Afro-American not because he is a despoiler of virtue, but because he succumbs to the smiles of white women."[21]

In 1919 the NAACP took the first steps toward securing the passage of a federal law against lynching. James Weldon Johnson, the secretary of the NAACP, worked hard to secure the support of senators and representatives. In 1921, Johnson succeeded in getting Representative L. C. Dyer of Missouri to introduce a bill in the House of Representatives "to assure to persons within the jurisdiction of every state the equal protection of the laws, and to punish the crime of lynching." Congressmen from southern states immediately began organizing to defeat the proposed bill but were not successful. The bill still passed, 230 to 119. The task in the Senate was more challenging, however. The NAACP published full-page ads in the *New York Times* and the *Atlanta Constitution* calling attention to the necessity for such a bill. These efforts failed when southern senators organized a filibuster that ultimately prevented a vote on the measure.

The NAACP was not deterred, however, and hired Walter White to go to the scenes of crimes and conduct a thorough investigation of the lynchings. In 1929, White brought out *Rope and Faggot: A Biography of Judge Lynch,* based on the findings of his lynching investigations covering a ten-year period. He concluded that reports linking lynchings to sexual assaults were baseless in the majority of the cases. Specifically, he found that only 19 percent of the victims were accused of rape. On releasing these findings, White characterized white women as "prone to hysteria" in their reactions to black men. He concluded further that "having created the Frankenstein monster," whites lived in constant fear of their own creation.[22]

One of the most glaring contradictions in the justification of lynchings as reprisals for sexual crimes was the fact that blacks were openly lynched for other alleged crimes as well. Luther Holbert, a black man who lived in Doddsville, Mississippi, had an argument with his white employer, whose corpse was found following their dispute. Holbert and his wife were captured and tied to a tree. According to the local newspaper, approximately one thousand whites stood and watched as the self-appointed executioners tortured, mutilated, and ultimately murdered the couple. Holbert and his wife were forced to hold out their hands while one finger at a time was chopped off. Their ears were likewise cut off. A large corkscrew was used to bore into the couple's arms and legs. When it was pulled out, large pieces of raw flesh were extracted. Two other blacks, mistaken for Holbert, were also slain by a posse.[23]

Furthermore, despite claims that lynchings were intended to punish rapes, black women were not exempt. When the number of lynchings between the years 1889 and 1918 was tabulated, it was found that 2,522 were perpetrated against blacks; fifty of the victims were women.[24] The barbarity of these acts is difficult to conceive. Upon hearing of the lynching of her husband, Mary Turner promised to find those responsible and avenge his death. She was in the eighth month of her pregnancy. Hearing of her threat, a mob of whites set out to "teach her a lesson." First, they tied her ankles together and hung her upside down from a tree. Next, they soaked her clothes with gasoline and burned them from her body. While she was still alive someone took a knife and cut open her abdomen. The infant fell to the ground and cried briefly. Someone from the mob crushed the baby's head with his leather boot. Finally, hundreds of bullets were fired into Mary Turner's body.[25]

The lynching and rape of a black woman in Columbus, Mississippi, was reported by *The Chicago Defender* on December 17, 1915:

> Thursday a week ago Cordella Stevenson was found early in the morning hanging to the limb of a tree, without any clothing, dead. . . . The body was found about fifty yards north of the Mobile & Ohio Railroad, and thousands and thousands of passengers that came in and out of this city last Thursday morning were horrified at the sight. She was hung there from the night before by a bloodthirsty mob who had gone to her home, snatched her from slumber, and dragged her through the streets without any resistance. They carried her to a far-off spot, did their dirt and then strung her up. The white mob simply claimed that a few months earlier Cordella Stevenson's son had burned down a white man's barn.

In future years the memory of lynchings would continue to be associated with the idea of alleged sex crimes, and black men would be remembered as almost the sole victims. In reality, men, women, and sometimes entire families were lynched; black women, in particular, became the forgotten victims of racial violence.

The unrelenting racial violence in the South further destabilized black families and was a major contributor to the increase in the number of families without fathers. Women whose husbands were lynched or run out of town by night riders were forced to either reach out to relatives and friends for their support or develop a great deal of self-reliance. A letter from one southern black farmer hoping to migrate to Kansas furnishes a glimpse of the distress that both black women and men were experiencing:

> We want to come out, and have no money hardly. We have to be in secret or be shot, and [are] not allowed to meet. . . . We have about fifty widows in our band and they are workmen and farmers also. The white men here take our wives and daughters and do [with] them as they please, and we are shot if we say anything about . . . We are sure to have to leave or be killed.[26]

In time, mob violence abated, only to be replaced by legally sanctioned forms of social control. Police and courts took over where the "night riders" had left off. One of the most notorious cases of legal lynching occurred in 1931 when nine black youths were indicted for allegedly raping two white girls on a train between Chattanooga, Tennessee, and Paint Rock, Alabama. The defendants became known as the Scottsboro boys because they were tried in Scottsboro, the county seat of Jackson County, Alabama. Although doctors examined the girls and testified that no rape had occurred, the nine young men were convicted, and eight were sentenced to die. After this decision was rendered, the International Labor Defense took over the case, and the appeals, reversals, and retrials continued until 1937. Twice the Supreme Court reversed lower court convictions, the first time on grounds that the defendants did not have adequate counsel and the second time on grounds of improper jury selection. Eventually, four of the nine were convicted, three were given seventy-five- to ninety-five-year sentences, and one was sentenced to die. Indictments against the other five were dropped.

The Scottsboro case illustrates how the legal system took over the function of social control by summarily convicting southern blacks of alleged sexual crimes and administering rapid and drastic punishment. The reign of terror was far from over—but now it was presided over by lady justice.

Preserving the "Sanctity" of White Women

While lynching was the most visible form of whites' efforts to "safeguard" the sanctity of white women, it was only part of an entire complex of customs and understandings that maintained the sexual taboo and that every southern black man grew up with. The imperative of every mother and grandmother who was raising black males in the South was to teach them that white women were off-limits to them.

Like most black men who grew up in the Jim Crow era in the South, Calvin Hernton vividly remembers his initiation into this societal taboo. The incident occurred when he was in grammar school. Hernton lived with his grandmother about four miles from school. Walking home from school, he met a white girl about his age traveling the same route. They became very close over time. One day his grandmother appeared on the sidewalk before them, and he could sense from the look on her face that something was "terribly wrong." His grandmother literally dragged him home, where she gave him the "beating of my life." When she finished "lashing my backside with her belt," she began to "lash me with her tongue." "Do you want to git yoself lynched? Messing around with a white gurl! ... Do you want to git me kilt? Git all the colored folks slaughtered ..." Hernton remembers his grandmother's words putting a "fear into me that I have never forgotten."[27]

Black males reared in the South were taught that they needed to exercise the greatest caution in their relations with white females. They were admonished that even casual encounters with white women and girls created potentially incendiary situations in which their lives could be abruptly ended. They were taught to avoid situations in which they might be alone in the presence of white women. If they passed a white woman on the street, they were to avoid eye contact by looking down or away. They were also warned not to brush up against white women when they passed them on the street or were in crowded situations with them.

Black mothers rearing sons in the South faced these challenges regardless of their income or level of education. Lugenia Burns Hope recalled coming home on a crowded streetcar with one of her sons. A white woman got on, and there were no seats on the streetcar. Her young son immediately got up and offered his seat to the woman. But even courteous gestures were taboo. According to Hope, her son's innocent action caused "a stir if not a racial 'incident.'"[28]

For black men the message was clear: They must stifle their human impulses and always remember to avoid acting as if they were equal to whites. Ralph Ellison remarked that parents needed to "adjust the child to the Southern milieu ... to protect him from the unknown forces within himself which might urge him to reach out for that social and human equality which the white South says he cannot have. Rather then throw himself against the charged wires of his prison, he annihilates the impulses within him."[29]

The taboo regarding interaction with white women was significant both in itself and for its symbolic value as the ultimate expression of whites' determination to maintain the system of social inequality. Beyond segregated facilities and the noxious "Whites Only" and "No Coloreds" signs that proliferated over parks, restaurants, bathrooms, and the like, an entire system of social control relied on a tacit understanding of what behavior was permissible and what was not. Generations of black children learned how to survive in a culture that viciously punished deviations from the prescribed norms. As late as the 1950s, Hylan Lewis, an African-American sociologist who studied the subculture in a southern mill town, found that black children, especially males, were socialized by black parents to "get along." Blacks employed various techniques to reduce "tension and frustration." In Lewis's view, two basic patterns of behavior emerged. The first was one of maintaining a studied reserve, wherein no genuine intimacy was possible between blacks and whites. The second pattern set limits on approved or even permitted behavior toward whites.[30]

Blacks reared in the North were not as tentative in their dealings with white women as those who came of age in the South. If they ventured to southern states, however, they were expected to modify their normal ways of acting. While a student at Fisk University, W. E. B. Du Bois accidentally brushed up against a white woman on a Nashville street. Immediately, "in accord with his New England upbringing," he raised his hat and apologized. The white woman was furious, and Du Bois was fortunate to escape without reprisal.

A black college president who, unlike Du Bois, was socialized in the South, related an incident that occurred to him at a railroad station in Atlanta. He heard a woman scream behind him—she had caught her heel on the steps and was falling headfirst. Instinctively, he raised his arms to catch her when he suddenly remembered where he was and dropped them to his sides. The white woman fell and suffered serious injuries—a victim of the customs she undoubtedly embraced.[31]

The landmark case of white male retaliation for black male sexual transgression against white women occurred in Leflore County, Mississippi. In 1955 a fisherman pulled the decomposed body of a dead black boy out of the Tallahatchie River. The corpse had been severely beaten, and the face was mutilated beyond recognition. A ring on one finger led to a positive identification of the victim, Emmett Till. Two white men, J. W. Millam and Roy Bryant, his halfbrother, were promptly arrested for Till's murder.

The facts in the Till case were never seriously disputed—not even by Millam and Bryant after a jury found them not guilty. Emmett Till, a fourteen-year-old visiting from Chicago, deviated from the southern racial codes by regaling the black youth of the small Mississippi town with tales of his exploits with white girls up north. He even proudly displayed a picture of one white girl that he carried in his wallet. Reared according to the social taboos in the South, his skeptical buddies dared the Chicago newcomer to walk into Bryant's general store and ask the lady who was alone behind the counter, Bryant's young wife, for a date. Till took the dare. Pistol in hand, Carolyn Bryant chased him from the store. As he retreated rapidly, in a gesture of adolescent grandiosity, Till "wolf-whistled" at her. For this "crime" Till was brutally murdered.[32]

Medgar Evers, who was later killed by a sniper's bullet, had recently accepted the position as field director for the NAACP. Evers organized blacks to boycott merchants as a protest of Till's tragic death.

The Emmett Till case is generally regarded as one of the critical events that paved the road to the civil rights movement. That same year Rosa Parks, a black woman in Montgomery, Alabama, refused to move to the back of a bus. Her action catalyzed the Montgomery bus boycott and the emergence of Martin Luther King, Jr. By the time four black students at North Carolina Agricultural and Technical College launched the sit-in movement at a segregated lunch counter in 1960, the stage was set for the beginning of the most profound changes in the status of African Americans since emancipation. One of these changes would ironically be the repeal of the antimiscegenation laws, making it possible for the first time for blacks, especially black men, not only to have sexual relations with whites but also to marry them.

The Outbreak of "Jungle Fever"

The attraction between black men and white women had been an issue since the times of slavery, but the passage of antimiscegenation laws prevented them from having legal marriages to each other. Before the passages of these laws there were notable examples of prominent black men marrying white women. Frederick Douglass had married a black woman, Annie Murray Douglass, the first time around. She was the mother of his two sons and reportedly made the suit he was wearing when he escaped from slavery.

When Annie Murray Douglass died in the summer of 1882, Douglass married Helen Pitts, a white woman, eighteen months later. In a ground-breaking new book entitled *Love Across the Color Lines,* Maria Diedrich has asserted that while Douglass was married to Annie, he had an affair with German journalist Ottilie Assing, a relationship that endured for twenty-eight years. Assing justified her relationship with Frederick by arguing that the "Douglass marriage had been over long before she entered the scene." When Douglass married Helen Pitts, someone twenty years Assing's junior, the following August she committed suicide with a dose of potassium cyanide.[33]

Ida B. Wells, once a guest in the Douglass home, was told by Frederick Douglass that only she and another black woman had treated his white wife with respect, the way "she has the right to be treated by her guest." Wells admitted that like other black women she would have preferred for Douglass to marry "one of the beautiful, charming colored women of my race."[34]

Another prominent black man, John Hope, the first black president of Atlanta University, a "race man" and close friend of W. E. B. Du Bois, was rumored to have extramarital affairs, "especially with white women."[35] Hope had a long-term marriage to a black woman, Lugenia Burns Hope, who had a distinguished career as a social work reformer. This is the same man who accused Atlanta club women of being "more masculine than feminine" and recommended that they model themselves after Florence Nightingale and Jane Addams, whom he commended for being "distinctively feminine."[36]

The issue of black/white intermarriage took a dramatic turn in the 1950s when Walter L. White, the executive secretary of the NAACP, divorced his black wife and the mother of his children to marry a white woman. Coincidentally, White's administrative assistant, Leslie Perry, was also married to a white woman. Vitriolic attacks were directed at White from the black community for his decision, and the *Norfolk Journal and Guide*, a black publication, even called for a "prompt and official announcement" of his resignation. The following year the NAACP lost 168,000 members, representing a 40 percent decline in its membership.[37]

At about the same time that two of the most visible black men in America were making nuptial commitments to white women, *Ebony* featured an article entitled "80,000 Negro Girls Will Never Go to the Altar." As black women searched frantically for suitable mates, roughly 50,000 black men were married to white women.[38]

The views of many black women that they were losing the most eligible black men to white women was captured in the words of a poem written by Langston Hughes:

> *Into the laps*
> *of black celebrities*
> *white girls fall*
> *like pale plums from a tree*
> *beyond a high tension wall*
> *wired for killing*
> *which makes it*
> *more thrilling.*[39]

For black women the loss of black men involved not only the men's attraction to white women but the behavior of white women themselves. If there was any doubt in the minds of black women that white women were in aggressive pursuit of black men, it was obliterated when a white woman wrote an open letter to the *Negro Digest* entitled "I Want to Marry a Negro." The anonymous woman noted that she found black men "exceedingly beautiful" and that in her view white men could not "match certain elements of the black man's beauty." She confessed that her attraction to black men has "deepened with every year."[40] The letter was followed by an article entitled "Are White Women Stealing Our Men?" This second piece was written by an anonymous but "socially prominent" black woman whose husband had deserted her for a white woman. She accused black leaders of practicing their own "happy doctrine of love thy neighbor." She added that although black men would not admit it, it "flatters" them to no end to have "white women prefer their bed and board" to that of a white man.[41]

Needless to say, black women were angry at black men for succumbing to the wiles of white women and were likewise angry at white women for being so aggressive in their attempts to "catch" a black man. E. Franklin Frazier, a highly respected black sociologist, infuriated black women further when he analyzed the competitive dynamics in this way:

> There is an intense fear of the competition of white women for Negro men. . . . The middle-class Negro woman's fear of the competition of white women is based often upon the fact that she senses her own inadequacies and shortcomings. . . . The middle-class white woman not only has white skin and straight hair, but she is generally more sophisticated and interesting because she has read more widely and has a larger view of the world.[42]

In the minds of black women, the preferences of black men reverberated in the lyrics of the "Negro punster" song:

> *She got to be white, Jack—*
> *'Cause white is right*
> *Both day and night!*
> *She got to be old and white,*
> *'Cause if she's old*
> *She's been white longer!*

133

She got to be big and white,
'Cause if she's big
She's much more white!
But listen, Jack—
If she just can't be white
Then let her be real light brown![43]

Between 1960 and 1997 interracial marriages increased sixfold, with twice as many black men as women marrying outside the race.[44] Given that black women greatly outnumber black men, many black women are infuriated by the loss of black males to white women, and they are giving expression to their ire in a myriad of ways. For example, in 1995 black women at Brown University inaugurated a "Wall of Shame" in a dormitory and listed the names of black men who dated white women.

Why do black men continue to marry white women at much higher rates than black women marry white men? M. Belinda Tucker and Claudia Mitchell-Kernan of the Center for African American Studies at UCLA have posited that women choose a mate based on earning capacity, whereas men are primarily concerned with physical beauty. The white-dominated media still present a largely Eurocentric standard of beauty exemplified by straight hair, light skin, and blue eyes.[45] Consequently, black men are drawn to choose as mates women who express this standard of beauty.

Charles V. Willie, a black Harvard University professor who is married to a white woman, has offered a different explanation. He has asserted that the attraction between black men and white women is related to their "separate but comparable vulnerabilities"—he in being a black male, she in being a female. The equality in the relationship, coupled with uncertainty about which party will dominate, generates sexual tension and excitement.[46]

Although these scholars are correct in pointing to some of the factors that influence men's and women's selection of mates, both analyses overlook a critically important point. Relationships between black men and white women can only be understood in the light of the social, psychological, and cultural context in which attitudes on interracial sex relations are formed. One frequently overlooked factor is the oppressive Jim Crow policies and practices developed by white men to preserve the "sanctity" of white women, thereby creating the "allure" [of forbidden fruit] and unwittingly establishing "conquests" of white women as a sign of black manhood.

Private Turmoil in Black Marriages

At the same time as the issue of black men marrying outside the race became highly public, black women's anxiety and insecurities were exacerbated by skyrocketing divorce rates among African Americans. Divorce rates were four times as high as those for whites during the 1950s and 1960s.[47] In April 1950, in an article entitled "Why Men Leave Home," St. Clair Drake, a black sociologist, identified the problem in black marriages as the male's "weakened" position due to his marginalized economic role within the family. The tone of this piece was Drake's concern that the black man was losing his patriarchal authority within the family.[48] The Pulitzer Prize–winning poet Gwendolyn Brooks wrote a rejoinder entitled "Why Negro Women Leave Home." Brooks asserted that black women leave not because of the black man's financial problems but because they are endeavoring to maintain "dignity and self-respect." From a black woman's perspective, women married to men with good incomes sometimes "resent dollar dole-outs," and some men make their wives "beg him for money." She closed by saying that a man who "respects" his wife as a person is not likely to lose her.[49] According to Brooks, it was not the size of a black man's paycheck that mattered so much as the respect he showed his wife.

Pauli Murray, an outspoken lawyer, black feminist, and Episcopalian priest, agreed with Drake that many black women had been "compelled to act as breadwinner and cementer of family relation-ships." Murray, however, blamed both black males and females for the emerging crisis in marital relationships. She faulted black men for their failure to stay in school, noting that as teenagers they "abandon their studies in droves" and "flounder about for years without vocational direction." As a result, black professional women had a "potential earning power" that far exceeded that of many black males. The emotional aspect of black marriages also con-tributed to their instability, Murray contended. In her view, a black man was unprepared to offer emotional support to his wife be-cause "he has rarely, if ever, known it himself." But while Murray charged black men with giving "vent to his resentments," she also characterized black professional women as the "most aggressive of the human species." She exhorted black men not to attempt to dominate black women or they would come "face to face with emotional disaster." Rather, black men must learn to treat black women as their equals and to end their "ruthless aggression" against them.[50]

Blaming Black Mothers

Ever since John Hope admonished the club women of Atlanta to "become more womanly," attention has been focused on deficien-cies in black women that supposedly contributed to black men's at-traction to white women. Frequently, black mothers were blamed. Calvin Hernton, a social scientist and author of the critically ac-claimed book *Sex and Racism in America*, reflecting on the effect that his grandmother's punitive child-rearing patterns had on him, realized that "there arose in me an incipient resentment towards my grandmother, indeed, towards all black women."[51] Richard Wright, reflecting the predicament of black families in the Jim Crow South, echoed Hernton's generalized rage at black mothers when he wrote of his first fight with white boys.

I sat brooding on my front steps, nursing my wound and waiting for my mother to come home from work.... When night fell my mother came from the white folks' kitchen. I raced down the street to meet her. I could just feel in my bones that she would understand. I knew she would tell me exactly what to do next time. I grabbed her hand and babbled out the whole story. She examined my wound, then slapped me.

"How come yuh didn't hide?" she asked me. "How come yuh always fightin'?"

I was outraged and bawled. Between sobs I told her that I didn't have any trees or hedges to hide behind.... She grabbed a barrel stave, dragged me home, stripped me naked and beat me till I had a fever of one hundred and two. She would smack my rump with the stave and while the skin was still smarting, impart to me gems of Jim Crow wisdom. I was never to throw cinders any more.... I was never, never, under any conditions, to fight *white* folks again.... Didn't I know that she was working hard every day in the hot kitchens of the white folks to make money to take care of me? When was I ever going to learn to be a good boy?[52]

Like Calvin Hernton, Price M. Cobbs and William H. Grier, black psychiatrists in private practice, accused black mothers of inflicting "senseless pain" on their sons. In their view the child-rearing practices of black mothers "blunted their assertiveness and aggression" and contributed to the black male's development of "considerable hostility toward black women." Black women experienced a "bottomless well of self-depreciation," and their child-rearing practices were derived not so much from concern for their children as from "personal frustration and self-hatred." Cobbs and Grier concluded by asserting that the concept of femininity is "only imperfectly grasped by most black women."[53]

Prominent white social scientists followed suit and likewise took aim at black women. Thomas Pettigrew, a renowned social psychologist at Harvard University who had written widely during the 1960s on the African-American family, accused the black woman of being so overwrought with her husband's financial dependence that her "rejection of him further alienates the male from family life."[54]

Pettigrew went further than any of the other social scientists when he declared, "Embittered by their experiences with men, many black mothers often act to perpetuate the mother-centered pattern by taking a greater interest in their daughters than their sons."[55] Whitney Young, the president of the Urban League, echoed Pettigrew's perspective when he accused black mothers of making "sure that if one of their children had a choice for higher education the daughter was the one to pursue it."[56]

An even harsher criticism of black women came from militant activist Eldridge Cleaver in 1968. In his book *Soul on Ice*, Cleaver expressed a viewpoint that was similar to that of Cobbs and Grier in describing black women as "subfeminine." Cleaver, however, laid the blame on white men:

> The myth of the strong black woman is the other side of the coin of the myth of the beautiful dumb blond. The white man turned the white woman into a weak-minded, weak-bodied, delicate freak, a sex pot, and placed her on a pedestal; he turned the black woman into a strong self-reliant Amazon and deposited her in the kitchen.[57]

While calling attention to the "myth of the beautiful dumb blond," Cleaver went on to acknowledge the effect that white women had on him:

> The Ogre [the white woman] possessed a tremendous and dreadful power over me.... I was at its mercy.... If I conquered the Ogre and broke its power over me I would be free.[58]

One of the most cogent analyses of what was going on in black relationships was presented by Nathan and Julia Hare, a husband-wife team of black psychologists. They viewed the black man as in a double bind, simultaneously admiring and fearing the black woman's strength. Like other social scientists, they traced this problem to the black mother—with a different twist. The Hares conceded that all men have to work through unresolved conflicts with their mothers, but what distinguished the black man's conflict was that his mother was in effect "both the mother and the father." In other words, the absence of the black father from so many homes meant that black mothers were having to be both mother and father to their children. These conflicts were then "fanned, inflamed, and distorted" by "white racism" and the "white feminist agenda."

The Hares also addressed the festering issue of black men's attraction to white women. In their view the problem wasn't that black women lacked femininity but rather that "cunning" white women did a better job of playing one role on the job and another at home. The black woman's dilemma was that she went into the workplace to "feel a higher sense of self-worth," while her "heart is in the home."[59]

The theme of blaming black women is not a new one. It first emerged during the retrogressionists' attack on blacks during Reconstruction. During that period black mothers were charged with not "fostering chastity" among their daughters and for exhibiting "sexual laxness." During the 1960s, the black man's anger at his mother was the reason given for his proclivity to white women, while black wives were characterized as "subfeminine." Reacting to these criticisms of black women, Pulitzer Prize winner Alice Walker would write, "Our plainer gifts, our labors of fidelity and love, have been knocked down our throat."[60]

The People Versus O. J. Simpson

In 1994 the complex dynamics of race, gender, and the "allure" of Miss Anne were played out before a nationwide audience in the murder trial of O. J. Simpson. How did the Simpson trial become "the trial of the century," the most extensively covered court case in American history?[61] One explanation points to the fact Simpson was a high-profile celebrity, an adored football hero who had retained a popular and even lovable image in movies and television commercials as well as in his role as a sportscaster. Yet some have argued that if this same beloved celebrity had been accused of murdering his first wife, Marguerite, who was black, the event would have faded from the public's attention rather quickly. What really made the case sensational, in this view, was that Simpson had been accused of murdering a white woman, his former wife, Nicole. The *Columbia Journalism Review* put it this way: "Simpson has been depicted as Othello, Richard Wright's Bigger Thomas, William Faulkner's Joe Christmas, and above all, as Emmett Till." These, of course, were all black men who had had purported liaisons with white women.[62]

Prior to his indictment for the murders of Nicole and her friend Ronald Goldman, Simpson had never achieved the celebrity status in the black community that he had in the white community. For most of his life Simpson was every black woman's worst nightmare. "O.J." grew up in a father-absent family in the Potrero Hill housing projects in San Francisco. His father, Jimmy Simpson, was gay and left his wife, Eunice, and their four children when O.J. was five.

Having a homosexual father was burdensome for a young black male growing up in the poor Potrero neighborhood in the 1950s and early 1960s. O.J. was reportedly teased mercilessly about his father's sexuality. Jimmy Simpson never left the Potrero community despite an environment that was hostile to a black man living an openly gay lifestyle with his lover. By 1985, Jimmy Simpson had full-blown AIDS. One year later he was dead. Simpson was a pall-bearer at his father's funeral one month to the day before his thirty-ninth birthday. Richard Majors, a psychologist and author of *Cool Pose: The Dilemmas of Black Manhood in America*, says that Simpson was abandoned by his father three times: "Once by his father leaving the home, ultimately by his father's death, and in between by the fact of his father's homosexuality."[63]

It seems that sex was never very far from Simpson's mind—even growing up. He would later brag, "If I saw a girl who looked good, I'd go right up to her and start rapping, even if she was with a guy."[64] Having achieved celebrity status as an adult, and believing the public relations propaganda that he was "colorless," Simpson had numerous affairs with white women, including the one who would become his wife. After a sexually passionate affair with eighteen-year-old Nicole, Simpson finally left Marguerite, his black wife of eleven years, and their three children.

The cracks in the relationship between Simpson and Nicole appeared shortly after their marriage. Their public profile, which exuded style and glamour, obscured Simpson's controlling behavior, jealous rages, violent outbursts, and continuing fondness for other attractive white women. The frightening history of Simpson's battering of Nicole and the fears she expressed for her life only became public after Nicole and Ron Goldman were murdered on June 12, 1994.

From the moment Simpson was arrested for the crime—compelling blood and trace evidence placed him at the scene of the crime, and he had no alibi for the time of the murder—the media went into a frenzy. Race was the subtext in discussions of the case in both the print and electronic media. By the end of the trial, the variable of race dominated the case, overshadowing the evidence, the law, and perhaps even the murders themselves.

Simpson's legal team, headed by black attorney Johnnie Cochran, based its defense on innuendo of a police conspiracy in which the motive was supposed to be Simpson's race. The defense sought to make this theory plausible by demonstrating the racism (and perjury) of Detective Mark Fuhrman. The notorious "Fuhrman tapes," which caught the detective using the word "nigger" more than forty times—he had sworn under oath that he had not used the epithet in the past ten years—were a godsend to Simpson and his attorneys. If anything, Simpson had always been treated with deference by the Los Angeles police. But Fuhrman's derogatory speech and his lies on the witness stand triggered black jurors' distrust of white policemen and their cynicism about the American system of justice, especially its historically inequitable treatment of black men. Amiri Baraka, an activist and poet, captured the sentiments of many in the black community when he said, "Simpson was the first black man to kill a white woman and get away with it."[65]

When the jury announced the "not guilty" verdict on October 3, 1995, the country seemed to fracture along racial lines. The jury, composed primarily of black women, had voted unanimously to acquit a black man of killing his white wife. In a poll taken immediately after the verdict, 85 percent of blacks agreed with the "not guilty" verdict, compared to only 32 percent of whites.[66] The black community's reaction to the verdict caught many white Americans by surprise. Blacks wearing Afrocentric apparel and African liberation colors were proclaiming victory and dancing in the streets. Whites viewed their television screens in horror and disbelief as both male and female law students at Howard University in Washington, D.C., were jubilantly exclaiming that the system had finally worked for a black man.

The prosecutors, Marcia Clark and Christopher Darden, a black man, were taken aback that their strategy of selecting black women jurors had backfired. Darden even broke down and cried in front of the television cameras as he responded to the verdict. The prosecution had mistakenly assumed that the black women jurors would find Simpson's abuse of Nicole both familiar and reprehensible and that they would identify with the victim even if she was white. Instead, blacks of both sexes rallied around an accused black man. The "genius" of Cochran's defense strategy was that he understood what Marcia Clark and Christopher Darden did not—that black women's identification with a black man is generally ensured when the black man's victim is a white woman.

Conclusion

Ever since slavery, the issue of black men's attraction to white women has contributed another disturbing element to the tensions between African-American men and women. The southern taboo that "protected" the chastity of white women against assaults by black men only contributed to the allure of Miss Anne by simultaneously putting her out of reach and unwittingly making the conquest of white women a symbol of black manhood. Southern whites' preoccupation with the sexual "crimes" of black men, together with their dismissal of black women as lacking in sexual morality and dignity, intensified the divisive symbolism of the white mistress.

Although blacks were lynched for any number of reasons in the Jim Crow South—women and children as well as men—lynching became identified with the sexual issue. One consequence was that in the American cultural memory black men became the primary symbolic victims of racism in its most barbaric form. The same dynamics worked to reinforce the identification of African-American progress with the advancement of black men.

The repeal of antimiscegenation laws in the era of civil rights brought the old issue of Miss Anne back to the surface as a disproportionate number of black men chose to marry outside the race. Coupled with the numerical shortage of marriageable black males and skyrocketing divorce rates among black couples, these interracial marriages increased black women's anxiety and anger.

Ironically, it was black women who were blamed by many commentators, white and black alike, for alienating their sons and husbands.

Despite these tensions, the O. J. Simpson case demonstrated once again that in the black community, race trumps gender. That same year Louis Farrakhan organized a "Million Man March" that convened in Washington, D.C., coincidentally about two weeks after the Simpson verdict was announced. Whites once again looked on in amazement as an estimated million black men moved in a peaceful and orderly procession from the Washington Monument to the Lincoln Memorial. Some have argued that the overwhelming response to the march was due in part to black men's strong identification with Simpson's vindication. The black community's reaction to the Simpson trial is just another indicator of the way the social memory of African Americans, shaped by the profound indignities of the past, can create solidarity on the basis of race even as it prevents men and women from coming to grips with the issues that continue to strain their relationships with each other.

6

Does Race
Trump Gender?

For years in this country there was no one for black men to
vent their rage on except black women. And for years black
women accepted that rage—even regarded that acceptance as
part of their unpleasant duty. But in doing so, they frequently
kicked back, and they seem never to become the "true slave"
that white women see in their own history.

—TONI MORRISON

Women in American society are held to be the passive
sex, but the majority of Black women have, perhaps,
never fit this model, and have been liberated from many
of the constraints the society has traditionally imposed on
women. Although this emerged from forced circumstances, it has nevertheless allowed the Black women the
kind of emotional well-being that Women's Liberation
groups are calling for.

—JOYCE LADNER, *Tomorrow's Tomorrow*

THE PERIOD SINCE THE LATE
1950s has been an era of rights
and liberation movements that have had a significant impact on
black women and on gender relations in the black community. On

the surface it might seem that the efforts to achieve equal rights for nonwhites and for women should have doubly benefited black women, but in fact the results have been ambiguous and frequently divisive. Although black men and women were comrades in the civil rights movement of the 1950s and 1960s, the explicit sexism within the movement added to tensions in gender relations. For its part, the women's liberation movement, essentially a white women's movement, failed to unite black and white women as it gave attention to certain aspects of black women's struggles while simultaneously neglecting others. Moreover, many blacks saw the women's movement as exacerbating the troubles in gender relations within their community. Nathan Hare, a highly respected psychologist, scholar, and author, gave expression to this view in his keynote address to the Fourth Annual Conference of Afro-American Writers in 1978. Hare accused the women's movement of "threatening unity between the black male and female."[1] More recently, affirmative action policies, which ostensibly were directed to both race and sex discrimination, have also produced ambiguous results for black women and for gender relations among African Americans.

In one respect these developments are nothing new. We have already seen how often black women in America have been presented with a Hobson's choice between their racial identity and their sexual identity, between standing with black men in the common struggle against racial oppression and standing up for their own interests as women both within and outside the black community. Typically, black women have opted for the only real alternative—to stand with their men. Yet we have also seen that for many black men the struggle for equality and self-assertion has been intertwined with an attitude of dominance toward black women that has only compounded black women's own battle with the dual challenges of racial and sexual oppression. Meanwhile, the debate over whether race or sex is the major source of oppression for black women has created tensions both between black women and black men and between black women and white women.

Thus it should come as no surprise that the twin swords of sexism and racism have frequently separated black women from their natural allies. Just as many black men have been oblivious to the particular forms of injustice encountered by black women, so, too, have many white women been blind to many of the struggles of black women. To further complicate these issues, black and white women have distinct histories that lead them to perceive the issues they confront in very different ways. White women have been perceived by black women as dependent creatures, relying on men for protection and support. In contrast, for many black women, working to support the family and asserting authority within the home have been integral parts of the female role. Consequently, while all women share certain interests on the basis of their sex, the agendas of white and black women are often significantly different.

The interrelatedness of race and gender has been an integral part of the historical dilemmas that have confronted black women in the struggles for political, social, and economic equality. Understanding these dilemmas is important not only for appreciating the issues faced by contemporary black women but also for achieving a deeper insight into the current tensions in gender relations in the African-American community.

Black Women and the Fight for Suffrage

The complexities of addressing simultaneously the issues of race and gender can be seen as early as Frederick Douglass's activism on behalf of woman suffrage in the nineteenth century. When women called their first suffrage convention in 1848 and invited all those who thought women ought to share equally with men in the affairs of government to attend, Douglass was the only man who came and stood up with the women activists. When asked why he chose to participate in the conference, Douglass replied that he "could not do otherwise"; women "were among the friends who fought my battles" when he first appealed to them for assistance in the antislavery cause.

Until his death, Douglass was an honorary member of the National American Women's Suffrage Association (NAWSA), and he was an honored guest at many of their gatherings. There was one notable exception, however, and it occurred when NAWSA had its annual meeting in the city of Atlanta in 1894. Knowing the feeling of the South about blacks, Susan B. Anthony specifically asked Douglass not to attend. In defending her behavior, Anthony stated that she did not want to subject him to humiliation, but more important, she did not want "anything to get in the way of bringing southern white women into the suffrage association."[2]

In discussing her actions with Ida B. Wells, Anthony admitted that when a group of black women asked for her assistance in forming a branch of the suffrage association, she declined to do so on the "ground of the same expediency." Anthony asked Wells whether she thought she was wrong in so doing. Wells replied, "Uncompromisingly yes," for "I felt that although she may have made gains for suffrage, she had also confirmed white women in their attitude of segregation."[3] But for Anthony, as for many later white activists, the women's cause came first.

Another source of disagreement between Wells and Anthony was the issue of whether women's getting the vote would make a difference in terms of the race question. In Wells's view, giving women the right to vote "would not change women's nature nor the political situation." This conversation between Ida B. Wells and Susan B. Anthony took place in 1894.[4] Anthony was president of the National American Woman Suffrage Association until she tendered her resignation in 1900. Her acquiescence to racism on the "ground of expediency" characterized her public stance on this issue during her tenure as president.[5]

One of the best examples of Anthony's willingness to capitulate on the race issue came when Lottie Wilson Jackson, one of the few black women admitted to the suffrage association, presented a resolution to the NAWSA conference in 1896. Wilson had traveled to the convention by train and suffered the humiliation of being forced to ride in the Jim Crow car. This car was often located next to the saloon or smoking car and was often occupied by offensive and brutish types of white male passengers. Her resolution to the conference was straightforward: "Colored women ought not to be compelled to ride in smoking cars, and that suitable accommodations should be provided for them."[6] Anthony, the conference's presiding officer, moderated the discussion of Wilson's resolution. Her remarks not only ensured the resolution's defeat but set the tone for acrimonious relations between black and white females for decades to come. Describing white women as a "helpless disenfranchised class," Anthony asserted, "Our hands are tied." She went on to say that "while we are in this condition, it is not for us to go passing resolutions against railroad corporations or anybody else."[7] W. E. B. Du Bois must have been referring to events such as these when he remarked that "the Negro race has suffered more from the antipathy and narrowness of [white] women both North and South than from any other single source."[8]

In spite of Ida B. Wells's disagreement with Susan B. Anthony on the issue of race, Wells went on to form the Alpha Suffrage Club, the first such club formally organized by a black woman. Following her lead, suffrage clubs begin to proliferate throughout the country in cities such as St. Louis, Los Angeles, Boston, New Orleans, and Tuskegee. A suffrage department was created in the NAACP, and influential black women such as Charlotte Hawkins Brown, Lucy C. Laney, Margaret Murray Washington, and Mary McLeod Bethune worked tirelessly for women's enfranchisement.[9]

Black women needed the vote even more than white women for numerous reasons, but one of the primary ones was their higher rate of participation in the labor force. Black women faced both economic and sexual exploitation in the workplace. It was Adelle Hunt Logan of the Tuskegee Women's Club who said that if "white women needed the vote to acquire advantage and protection of their rights, then black women needed the vote even more so."[10]

While the suffrage movement fractured along racial lines, it also led to tensions between black women and men. Like the late-nineteenth-century white reformers, black women suffragettes affirmed the popular belief that women were more nurturing, moral, and altruistic than men. Although Frances Ellen Watkins Harper, a suffragette, chastised black men for their "greed for gold" and their "lust for power," her vision of black men and women was that of a working partnership. She advocated enfranchisement for black women in order for them to be a "sharer in the social and moral development of the race."[11] Club woman Anna Julia Cooper echoed this theme and viewed gender equality as a consequence of the denial of the franchise to the race as a whole. In Cooper's view, black men had been driven from the polls by repression while black women had never been given the vote. Cooper accused southern black men of selling their vote "for a mess of potage." She declared further that a black woman would never do something like this, being ever "orthodox on questions affecting the well-being of her race."[12]

Although several influential clerics and ardent feminists such as W. E. B. Du Bois supported woman suffrage, other influential black men came out against it. In an 1888 article in the *African Methodist Episcopal Church Review* entitled "Shall Our Girls Be Educated?" Reverend R. E. Wall conceded that "divine law makes no distinction between the sexes," yet maintained that when it comes to politics, "it may not be expedient to make them [women] equal."[13] During this period the Baptist clergy were even more conventional than the Methodists in their view of women's role in the public sphere. According to an editorial in *The Women's Era,* a series of articles published in Baptist periodicals endeavored to prove through biblical authority that the "only place for women in the church is that of a singer and a prayer." Women who preached or taught were acting "contrary to divine authority," and suffrage would be a "deplorable climax to these transgressions."[14] Mary Church Terrell, the only black woman invited to speak before the mostly white National American Women's Suffrage Association in 1898—she was invited to return in 1900—spoke for many black women when she asserted, "For an intelligent colored man to oppose suffrage is the most preposterous and ridiculous thing in the world."[15]

These exchanges highlighted the fact that the fight for the women's vote ran against the prevailing patriarchal ethos in the black community. In 1914 the Illinois legislature was considering the question of enfranchising the women voters of the state. Ida B. Wells organized the Alpha Suffrage Club to get black women interested in using their vote for the "advantage of ourselves and our race." When black women in Chicago organized into neighborhood blocks and began to work aggressively to register women to vote, they were derided by black men. The women working in Wells's Alpha Club reported that the men "jeered at them and told them they ought to be at home taking care of their babies." Other men accused the women of "trying to take the place of men and wear the trousers." Wells, a smart political strategist, advised the women to tell the men that they wanted to register black women so they could "put a colored man in the city council." According to Wells, this line of reasoning "appealed very strongly" to black men. The work of the women was so effective that her ward had the sixth highest women's registration in the city. What amazed Wells is that not one of the black male politicians, not even the ministers, had "said one word to influence the women to take advantage of the suffrage opportunity."[16] As a result of the black women's steadfast efforts, Oscar DePriest sought the Alpha Club's support for his candidacy. DePriest went on to beat his two white opponents, becoming in 1915 the first black alderman in the city of Chicago. DePriest went on to the House of Representatives in 1928, making him the first northern black elected to Congress.

Black women's efforts to secure voting rights are one more example of their historic dilemma of being caught between the opposing issues of gender and race. Although many black feminist historians have highlighted how white suffragettes such as Susan B. Anthony acquiesced to racism on the "grounds of expediency," much less attention has been given to black men's effort to repress black women's political participation. The irony is that once black women secured the vote, black male politicians were the first to benefit from their labors.

A Second Divisive Issue: Domestic Service

For decades most black women found themselves relegated by virtue of their gender and race to domestic service as their main opportunity for employment. In the postemancipation South, domestic service represented a recapitulation of conditions during slavery when black women's responsibilities to the white household took precedence over their responsibilities to their own families. Black domestics were so prevalent that, in the words of T. J. Woofter, a scholar who studied the employment patterns of blacks, "the broadest and most intimate point of contact between the races in the South is through domestic service, and the attitude of the servant to the housewife, and the housewife to the servant, had much to do with the attitude of the races in general."[17]

Domestic service was truly an integral part of the system of racial subordination, since white women in the South systematically rejected this line of work. Distinctions based on race overwhelmed any sense of common interests among women. A Georgia domestic observed that more than two-thirds of the black women in her town were forced to hire themselves out as cooks, nursemaids, washerwomen, and chambermaids, and were caught up in conditions "just as bad as, if not worse than, it was during slavery."[18]

As African Americans migrated from the rural South to the urban North, black women were making occupational shifts from farm labor to working in private households. The few white women who worked as domestics outside the South were generally European immigrants. Mary Ovington, a close friend of W. E. B. Du Bois, studied the economic conditions of blacks at the turn of the century. She found that among the "laboring classes" in New York City, seven times as many black women as white women were engaged in what she called "self-supporting" work and noted that 90 percent of the black women were in "domestic or personal service."[19] Claudia Goldin, a labor economist, conducted a rigorous national analysis of gender gaps in earnings and occupations, and found that in both 1890 and 1930, fully 90 percent of all black women who worked for wages were found in only two sectors— personal service and agriculture. She also found that as late as 1940, fully 60 percent of all employed black women were servants in private households, and in 1940 black females earned only two-thirds as much as comparable service workers. Goldin concluded that the "ratio of black to white female earnings must have decreased from 1890 to 1940, an inference that is consistent with the formidable restrictions on black women's employment during this period."[20]

The onset of the Great Depression in the 1930s brought formidable challenges for all workers, but especially domestic workers. The economic upheavals during this period created "slave markets" in northern cities wherein middle-aged black women wearing thin, shabby clothing stood on street corners waiting for white women to drive up and offer them a day's work. Housecleaning services were offered for the nominal wage of thirty cents an hour— but on some days women on the corners would "run off" those women who accepted a lower hourly rate. One black domestic shared her feelings with a federal interviewer about the people she worked for: "Dey's mean, an' 'ceitful; but what ah'm gonna do? Ah got to live—got to hab a place to steh."[21]

Following the outbreak of World War II, local economies expanded, and large numbers of men went into the armed services. The resultant labor shortage opened up many traditionally male fields to women. The wartime expansion of the economy brought many changes in the labor force participation of both black and white females. Black women took advantage of the newly created war industries in such large numbers that nearly half of all white housewives lost their black domestics.

The eagerness of black women to leave domestic work, even to accept jobs in factories, was reflected in a Roper poll conducted in 1943. This poll found that three out of four black women were willing to take factory jobs, whereas only one in eight white women found factory work acceptable.[22] One black domestic who left work for a higher paying factory job put it this way: "Lincoln freed the Negroes from cotton picking and Hitler was the one that got us out of the white folks' kitchen."[23] But industrial jobs did not obliterate distinctions based on race. The few white women who found factory work acceptable were assigned to the most desirable jobs.

The wartime economy improved both the South and the economic conditions of many black women. The black domestics who were still willing to work in white households during the war charged twice as much, were less willing to live in, and refused to do many of the chores (such as window washing) they had done before the war. Domestic workers who found better-paying jobs in factories, offices, and service industries "enjoyed the higher wages and better conditions as well as the independence, social contacts, and 'self-respect' that attended their new occupations."[24] Even with these changes, however, Charles S. Johnson, a black sociologist, observed that black women remained in the "most marginal position of all classes of labor."[25]

After the defeat of Germany and the surrender of Japan, employment in defense industries was cut in half. Nine million men and women in the armed services were discharged, and the government canceled contracts worth more than $35 billion, further weakening the position of the black worker. Nevertheless, there were high hopes that postwar prosperity would bring a permanent improvement in the conditions of black women. In March 1947 a feature in *Ebony* entitled "Goodbye Mammy, Hello Mom" pointed out that black women had never historically had the opportunity to devote their full attention to their families, but now for the first time "since 1619" they would enjoy the benefits derived from their husband's high wages. The article ended by noting that "the cooking over which the 'white folks' used to go into ecstasies is now reserved for her own family and they really appreciate it."

Ebony was overly optimistic. In most major northern cities the jobless rate for black women was three to four times higher than for foreign-born white women, and many were thrown back into domestic service. For those black women who were fortunate enough to find jobs, the disparities between their wages and those of white women were alarming. Whereas white women made sixty-one cents for every dollar made by a white male, black women made only twenty-three cents. In 1950 the percentage of black women in domestic service was even greater than it had been in 1940.[26]

The war represented a turning point in the employment prospects and the income of black men, and their income relative to that of white men grew from just 41 percent in 1939 to 61 percent by 1950. The defense industry recruited heavily among southern blacks, mainly to reduce the tremendous labor shortage in the urban North during World War II. In the 1940s and 1950s the new black male urban workers enjoyed job opportunities and wages unknown to them in the declining agricultural economy of the South. Nevertheless, even with husbands present, 30.2 percent of black wives worked, compared to only 19.6 percent of their white counterparts.[27]

These conditions perpetuated black women's antipathy toward white women. One domestic remarked on the difference between the oppression experienced at the hands of black men and that suffered at the hands of white women:

> Black men will make a fool out of me if I let them, but it was a white woman who had me crawling around her apartment before I was thirteen years old, cleaning places she would never think of cleaning with a toothbrush and toothpick.[28]

Toni Morrison elaborated further on the mistrust between black and white women when she observed:

Black women have no abiding admiration of white women as competent, complete people. Whether vying with them for the few professional slots available to women in general, or moving their dirt from one place to another, they regarded them as willful children, pretty children, mean children, ugly children, but never as real adults capable of handling the real problems of the world.[29]

As tensions and mistrust escalated between black and white women, there were high hopes that the economic boom due to World War II would benefit black women. They were hoping to derive benefits from their husbands' improved job prospects and devote more time to their families. But the enhanced economic prospects for black men would be short-lived. Despite the unprecedented economic opportunities for black men in the cities, black men's economic disadvantage relative to white men persisted. Black men were often temporarily hired, squeezed into the most insecure and dangerous unskilled jobs, and frequently laid off and fired. Black wives remained in the most marginal position in the workplace. Their families' reliance on their incomes, however, did not abate.

The Civil Rights Movement:
Catalyst for Feminism

Just as the movement for woman suffrage in the nineteenth century grew out of women's involvement in the abolitionist struggle, so, too, the emergence of the quest for women's rights in the 1960s received its impetus from the civil rights movement.[30] On February 1, 1960, four black college students set out to integrate a lunch counter in Greensboro, North Carolina. The students refused to leave until they were served; after an hour, management closed the counter. Even though the students left peacefully, the civil rights movement was launched that day. The principal organization to emerge from the student sit-ins was the Student Non-Violent Co-ordinating Committee (SNCC). By the winter of 1965, SNCC had grown from a small group of 16 to a staff of over 180, of whom 50 percent were white.

The sit-in movement had a galvanizing impact on northern liberal culture. One result was that hundreds of young white women from middle- and upper-middle-class families went south between 1963 and 1965, and this experience marked a turning point in their lives. Such political and social activism was uncharted territory for most white women, and like the abolitionists a century earlier, they would later use what they learned on behalf of women's issues. The presence of white women in SNCC, however, heightened the tension between black men and women in the organization because it was the first time many of the men had sexual access to white women. Sexual relationships between black men and white women became increasingly prevalent and created a backlash among black women, who were becoming a powerful force within SNCC.[31]

Black women's anger over the relationships between black men and white women was even greater because many of the white women were not considered attractive by white standards of beauty. Rather, they were sexually appealing for the first time simply by virtue of their white skin. One white woman described these dynamics:

> My sexuality for myself was confirmed by black men for the first time ever in my life, see. In the white society I am too large . . . so I always had to work very hard to be attractive to white men. . . . Black men . . . assumed that I was a sexual person . . . and I needed that very badly. . . . It's a positive advantage to be a big woman in the black community.[32]

According to Staughton Lynd, director of the freedom schools, "Every black SNCC worker with perhaps a few exceptions counted it a notch on his gun to have slept with a white woman—as many as possible."[33]

Antagonism over these interracial relationships involved issues of status as well as sex. One black woman upbraided black men for having different sets of duties for black and white women. White women were performing the domestic tasks "in a feminine kind of way, while [black women] . . . were out in the streets battling with the cops. So it did something to what [our] femininity was about. We became amazons, less than and more than women at the same time."[34]

If there was resentment between black and white women, both groups also took issue with their treatment by the men in the organization. During the period when relationships between black men and white women were becoming more frequent, black women began to assert their power within the organization and white women began describing themselves as being in "positions of relative powerlessness." But a black woman observed, "If white women had a problem in SNCC it was not just a male/woman problem . . . it was also a black woman/white woman problem. It was a race problem rather than a 'woman' problem."[35]

With SNCC exhibiting multiple fissures along racial and gender lines, a staff retreat was held in November 1964 at Waveland, Mississippi. Thirty-seven papers were written on staff relations. Catalyzed both by the growing strength of black women within SNCC and the heightening tensions between black and white women, two white women wrote a paper entitled "SNCC Position Paper (Women in the Movement)" but were "reluctant and even afraid" to sign the document. The paper opened by denouncing SNCC for treating women the same way corporations treated token blacks. "The woman in SNCC is often in the same position as that token Negro hired in a corporation. The management thinks it has done its bit. Yet, every day the Negro bears an atmosphere, attitudes, and actions which are tinged with condescension and paternalism . . ." The paper went on to document eleven specific examples of paternalistic behavior, including relegation of women to clerical work and exclusion of women from decision-making groups and leading positions. The anonymous authors pointed to the source of the problem as the "assumption of male superiority . . . as widespread and deep rooted and every much as crippling to the woman as the assumptions of white supremacy are to the Negro." The prescience of the paper was reflected in its conclusion:

> The whole of the women [sic] in this movement will become so alert as to force the rest of the movement to stop the discrimination and start the slow process of changing values and ideas so that all of us gradually come to understand that this is no more a man's world than it is a white world.[36]

Except for some speculation about who may have authored it, the paper went relatively unnoticed at the Waveland conference. What was remembered, however, was the late Stokely Carmichael's caustic rejoinder: "The only position for women in SNCC is prone." As feminist historian Sara Evans has observed, the significance of the Waveland conference was that for a "moment black and white women had shared a feminist response to the men in SNCC" although they "lacked the trust and solidarity to call each other 'sister.'"[37] While the civil rights movement would help to catalyze the cause of feminism, the racial fissures within SNCC were a sign of the coming failure of black and white women to unite in a common cause.

Black Women: The Reluctant Feminists

The escalating tensions between black men and women in the civil rights movement and the moment of "solidarity" between black women and white women at the Waveland conference did not unify women. When feminist Betty Friedan was unsuccessful in her attempts to recruit black women, she went to SNCC headquarters. Friedan was dismayed when they told her that they were not interested in joining the feminist movement but rather in helping black men get "the rights they had been denied so long."[38] In 1974, Aileen Hernandez, a black feminist who was a founding member of the National Organization for Women (NOW) and its second president, explained black women's lack of visibility in the feminist movement:

> They have been asked to step to the back of the civil rights movement by some who believe it is the black man's time. They have been largely absent from the feminist movement because some black sisters are not sure that the feminist revolution will meet their current needs—and the wounds of racism do not heal easily.[39]

Whereas Hernandez emphasized black women's own interests, Dorothy Height, president of the National Council of Negro Women, provided a perspective that was based on the needs of black men:

> If the Negro woman has a major underlying concern, it is the status of the Negro man and his position in the community and his need for feeling himself an important person, free and able to make his contribution in the whole society in order that he may strengthen his home.[40]

This statement is consistent with Height's patriarchal ideology in which primary attention is directed to the black man's role within the family and the larger community. With the black community's antagonism and ambivalence toward black feminism, it is not surprising that Height, like her predecessor, Mary McLeod

Bethune, was often the only woman in attendance at meetings that brought major civil rights leaders together.[41]

What perplexed white feminists like Friedan was that black women seemed to be reluctant to participate in the feminist movement even though surveys showed that their attitudes were more "feminist" than those of white women. When a Louis Harris–Virginia Slims poll conducted in 1972 asked whether women favored "efforts to strengthen or change women's status in society," 62 percent of the black women respondents agreed, compared to only 45 percent of the white women. Even more surprisingly, 67 percent of black women expressed "sympathy with the efforts of women's liberation groups," compared with only 35 percent of white women. This poll was conducted during a period when a survey found that African Americans made up only 5 percent of the NOW membership.[42]

The attitudinal differences between black and white women toward the goals of the feminist movement were partly a function of economics and the disparities in income between black and white families. The median annual income during this period for black families with both husband and wife employed was $7,782, whereas the median income of white families with only one wage earner was $8,450. Black women's income was lower than black men's, $3,008 and $5,194 respectively, and black women's earnings were crucial to her family's well-being.[43] Given that the major goals of the liberation movement included equitable pay and provisions for child care, it is not surprising that black women were more likely than white women to express "sympathy with the efforts of women's liberation groups."

Nevertheless, black women continued to absent themselves from the dominant women's organizations. The resulting confusion among white feminists regarding black women's perspective on women's liberation led Toni Morrison to write a cover story for the *New York Times Magazine* in 1971 entitled "What Black Women

Think About Women's Lib." Morrison maintained that black women are different from white women because they "view themselves differently, are viewed differently and lead a different kind of life."

> A Black woman did the housework; . . . she reared the children, often alone, but she did all of this while occupying a place on the job market, a place her mate could not get or which his pride would not let him accept. And she had nothing to fall back on; not maleness, not whiteness, not ladyhood, not anything . . . so she combined being a responsible person with being a female— and as a person she felt free to confront not only the world at large (the rent man, the doctor and the rest of the marketplace) but her man as well. She fought him, she nagged him—but knew that you don't fight what you don't respect (if you don't respect your man, you manipulate him, the way some parents treat children and the way white women treat their men).[44]

While black and white women did not unite under the banner of one mainstream feminist organization, some black women formed their own associations. The major black feminist organization to emerge during the 1970s was the National Black Feminist Organization (NBFO). Organized when Dorothy Wright assembled a meeting of thirty women in May 1973, it was inaugurated at a press conference on August 15 and convened its first conference in November. The NBFO's statement of purpose encapsulated the unique challenges faced by black women in America. Launching a frontal assault on sexism and racism, the statement asserted that black women "have suffered cruelty in this society from living the phenomena of being black and female, in a country that is both racist and sexist. . . . We, not white men or black men, must define our own self-image as black women." The statement closed by declaring, "We must together, as a people, work to eliminate racism from without the black community" and at the same time "remember the sexism destroying and crippling us from within."[45]

Like white feminist organizations, the NBFO used consciousness-raising sessions as its primary organizing tool. These sessions were generally small discussion groups, with topics focused on issues that black women were grappling with. When Brenda Eichelberger, chairperson of the Chicago chapter, was asked what subjects came up in the sessions, the first one she mentioned was relationships between black men and white women. Eichelberger went on to say that "this problem is a thorn in the side of black women, the fact that some black men date and marry white women, especially when there are so many fewer black men than black women to begin with." Other topics included issues of black women's self-image, the greater opportunities for white women, the myth of the black matriarchy, and the prevalence of rape and crime in black communities.[46]

NBFO shared some of the same goals as white feminist organizations, such as abortion rights, child care, the ratification of the Equal Rights Amendment, and support for the rights of black lesbians. This agenda led to accusations that the organization was putting gender ahead of race. The harshest criticism came from Brenda Verner, a professor at the University of Massachusetts and staff writer for *Encore* magazine. She charged the women of NBFO with yielding their "cultural and political unity as an ethnic segment . . . for some vague, emulative form of white feminism." After attending one of the NBFO meetings, she escalated her criticisms by focusing on the physical appearance of some of its members. Verner described one woman who "wore a man's tan corduroy suit with a black turtle neck," and another woman who was "wearing a full Afro, mustache, man's sweater, pants and ankle boots." Verner understood, it seems, that homophobia had deep roots in the black community. According to historian Deborah Gray White, these criticisms "not only tapped some of the deepest fears and anxieties of black America, but it made the organization appear to be opposed to black liberation."[47]

Dissension from within the organization, coupled with charges from outside that it was controlled by white feminists, created organizational conflict and confusion that ultimately led to the resignation of its president, Margaret Sloan. By July 1974 a majority of the board had resigned, and by the end of the year the New York chapter was no longer in business. Some NBFO chapters continued to operate, however. For example, the Chicago chapter changed its name to the National Black Feminist Alliance and in spite of financial difficulties persevered until 1981. But that marked the end of the NBFO and its successors. In the intervening years no sizable black feminist organization has emerged to take the place of NBFO.

Despite the collapse of black feminist organizations, a *New York Times* survey confirmed findings from the earlier Louis Harris–Virginia Slims poll about black women's identification with the goals of the women's movement. Eighty-five percent of African-American women questioned supported the movement, compared to only 67 percent of white women.[48] Yet black women's participation in the white feminist movement remained minuscule, while the principal black feminist organization was short-lived. The NBFO, like other organizations that have not placed race at the forefront of their agenda, has historically not received widespread support in the African-American community. The prevailing viewpoint remains that expressed by psychologist Nathan Hare—namely, that feminism only threatens the unity of black women and men.

The Ghettoization of Black Professional Women

Many observers, focusing on the advances made by black women in the workplace, have made the claim that black women have an economically superior position relative to black men and that this position has complicated gender relations. The reality, however, is much more complex.

Despite the restricted opportunities for black women that led so many of them to work as domestics, black women had a strong tradition of education and professional employment. From 1940 to 1960 there were significant shifts in their occupational achievement. Black women's participation in domestic service dropped from 60 to 35 percent, and their socioeconomic index, a measure of both social and economic factors, increased from 13 to 21. The scores on this scale range from a high of 74 points for professionals to a low of 7 points for domestic service. Although the socioeconomic index for white women was almost three times that of black women in 1940, their index remained unchanged from 1950 to 1960, resulting in a relative gain for black women.[49]

In the mid-1960s two relatively unknown white sociologists published findings on the black family and came to similar conclusions. Daniel Patrick Moynihan characterized the black family as "matriarchal" and argued that black women suffered less from racism than black men.[50] Jessie Bernard asserted that black women's "natural superiority" as women had been buttressed by the social and cultural environment.[51]

Bernard documented the higher levels of formal education found among black women, noting that in 1960 black women constituted 60.8 percent of the black professional class, whereas white women constituted only 37.2 percent of the white professional group. (When these figures were re-examined thirty years later by Andrew Hacker, black women had increased less than 5 percentage points, to 65.1 percent, whereas white women had increased 15 percentage points, to 52.6 percent.[52]) Bernard went on to discuss the implications for these differences in the "relations between the sexes," arguing that the responsibilities imposed on black women "are not always congenial to the feminine role vis-à-vis the masculine role."[53] In other words, the very success of black women in the professions made it harder for them to maintain the traditional feminine role in relationships with their men.

Two surveys conducted during the 1960s found differences between black and white women in their expectations about employment after marriage. The proportion of black women who expected to combine full-time employment with the traditional role of mother and wife was roughly three times greater than that of white women. Conversely, the ratio of white to black women who wished to be full-time homemakers was two to one. Black women's expectations about having to combine the role of wife and mother with occupational roles were consistent with the realities they were likely to encounter after marriage.[54]

To the extent that black women formulated high career aspirations, their motivation was often not based on achieving personal fulfillment. An investigator who examined the career aspirations of black and white female college students encountered some unanticipated findings. For black women, high career expectations were related to their perceptions of the expectations and desires of friends and family. They thought their mothers and the men they knew expected them to have more work involvement. In contrast, white women with high career aspirations were more likely to be in search of personal and/or professional fulfillment. The researcher concluded that the black women's high career expectations derived not so much "from an achievement ethic as from a sense of responsibility."[55] Another study found that black women displayed lower mobility aspirations than white women and aspired to stereotypic occupations with lower prestige, ability demand, and financial compensation. These findings support the idea that black women worked out of economic necessity and a sense of obligation to their families, not to find personal fulfillment.[56]

When black women's professional status was reexamined in the 1970s, it was found that only 10 percent of black women were professionals, whereas 15.5 percent of white women had attained professional status. Furthermore, the earnings of black women were still only 60 percent of those of black men, even though their educational achievements were comparable in the years from 1952 to 1970 (3.9 years of college for black men and 4 years for black women).[57]

Although black women's educational attainment was impressive compared with black men's, the great majority of professional black women (88 percent) chose traditionally female professions such as elementary and secondary school teaching, clerical jobs, nursing, and social work. Of the black women classified as professionals, 54 percent were teachers, compared to 39 percent of white women. Typically, black women professionals were employed in teaching in public schools, nursing in public hospitals, or working with heavy caseloads for the department of public welfare. Contrary to the perception of black women's "natural superiority," in 1960 black women were the least likely of all race/gender groups to be employed in male-dominated professions. The low number of black women who did enter male-dominated professions tended to work in public defender's offices, city-operated hospitals, dental clinics, and minority relations in corporate offices.[58]

Up to this point the reports on the educational achievements of African Americans focused attention on women's higher aggregate accomplishments relative to men. The number of black colleges had increased from one in 1854 to more than one hundred by the middle of the next century. The enrollment of African Americans increased steadily in these institutions in the years following World War I, and 97 percent of these students were attending colleges in southern states. The attainments of black men at the highest educational levels outstripped those of black women, but discrepancies went unnoticed by social scientists such as Moynihan and Bernard. Jacqueline J. Jackson, a black sociologist, was one of the first social scientists to verify black women's underrepresentation in male-dominated professions. Jackson analyzed blacks in higher education in the 1970s and found that although a greater proportion of black women than men were enrolled in colleges and universities, the men were more likely than black women to obtain degrees beyond the master's level. In the combined fields of medicine, dentistry, law, veterinary medicine, and theology, 91 percent of the degrees went to men, including 85.6 percent of the M.D.s and 90.4 percent of the law degrees.[59] Black women fared somewhat better in a survey of blacks with doctorates in all fields from all institutions in 1969 and 1970. These surveys suggested that black women held roughly 21 percent of the advanced degrees.[60]

By the mid-1980s for the first time black women received more than half of all doctorates awarded to blacks, even in the traditionally male-dominated fields of science and engineering. However, only 6 percent of all science degrees awarded to black women were in the higher paying and more prestigious areas of engineering, mathematics, and physical science, where black men were predominant. Black women, on the other hand, were dominant in the less lucrative social and behavioral sciences.[61]

Natalie Sokoloff contributed to a fuller understanding of the relative achievements of black women by constructing an index to measure their representation in the professions and technical fields from 1960 to 1980. The professions were divided into five areas: male professions (elite and nonelite), gender-neutral professions, female professions, male technical fields, and female technical fields. Black women gained more than a half-million new jobs in the professional and technical arenas between 1960 and 1980, but of these jobs fewer than 10,000 were secured in the elite male professions. Black women secured fewer than half as many new elite jobs as black men, 9,332 and 20,924 respectively. (In contrast, white men gained more than a half-million new elite jobs.)[62]

Another professional area in the black community where gender discrimination is especially apparent is among the traditionally male clergy. Although women numbered as many as one-third of all black ministers in some of the historically black denominations in a survey conducted in 1977, black women reported that they were rarely allowed to achieve their own pulpits. Many black women have gotten around the male domination of churches by opening new churches of their own. What has intensified the struggle of many black female clergy is that the church has conventionally been the "primary vehicle for black men to exercise both religious and political power."[63]

In sum, what the findings of the past thirty-five years demonstrate is the ghettoization of black professional women. In highlighting the educational and professional achievements of black women relative to black men, social scientists generally overlooked the fact that black women were virtually absent in the elite male professions. Black women's educational achievements helped them secure jobs primarily in traditionally female professions, such as teaching, social work, and nursing. Even though black women had more education than black men, they were paid less than black men and were the least likely of any race/gender group to be employed in the better paying male-dominated professions.

Pay Equity—an Elusive Goal

A significant shift in trends in the higher education of African Americans became noticeable in the second half of the twentieth century. Prior to World War II it was most unusual to find black students attending predominantly white institutions of higher learning. Beginning in the 1960s the numbers increased steadily, and by 1977 there were 1.1 million African Americans enrolled in colleges and universities throughout the country, with about half of these students enrolled in historically white institutions. The increased enrollment of black students in predominantly white colleges was due in part to policies created by universities to comply with requirements set by the Department of Health, Education, and Welfare in the 1970s. In addition to increasing the enrollment of black students on historically white campuses, affirmative action policies expanded public and private sector employment opportunities for racial minorities considerably in the 1970s and 1980s.[64]

What were the effects of these policies on gender and race

differences in the workplace? One carefully controlled survey suggested that affirmative action had a noticeable effect on opportunities for black men and women, with women benefiting more than men. Sixty-eight thousand firms that had government contracts and were required to emphasize minority hiring reported that the employment of black men rose by 6.5 percent and that of black women by 11 percent.[65]

One of the most comprehensive accounts of the effects of affirmative action from 1982 to 1992 was based on data submitted by thirty-eight thousand businesses that report to the U.S. Equal Opportunity Commission. Before comparing men and women it is important to note the paucity of blacks in the category designated as professionals in EEOC companies—only 5.9 percent of all professionals and 5 percent of officials and managers in 1992. According to this analysis, in 1982 there were 1.2 black women for every black man in the professional category; by 1992 there were 1.8. Although the hiring of black women had outpaced that of black men, black women's salaries trailed those of black men by 14 percent.

In this survey, black men outnumbered black women in only one area in 1992, and that was the higher ranks of corporate America. In the category EEOC calls "officials and managers," black men held about 146,000 jobs, while black women held 113,000. Black men's plurality in the managerial ranks is one explanation for their higher salaries compared to black women. From 1982 to 1992 black men increased their numbers in management by 22 percent, whereas black women increased their numbers by 64 percent. The fact that black women continue to lag behind black men, in spite of their substantial increases, is one indicator of the extent to which black men dominated the management field prior to the implementation of affirmative action policies. Although black women made progress in securing managerial positions, those who did frequently suffered from isolation and lack of mentoring. Moreover, many were disproportionately bypassed for promotions and were thereby more vulnerable to corporate streamlining.[66]

One of the clearest examples of the games played by corporate America was chronicled in the book written by Bari-Ellen Roberts. During her tenure as a senior financial analyst at Texaco from 1990 to 1997, Roberts experienced numerous insults, including being referred to as a "little colored girl" by her white coworkers and having to watch her boss in a Sambo costume at the annual Halloween party. She endured the harshest indignity, however, while presenting a plan with a coworker for enhancing ethnic diversity at Texaco. The vice president of Human Resources exploded:

> You people must have lost your minds! I think you're a bunch of militants! I've been here for thirty-three years and I can tell you right now that Texaco will not even consider any of these crazy proposals. We'll never do any of these things! The next thing you know we'll have Black Panthers running down the halls or around the circle in front of the building! . . . As far as I'm concerned this meeting is over.[67]

Roberts brought a suit against Texaco for racial discrimination and won a $176 million class-action settlement. One of the primary reasons she ultimately secured the settlement is that she had the help of a justice-oriented white executive, Richard Lundwall, who went public with taped racist remarks made by his white colleagues.

The study of EEOC data from 1982 to 1992 indicated that, in addition to management, black women experienced increases in other sectors as well. For example, in the "white collar" domain, excluding clerical workers, the number of black women increased 90 percent, whereas the number of black males grew by less than 50 percent. A Detroit utility company reported that the number of black women professionals grew 90 percent, compared to 16 percent for black men.[68]

Black women outnumber black men in corporate America in every sector except management. Several explanations have been offered for this. The major one is education: More black women than men graduate from college and professional schools. (See Figure 3 in Appendix.) Approximately 14.3 percent of black women in the civilian workforce have bachelor or postgraduate degrees, compared to 11.9 percent of black men.[69] Harry Holzer, an economist, conducted an in-depth analysis of white employers' decisions to select black women and found that in positions requiring cognitive-interactive skills without a college education, less qualified black women were consistently hired over black men.[70] However, since black men command higher salaries, on average, than black women, it is also possible that women are more likely to be hired because their salary requirements are lower than men's. Their very "success" may be a by-product of discrimination based on gender.

Although black women have fared better numerically in corporate America than black men, it is important to point out that black men have fared better as business owners. In 1996 black men owned 2.4 businesses for each one owned by a black woman.[71] Because affirmative action policies have been so controversial, one study set out to examine the long-term consequences of college admissions criteria based on race. This study focused attention on the differences between blacks and whites by analyzing the academic, employment, and personal histories of more than forty-five thousand students of all races who attended "selective" universities between the 1970s and 1990s and compared these graduates with B.A. recipients nationwide.[72] One of the obvious differences in the two groups is that black graduates from "selective" universities are more heavily represented than college students nationally in the fields of medicine, law, and higher education. Black women graduates of the elite colleges were five times more likely than national graduates as a whole to work in higher education, six times more likely to be lawyers, and eight times more likely to be physicians. The ratios for black men are comparable.[73] (See Figure 4 in the Appendix.)

With respect to the economic prospects for graduates, the mean earned income for black men from elite colleges and universities was $85,000, while for black women it was $64,700 (76 percent of men's); for white men it was $101,900 and for white women it was $66,000 (65 percent of men's). The corresponding figures for white men and women were $98,000 and $64,100 (65 percent of men's). With respect to the elite professions of law and medicine, some interesting patterns emerged among students who attended "selective" universities. Among black men, 15 percent went into medicine, with a mean annual earned income of $155,000, whereas 8 percent of the black women became medical doctors and earned an average of $138,000 (89 percent of men's) annually. Surprisingly, the pattern shifted for the profession of law, where gender differences were somewhat neutralized. Twelve percent of the black women went into law, compared to 11 percent of the black men, and their average salary of $74,000 was 95 percent of men's ($78,000). Within the elite professions, black women physicians enjoy the highest salary premiums, and black women attorneys have the lowest—primarily because so many of them work in the not-for-profit and the government sectors.

In business, 17 percent of black male graduates of elite universities were in the executive sector, 9 percent in the financial sector, and 6 percent in marketing. Black women's specializations were comparable. The income differences between black men and women were more dramatic in these areas. Black men's average earned income was $80,000 in the executive arena, $124,000 in finance, and $57,000 in marketing. The comparable figures for black women were $61,000 (70 percent of men's salaries), $75,000 (60 percent of men's salaries), and $72,000 (126 percent of men's salaries). Only in the marketing area did black women's salaries exceed those of black men. Although the income gap between black males and females narrowed among those who were not graduates of elite universities, the salaries of black males exceeded those of black females in all areas, including marketing. The dramatic difference in the salaries of black men and women in the business sector speaks to the preeminence of maleness in the corporate world.[74] (See Figure 5 in Appendix.)

Conclusion

Black women have been systematically portrayed in the social science literature and in the media as having "superior" status vis-à-vis black men, and the major catalyst for this depiction was the infamous 1965 Moynihan Report.[75] This persistent myth has not been supported by the data, however. Psychologists Nathan and Julia Hare have asserted that "the positive virtues of being a black woman—easier access to jobs and financial favors compared to black men—have negative consequences in that they depreciate the black male."[76] Black men have unquestionably endured tremendous economic hardships, but it is not the "positive virtues" of black women that depreciate the black men—it is racism and the subjugation of black people.

The late Pauli Murray—lawyer, ordained priest, civil rights activist, and a significant figure in the emergence of the modern women's movement—responded in this way to those who contended that black women have superior status:

> The notion of the favored economic position of the black female in relation to the black male is a myth. . . . In the face of their multiple disadvantages, it seems clear that black women can neither postpone nor subordinate the fight against sex discrimination to the black revolution. . . . While efforts to raise educational and employment levels for black males will ease some of the economic and social burdens now carried by many black women, for a large and growing minority these burdens will continue. As a matter of sheer survival black women have no alternative but to insist upon equal opportunities without regard to sex in training, education, and employment.[77]

The era of civil rights and women's liberation has brought mixed results for black women and has sometimes intensified issues in gender relations in the African-American community. Ever since the fight for suffrage in the nineteenth century, black women's efforts to stand up for themselves as women have been interpreted as harmful for African Americans as blacks. Further, although black women identify strongly with the goals of the women's rights movement, they have not united with white women to achieve these goals. Both inside and outside the black community, with respect to black women's struggles, race has trumped gender.

The civil rights movement and affirmative action policies have benefited all African Americans, but for black women the benefits have frequently come at a price. Sexism within the civil rights movement continued the legacy of the "new manhood" movement earlier in the century, preventing black men and women from standing shoulder to shoulder as equals in the fight against racism. Efforts to legislate equal opportunity and pay equity on the basis of race and gender have resulted in gains for African Americans of both sexes, but the divisive notion that black women have enjoyed an economically superior status to black men is unfounded. Even when they outnumber black men in more elite occupations, black women are disproportionately represented in lower-paying careers and jobs.

The struggle will continue in the twenty-first century to achieve equality in economic and social opportunity for all men and women in America. It is a mistake to think that success in this struggle requires choosing between fighting racism and fighting sexism. African Americans can unite only when they recognize not only the common foe of racism but the specific challenges that they face as black men and women. It is not our common interests that divide us as women and men, it is what oppresses either of us that must surely contribute to the oppression of the other.

7

The Path to
Healing

The wounds inflicted by men and women on each
other constitute the fundamental fault line running
beneath all other human conflict.

—JOHN DAWSON, *Healing America's Wounds*

If one ignores "differences" one distorts reality. If one
ignores the power relations built on differences one
reinforces them in the interest of holding power. . . .
What we are trying to do is create a holistic history in
which men and women, in various aspects of their lives,
interact in various ways, reflecting the differences
among them. The textured richness of such a reconstruction of the past depends on our ability to
embrace difference, hear many languages, and see
interdependence rather than separation.

—GERDA LERNER, *Why History Matters*

H ISTORICALLY, THE ISSUES
of gender discord have been so
painful to African Americans that they have largely hidden them
not only from each other but also from the public's view. This pattern changed in the 1990s as tensions between black men and

women came to the public's attention in several highly publicized events. First came the visible and vocal support given to heavyweight fighter Mike Tyson during and after his 1991 trial on charges of raping a young black woman. Later that same year came the Senate confirmation hearings of Supreme Court nominee Clarence Thomas and the attacks on Professor Anita Hill, the black woman who accused Thomas of sexual harassment.

Finally, two national marches of African Americans called attention to gender issues. First was Louis Farrakhan's "Million Man March" in March 1995, in which hundreds of thousands of black men came together for a day of speeches, prayers, and "atonement" emphasizing themes of black male responsibility and black self-reliance. While some black women applauded the goals of the march, the mass media noted that the very idea of a million-man march alienated others. *USA Today* quoted Kimberle Crenshaw of the group African-American Agenda 2000: "No one seems to notice that the gender exclusion is just as much a problem as what everybody in the march wanted to talk about, which is racism. . . . A unity purchased through the exclusion of the interests of specific obstacles facing 50 percent of the community is ill-begotten unity."[1]

Two years later, tens of thousands of women converged on Independence Mall in Philadelphia for a "Million Women March" dedicated to "healing." "There are a million reasons to be here," said Ms. Bartell, who arrived at the march from Detroit, "but I think healing is the number one thrust that has jelled the women to say I want to be a part of this. Healing mentally, physically, spiritually."[2]

These events took place even as the evidence continued to mount of how much healing was needed in the relationships between black women and men. A significant barometer of gender relations for any group is the state of marriage. One gauge of the crisis in gender relations among African Americans is the proliferation of divorce. Since 1960 the divorce rate for blacks has increased fourfold; currently it is double that of the general population. Black women today are less likely to marry, stay married, and to re-marry than their white counterparts.[3]

Marriage patterns are not the only indicators of the crisis in the gender relations of African Americans. As marital relationships have deteriorated, there has been a resurgence in black national-ism, also referred to as Afrocentrism, with its male-centered ca-dence. Angry debates between black women and men followed the release of literary works by black feminists such as Michelle Wal-lace's book *Black Macho and the Myth of the Superwoman,* Ntozake Shange's play *For Colored Girls Who Have Considered Suicide,* and Alice Walker's Pulitzer Prize–winning novel *The Color Purple* (which was also made into a film in 1985 directed by Steven Spielberg). Black men's rabid reactions to these and other literary releases were an indication that the war between the sexes was es-calating in the black community.[4]

Yet there is a potential gain, because the strains of discord are now being heard openly both inside and outside the black commu-nity. It is a commonplace that in every crisis there is opportunity for growth and change. Open discussion, even if it begins in acri-mony, can eventually lead black men and women to confront the issues troubling their relationships, understand the sources of these issues, and find the path to healing.

The People Versus Mike Tyson

Desiree Washington took a courageous stand when she decided to press rape charges against Mike Tyson in July 1991. Desiree, a for-mer Miss Teenage Black America, was eighteen years old at the time of the rape. In March of that same year a prominent white man, William Kennedy Smith, had been acquitted of the charge of rape brought against him by a woman named Patricia Bowman.

One of the striking differences in the two cases was the credibility of the women involved. Patricia Bowman was much less credible than Desiree Washington. When Bowman was on the witness stand, she seemed confused and appeared not to remember details about the evening of the alleged rape. Desiree Washington, on the other hand, was poised and well spoken throughout the trial. She was articulate and had a consistent memory of the details of her encounter with Tyson.

In addition to a history of violence and abuse toward women, one of the strongest pieces of evidence against Tyson was a quotation taken from his biography: "You know something, I like to hurt women when I make love to them. . . . I like to see them scream with pain, to see them bleed. . . . It gives me pleasure."[5] Few should have been surprised when an Indianapolis jury convicted Tyson.

The headline in *People* magazine captured the perspective of most white Americans on Tyson's conviction: "Judgment Day: Payback Comes to Sexual Predator." In the African-American community, however, the message of the Tyson conviction was quite different. Tyson's conviction and Smith's acquittal were just another indication of the double standard in the nation's judicial system. Blacks blamed Tyson's conviction on everything from a racist jury to his inept legal representation.

What many whites may have found even more surprising, however, was the treatment given Tyson and his victim by many members of the black community. The strongest attacks were directed not at the convicted rapist but at Desiree Washington, who was vilified and demonized. Desiree's decision to press charges against Tyson caused considerable consternation among self-conscious African Americans. Many of her detractors rationalized that she "got what she deserved" when she decided to accompany Tyson to his hotel room. Four years later the O. J. Simpson double-murder trial revealed much of the same "closing ranks" reasoning as did the initial reaction of much of the black community to the Tyson rape trial.[6]

In an effort to give Tyson support following his release from prison, Reverend Al Sharpton headed an organizing committee whose members included boxing promoter Don King, New York congressman Charles Rangel, Wyatt Tee Walker of Harlem's Canaan Baptist Church, Conrad Muhammed from the Nation of Islam, and singer Roberta Flack. Headlines in the black-owned *New York Amsterdam News* detailed the planned event for Tyson, reporting "Stars, a Parade, a Street Festival for the Champ."[7]

Upon hearing of the planned Tyson Fest, African-American women in the New York area mobilized a response. A coalition of women and men formed, calling themselves African Americans Against Violence. The group's initial goal was to stop the parade and rally, and to bring attention to the message the Tyson Fest was sending by conferring "hero" status on a convicted rapist and abuser of women. The only elected officials who supported the group's efforts were City Councilwoman C. Virginia Fields and Assemblyman Keith L. T. Wright. Reverend Calvin O. Butts, pastor of the Abyssinian Baptist Church, was the only member of the black clergy in the New York area who supported their efforts. Bob Herbert, columnist for the *New York Times,* pointed to the disturbing message such a show of support for Tyson would send: "For black women in particular, any kind of celebration of Mike Tyson is an act of contempt. It gives comfort and support to the idea—expressed so frequently in the rap culture and acted out so tragically in the real world—that women are here primarily for two reasons: to serve men as vessels of pleasure and as objects to be brutalized."[8]

The reaction to the Tyson trial brought into the open the discord between men and women in the black community. In addition, this incident once again directs attention to the difficulties faced by black women when they break their silence. In the black community the challenges facing the black man have become the symbolic representation of racial injustice. By comparison, black women like Desiree Washington who step forward to "speak their truth" are vilified by many African Americans. The Anita

Hill/Clarence Thomas debacle would once again point to these historic patterns in the black community.

Anita Hill and the Denigration of Black Women

Another black female victim who garnered even more attention than Desiree Washington was college professor Anita Faye Hill. When the Senate confirmation hearings of Clarence Thomas opened in the fall of 1991, Anita Hill was a little-known figure to most Americans. Claiming to have been sexually harassed by Thomas a decade earlier, Hill came forward reluctantly when approached by the Senate Judiciary Committee. She held a press conference on October 7, 1991, responding to speculation about her motives. She subjected herself to nearly an hour of questioning from members of the press, discussing her reasons for coming forward.

Hill was catapulted into national visibility after being subjected to a grueling cross-examination by fourteen white male members of the Senate Judiciary Committee. Two primary weapons were employed in the assault on her credibility: race and gender. Since race has historically trumped gender in the black community, if Hill spoke out about her harassment as a woman by a black man, even if he was a conservative, she would alienate many African Americans.[9]

One of the most dramatic moments during the Senate hearings occurred when Clarence Thomas angrily characterized them as a "high-tech lynching." This strategy caught the white senators on the Judiciary Committee off guard, and no one marshaled the courage to challenge him. In the minds of white and black Americans alike, Thomas's well-chosen metaphor invoked images of countless black men whose lifeless bodies dangled from trees. Almost immediately, a man accused of crude sexual harassment was metamorphosed into a victim of racial bigotry, not only eclipsing his alleged victim, Anita Hill, but somehow making this distinguished and articulate black woman a party to a heinous racial crime. This tactic played very well in the black community: Thomas's favorability ratings soared from 54 percent to nearly 80 percent following his remarks.[10]

There was another less prominent black woman who was also victimized during Thomas's ascent to the highest court in the land—Thomas's sister, Emma Mae Martin. Thomas captured the attention of prominent Republicans when he made a speech to black conservatives and denounced the effects that welfare had on poor African Americans. He personalized his remarks by making reference to his only sister: "She gets mad when the mailman is late with her welfare check, that's how dependent she is. What's worse is that now her kids feel entitled to the check, too. They have no motivation for doing better or for getting out of that situation."[11] When an investigative reporter for the *Los Angeles Times* examined Martin's story, new facts emerged that contradicted Thomas's account. Martin received welfare assistance only once in her life, for one four-and-a-half-year period during which she was caring for an aunt who was disabled by a stroke. During Thomas's years at Yale, Martin, a divorced mother, was holding down two minimum-wage jobs to support her three small children. At the time of the Senate hearings, Martin was working as a cook on the night shift at the hospital in a town where many poor black women earn their living picking crabmeat.[12]

Kimberle Crenshaw offered a pungent analysis of Thomas's ascent: "My sense of Clarence Thomas is that he doesn't represent the much-heralded phenomenon of pulling oneself up by one's bootstraps. The story instead is how he climbed over the body of his sister—and metaphorically the bodies of the very black women he insults with his willingness to demean us for his own political gain." Crenshaw went on to contrast the life stories of Thomas and his sister: "The real story . . . is a story of gender and class. Namely, he was sent to school to be educated. She wasn't. She took care of people. He didn't."[13]

Crenshaw's view of Thomas deviated from that of many African Americans, including many black women on the liberal end of the spectrum.[14] Two noted black women who came to Thomas's defense were Dr. Maya Angelou and Dr. Niara Sudarkasa, formerly a president of Lincoln University in Pennsylvania. These women were joined in their support of Thomas by such prominent black men as Stephen Carter, a law professor at Yale University; Orlando Patterson, a sociology professor at Harvard University; Juan Williams, author of the documentary history of the civil rights movement *Eyes on the Prize* and, ironically, someone who had sexual harassment complaints made against him by at least seven female employees at the *Washington Post*;[15] and William Raspberry, columnist for the *Washington Post*. Once again the symbolism of a victimized black male trumped the victimization of a black woman.

But Thomas could be defended only if Anita Hill was in some way discredited. One of the most resolute attacks came from Nathan and Julia Hare in an article in the Nation of Islam newspaper *Final Call* entitled "The Many Faces of Anita Hill." The Hares linked Hill to other black women who had violated the code of silence by speaking out publicly on issues of sexism within the black community. Not surprisingly, they began by attacking feminist authors Michelle Wallace, Ntozake Shange, and Alice Walker for writing "white-promoted" fiction that "exorcised" the black male. They went further than the critics who preceded them, however, when they attacked Congresswoman Maxine Waters for "following the script of the white pro-choice feminists" during the 1984 Democratic campaign; Faye Wattleton for being "Planned Parenthood's puppet black mannequin"; and Margaret Bush Wilson, chair of the NAACP, for opposing Thomas's nomination on the basis of his anti–affirmative action stand. The Hares concluded with an unmistakable warning to black women presumed to embrace some "white feminist scheme": "We will be watching you."[16]

Despite the admonition of the Hares and others, the cat was out of the bag. No longer content to remain silent about the issues confronting them, a number of black women mobilized a response to the hearings. In a statement entitled "African-American Women in Defense of Ourselves," these women declared that the "malicious defamation of Professor Hill insulted all women of African-American descent." The statement went on to say, "Throughout U.S. history, black women have been stereotyped as immoral, insatiable, perverse; the initiators in all sexual contacts—abuse or otherwise. . . . As Anita Hill's experience demonstrates, black women who speak of these matters are not likely to be believed."

The campaign's organizers used letters, faxes, and phone calls to contact black women across the country, and responses poured in at a rate of more than several hundred a day. The campaign had three announced goals: (1) to oppose the sexual abuse and degradation of black women, (2) to condemn the misogynist and reactionary policies and practices of Clarence Thomas, and (3) to dispel any notions that Thomas enjoyed ubiquitous support among black women. An ad carrying the group's statement ran in the *New York Times* on November 17, 1991, signed by 1,603 black women. It also appeared in seven African-American newspapers across the country and was reprinted in *Essence* and *Black Scholar*.

This campaign was a landmark in black women's political history because it was the first time black women mobilized so quickly and broadly in connection with an event that affected their lives. But while it revealed many black women's willingness to bring their concerns into the open, the very need for such a response to the Clarence Thomas hearings showed how far the black community was from confronting and resolving divisive gender issues.

The Marriage Squeeze

Even as the accumulated tensions between black men and women became increasingly visible in the 1990s, gender relations were further strained by a factor demographers call a "marriage squeeze."

This occurs when a decrease in the availability of eligible partners leads to lower marriage rates, especially among women. Nationally, the overall ratios in the black population rose during the decade of 1830, a period when Blacks were in slavery and the ratio was 100.3 men to 100 women. From that year the ratios fell consistently until 1990, when they reached 88.2 men for every 100 black women (and this figure doesn't take into account factors such as unemployment and incarceration). In contrast, the corresponding figure for whites is 96.[17]

Despite the challenges they face in their relationships with men, black women have displayed a strong interest in marriage since emancipation, and like most women, black women today remain vitally interested in marrying. Yet a recent census analysis found that 44 percent of black women aged thirty to thirty-four were never married, compared to only 15 percent of white women.[18] Another estimate found that over a thirty-year period the proportion of time women can expect to spend married has declined dramatically. For white women this amount of time declined from 54 to 43 percent, whereas for black women it has plunged from 40 to 22 percent—the same proportion of life that the average college-educated person spends attending school. For women born in the 1950s these estimates suggest that 91 percent of whites, but only 70 percent of blacks, will ever marry.[19]

At the same time as the number of never married black women has been increasing, the average age of marriage for both African-American men and white men has been rising. Furthermore, around 1950 African American men began to marry later than white men, and they continue to do so.[20] Clearly, one factor in this trend is the difficulty black men have in gaining employment.

What generally determines a man's eligibility for marriage is employment, and many scholars concerned about the decline in black marriages have focused specifically on the economic causes. Black unemployment rates have consistently been twice as high as those of whites, and the earnings of black men have decreased in real terms in recent decades. The impact of these changes has been so dramatic that there are now more black women in the labor force than black men. In 1950, for example, 6.4 percent of wage earners were black men and 3.4 percent were black women. By 1990 the proportion of wage earners who were black men had declined to 5 percent, while the percentage who were black women had increased to 5.4 percent.[21] A number of analyses have found that men delay marriage when they are not employed. But the lack of jobs does not seem to be the whole answer. One analysis specifically found that declining employment for black men explained only 20 percent of the change in the average age of marriage.[22]

A second contributing factor is the migration of blacks to the North. Before World War II, African-American men had lower labor force participation rates and earnings than white men, yet they married earlier, on average, than their white counterparts. In the South, African-American men were employed in tenant farming, a system that encouraged men to marry early because an entire household was under contract and every able-bodied person was needed—including wives and children. With the mass northern migration of blacks through the 1950s, African-American men were relocated to an industrial economy that decreased the economic benefits for marriage.[23]

Besides economic factors, the delay in marriage of African-American men in the last half of this century reflects attitudes and behaviors that stem from the numerical shortages of marriageable males in the black community. These shortages have inflated the value of eligible men, allowing them to be more selective when picking a marital partner. As a result, black men prolong their dating years. Evidence for this explanation was provided by a survey that asked single men to select from a list the reason(s) they had not married. Whereas 27 percent of the white respondents indicated that "there were not enough women who met their standards," 47 percent of the black respondents chose this answer.[24] Another study found that although both black men and women were significantly less desirous of marriage than their white counterparts, young unmarried black men were much less enthusiastic than black women. Black men anticipated less improvement in their sex lives and personal friendships after marriage than their white counterparts.[25]

As a result of these trends, black women who are looking for a committed relationship find that many potential partners have become rather arrogant about their "preferred status." And, of course, because they are outnumbered by black women, black men have many more potential dating partners. Consequently, many black men date a lot of different women, while at the same time maintaining that they can't find women who meet their standards. Blair Underwood, a lead actor on several popular television shows, voiced a common attitude among black men on the *Oprah Winfrey Show.*

BLAIR UNDERWOOD: For me, I, like a lot of men, ran women and dated a lot, and I had to go through that process.

OPRAH: When you say "run women," Blair, what's that mean?

BLAIR UNDERWOOD: Run—dating a lot of women.... For me, I, like a lot of brothers, especially, you know, ran women and—dated a lot, and I had to go through that process of realizing that it is wrong and really taking a—a, you know, account of what I was saying and doing....

OPRAH: No, but really, I was just clarifying for all people—you know, like you, you mean you were dating a lot of women.

BLAIR UNDERWOOD: Yeah and for—you know, society almost allows, in fact, it does allow you as a man to say it's OK to have five, six different women.[26]

Black men's propensity to be involved in interracial dating and marriage further reduces the pool of marriageable black males and contributes to the decline in marriage among African Americans, since black women are much less likely to date and marry outside of the race. Black women's reluctance to have romantic relationships with white men is rooted in their history. For example, bell hooks described her experience when she arrived from the South on a predominantly white college campus with few black men to date:

> You couldn't grow up in the apartheid south and not know that the average white man looked at black women as sexual savages, wild things, bush mamas; mammy, whore, or prostitute, take your pick; that's the way it was. No wonder most black women felt they had to stay away from white men. She would have loved to have had black men with good hearts standing in line, longing to be close to her.[27]

Hooks went on to discuss the black community's double standard concerning interracial dating:

> I used to hang out with the street black men who came on campus to sell their wares, with some of the Muslim brothers. They would rant and rave about a sister who would do it with a white man. That sister was a traitor to the race. Of course the brother doing it with a white woman was not betraying the race in their eyes, he was just getting some pussy. Pussy had no power, no color, but dick now that was tied to meaningful manhood, to notions of privilege and choice and power.[28]

Given the realities of the dating market for black women, there are no easy answers for black women caught in the marriage squeeze. But for black women the inescapable reality is that they must also spread the "dating net" as widely as possible and not limit their dating opportunities to African-American men. For black women who are serious about maximizing their dating options, the best approach would probably be to remain open and not prejudge potential suitors based on such external characteristics as race or ethnicity and focus more attention on the inner person.

Personal Troubles as Public Issues

The late C. Wright Mills, in his classic *The Sociological Imagination*, distinguished between individuals' personal troubles, such as being unable to find a job or getting a divorce, and public issues, such as patterns of widespread joblessness or high rates of marital dissolution. Mills argued that the "sociological imagination" allows us to see the interconnection between individuals' troubles and large-scale patterns in society.[29]

The increasingly visible conflicts between black men and women are a case in point. Behind this public issue are countless individual stories of troubled relationships and marital breakups, events that seem private and personal to the men and women involved. When we stand back and look at events on a larger scale, however, we can detect patterns that reveal some of the broad social factors at work in black marriages. Understanding these factors can shed light on the unique experience of individual men and women.

As I indicated earlier, marital patterns are one good index of the state of gender relations in the African-American community. The social science and public policy literature has given attention primarily to poor black families. Here we focus on the relatively neglected patterns in middle- and upper-income marriages. The data on these marriages suggest that black marriages are subject to a complex set of strains and tensions.

Statistics from a national data set of college graduates provide one window into marital breakups among middle-class blacks. For women, nearly twice as many black college graduates were divorced or separated as white graduates (21 percent versus 11 percent). For male college graduates, the rates of divorce and separation were somewhat lower, 15 percent for black men and 9 percent for white men. Of these four groups, then, black women had the highest rate of marital breakups.[30]

Household income may provide a clue to the greater strains placed on the marriages of college-educated black women. Data on the income of graduates from elite colleges and universities show that white married women's household incomes were higher than those of black married women graduates and that the white women graduates were married to men who made substantially more money than the husbands of the black women. What may be more surprising is that black women graduates from elite colleges and universities earned considerably more money than their husbands—exactly the opposite of the pattern for the white women graduates. The black women graduates, on average, earned $58,500, compared to $34,300 for their husbands; the black women thus contributed 63 percent of the household income. In contrast, the white women graduates earned an average of $46,800, or 40 percent of the total household income of $116,700. Interestingly, although the household income of black male graduates was less than that of white male graduates ($107,800 and $125,200 respectively), the spousal income for both groups of men was the same ($26,000).[31]

In part these differences in spouses' contribution to household income suggest exactly what classic exchange theory predicted: Traditional marriage is an exchange of a male's economic resources for a female's social and domestic services.[32] In our supposedly postmodern society, it seems that the best-educated black and white males continue to exchange their higher socioeconomic status for spouses who conform to more traditional gender-role behavior. What is less clear is what is involved in the barter between women graduates from elite universities and their spouses. Although white women graduates enjoyed higher household incomes than black women, their own earnings were $10,000 less than those of the black women and considerably less than their husbands'.[33] What this suggests is that white women graduates may voluntarily elect to "downsize" their careers and increase their commitment to their families, an option black women feel they do not have because of their husbands' lower earnings.

For black women, then, the traditional exchange model does not apply. Even the best-educated black women continue to fulfill the dual roles of homemaker and wage earner. In fact, in a competitive market with a depleted pool of marriageable males, a college education probably increases the chances of a black woman's getting married. Figures from the National Health and Social Life Survey 1992 suggest this hypothesis by indicating that black women on the high end of a seven-category income scale are 77 percent more likely to get married than black women at the lowest end of the scale. (In contrast, high personal income had no significant impact on the odds of black men's ever being married.[34]) But with a divorce rate that is more than twice as high as white women's, there is clearly more instability in black women's marriages.

Not only are black women deprived of the "benefits" of the traditional exchange between white women and their husbands, but there has historically been less consensus among black men and women about what constitutes appropriate gender roles. This lack of agreement on what is "appropriate" for men and women adds to the strain on black marriages. In particular, a nationwide survey conducted in 1997 found dramatic differences in the attitudes of black men and women regarding the effect on their marriages of women's working outside the home. Whereas 51 percent of black men believed women's increased participation in the labor force made it easier for marriages to be successful, 67 percent of black women believed that their participation in the workforce made it more difficult for their marriages to succeed.[35] What this suggests is that black women are only reluctantly shouldering the historical double burden of work and family responsibilities in their marriages, and either they are not communicating the weight of this burden to their husbands or the husbands aren't listening. At the same time, black women's willingness to continue combining work

THE PATH TO HEALING

and family duties may reflect the "tight" marriage market wherein black women feel lucky to be married at all.

Black women's choices may be limited, but that does not mean they are content with them. The disparities in the incomes of the black college-educated women and their spouses—and the apparent lack of discomfort on the part of black men with their "lighter load"—enhances our understanding of a 1993 research study which found that black women placed "greater emphasis on economic support" than the white women surveyed. In addition, compared to white women, black women were more resistant to marrying someone with fewer economic resources.[36]

The strains on black marriages are reflected in the attitudes of black men and women toward the costs and benefits of being married. Mark R. Rank and Larry E. Davis conducted a rigorous investigation of how spouses perceived the effects of marriage on their prospects for happiness, a question that had been virtually ignored in the literature of black and white family life. Utilizing a nationally representative sample of 13,017 individuals, they asked currently married men and women what their level of happiness would be if they were separated from their spouse. The analysis uncovered sizable racial differences. Both black wives and husbands were considerably more likely than their white counterparts to say that their level of happiness would be higher if they were not married. Whereas 45 percent of white wives and 36 percent of white husbands felt that their level of happiness would be much lower outside of marriage, only 22 percent of black wives and 20 percent of black husbands reported similar perceptions. More specifically, black husbands and wives were more likely than whites to feel that their standard of living, career opportunities, social life, sex life, and even their life as a parent would be more favorable outside of marriage. The widest differences between white and black wives were in terms of their standard of living, sex life, and being a parent; for husbands, the differences were greatest in terms of sex life and being a parent. These findings are consistent with those from an earlier study which reported that the majority of residents in an exclusively middle-class African-American neighborhood in Atlanta described their marriages as "weak." These research data on married couples' attitudes and perceptions suggest that something much deeper is going on in black marriages than is explained by such structural factors as black men's employment.[37]

In recent investigations comparing white and black married couples, four factors have emerged to explain the greater marital instability among African Americans. First, compared to white husbands, black husbands do have greater anxiety concerning issues of job stability and financial security.[38] Second, an ideology of male dominance continues to prevail among black men whose "traditional" views on issues of gender equality are generally not shared by their black spouses.[39] Third, the imbalance in the ratio of men to women in the black community contributes to a "buyer's market" for black men and weakens their resolve to work out marital conflicts.[40] Finally, the proportion of black men who admit to being unfaithful to their wives (44 percent) is almost double the figure for white men. In contrast, the differences between black women and white women are minuscule (18 percent and 15 percent respectively).[41]

When psychologist John M. Gottman conducted research in an effort to determine what constitutes a successful marriage, he may have identified the missing link for many black couples. His research contradicts the Mars-Venus school of relationships and found that equal percentages of men and women in his study sample said that the quality of the spousal friendship was the most important factor in marital satisfaction. Given the historic conflict between black men and women, it seems that the greatest challenge facing black couples is becoming friends.[42]

The various findings on black marriages suggest that these relationships are strained by a complex interaction between black couples' attitudes and expectations and their objective circumstances. In particular, both black men and women may be affected by the traditional ideas about marriage and gender roles that are prevalent in white society even when their own situations force them into behaviors that depart from these "ideals." Given the limited opportunities for many black men to secure high-paying jobs, the traditional exchange theory between men and women, whereby women trade their roles as homemakers and mothers for their husbands' status and financial support, is out of reach for many black couples. Yet both parties may have conflicting and ambivalent attitudes about their inevitable compromises within this traditional model. While a majority of black men may not see their wives working (and doing "double duty") as problematic for their marriages, many of the same men continue to subscribe to the "ideal" of male dominance. In effect, they expect their wives to be at once feminine and submissive yet strong enough to shoulder their double burden of family responsibilities and work. Furthermore, at a deeper level, men's financial dependence on their wives may trouble both spouses.

The experiences of a man named John illustrate the effects that a husband's job instability can have on even a ten-year marriage:

John, a 42-year-old factory worker, grew up in a working-class nuclear family with five older sisters. John's father worked in a factory and his mother was employed as a domestic servant. John's comments give us some insight into the quality of his parents' marriage. "My parents were married for 40 years. They were poor, but loved each other. We had a lot of love in our family and that kept us close." Although John's father had a sixth-grade education, he emphasized the importance of a college education.

John graduated with a bachelor's degree in sociology from a historically black college, where he met his wife. Although she already had a child, she had never married. In recollecting the decision to marry, John reported: "We got married 'cause we wanted to, she was not pregnant. I thought we could make it 'cause she handled money wisely and worked hard. . . . She earned an accounting degree, and I considered her daughter my own biological daughter. At age 36, we owned two houses." John described the period prior to his marriage as "the happiest time of my life" and described the roles of husband and father as sources of contentment and stability. Even though John had a college degree, he worked as a factory laborer just as his father before him, who only had a sixth-grade education.

When the company John worked for downsized, he was laid off. During his period of unemployment, he was a househusband, while his wife worked two jobs. He describes the frustration he experienced during that period in the following comments: "I just couldn't keep living like that. . . . I hated to see my wife support the family by working two jobs. . . . I felt like a failure." He eventually moved his family to another city where he found better employment opportunities, and worked constantly to decrease the debts accumulated over the years. Considerable tensions built up in his marriage during those years and when he divorced, he attributed the divorce to that layoff. "Before I was laid off, we took vacations and entertained friends. I was making good money when the company closed. During that time, my son was born and we purchased a home. We also had a two-year-old daughter. When our lifestyle changed, our marriage fell apart. . . . I worked three jobs to try and stabilize the family financially, but we couldn't get the marriage on track after the layoff. . . . I promised myself to have enough money saved for future layoffs."[43]

For their part, black women who assume the double duty of work and family responsibilities may do so only reluctantly, harboring resentment even while being proud of their ability to contribute to the family's support. Furthermore, black women's historic role as wage earners and pillars of the family contributes to a sense of strength that is not easily reconciled with a traditionally "feminine" stance of submissiveness toward their husbands. One black woman described how her quest for personal growth collided with her own and her husband's expectations about gender roles in marriage:

My husband had quite conventional ideas about spousal relations and in the beginning, trying to be the proper wife, I accepted his logic without question. After all, I reasoned, I wanted to be like my mother, a good wife, and to do what I had to keep peace and harmony in my marriage. My husband and I rarely argued, mainly because he acted on whatever decision he made and generally told me about it afterward, and as he so candidly told me in the beginning of our relationship, I could either accept it (his decision) and get mad, or not accept it and get mad; either way it was up to him.

But as I moved more into a place of self-growth and discovery I started taking figurative swings at this form of subtle control by following his example. I started making my own decisions, and then telling him about them. "Why didn't you ask me first?" he would inquire. "You never ask me about decisions that you make," I would respond, and the argument was on. Sometimes I felt the need for support and called Momi, but as it was with my brother when I was younger, Momi would reply in a soft voice, "Well now, baby, he is your husband." Again, not the response I wanted or needed to hear. . . .

Sometimes when my husband and I could talk rationally about things he would state his concern about changes I was making in myself. "You never acted like this before; you're changing and I don't know if I like it." In all fairness, he was right. I was changing, and while I wasn't sure if I totally embraced all the aspects of my changes, at that time in my life, I did know that I wanted to experience and enjoy a certain kind of emotional freedom.

"What type of emotional freedom are you talking about?" he would ask suspiciously. "I'm not really sure, but I don't want to give up learning about and expressing myself. I'd really like to

197

have your support, not your approval or disapproval, but just
some support."

We were divorced a year later. Enough said.[44]

The Chains of the Past

While such immediate circumstances as gender ratios and employment opportunities contribute to the strains on relationships of
black men and women, they do not of themselves fully explain what
is going on in gender relations in the African-American community. As we have seen, at least equally important are the attitudes, expectations, and values that individual men and women bring to
their relationships. These "inner" variables are strongly influenced
by what happens to us in our growing up years, when we learn what
marriages and families are about, what it means to be a man and a
woman, and what to expect from individuals of the opposite sex.

For African Americans, as for all people, the formative experiences of childhood are conditioned by history. The experiences of
one generation shape the legacy passed on to the next. Just as the
development of human babies in the womb repeats in miniature
the evolutionary history of the human race, so, too, the personal
stories of contemporary African Americans reflect and recapitulate
the history of blacks in America. While in some ways this history is
a source of strength, in other ways it has forged inner chains that
black men and women must learn to cast off if they are to find the
path to healing.

For example, a primary reason for black couples' marital tensions is the husband's need to be dominant in the marriage. What is
the underlying issue in this need for dominance in romantic
relationships? Two psychologists at the University of California at
Berkeley, Carolyn Pape Cowan and Phillip A. Cowan, have been
conducting a long-term study that evaluates what happens when
partners become parents. The wealth of research evidence they have

amassed suggests that "good things" and "bad things" cycle through the generations. In particular, the patriarchal ethos that emerged in the black family after emancipation has been transmitted across the generations and today translates into male dominance.[45]

The story of Malcolm X is an example. He was six when his father was brutally murdered. Some of Malcolm's most vivid memories of his parents' marriage were of the friction between them. His father was the controlling force in the marriage and often beat his mother. It is not surprising that Malcolm carried his attitudes of dominance toward women into adulthood, attitudes that he consciously identified and strove to overcome:

> I taught brothers not only to deal unintelligently with the devil or the white woman, but I also taught many brothers to spit acid at sisters. They were kept in their places—you probably didn't notice this in action, but it is a fact. . . . If the sisters decided a thing was wrong, they had to suffer it out. If the sister wanted to have her husband at home with her for the evening, I taught the brothers that the sisters were standing in their way; in the way of the Messenger, in the way of progress, in the way of God Himself. I did these things my brother, I must undo them.[46]

While some black men have learned an attitude of dominance toward women from the example of their fathers and other male adults, others have acquired it from growing up in families where there is no male role model and a woman is the dominant figure. Psychology suggests an explanation for this seeming paradox. A male's attitude toward women is deeply rooted in how he experienced his female caregivers as a child. In order for a boy to develop into a man, he should ideally give up his attachment to his first love—his mother. Part of the process is learning to identify with the male parent. If the father is either absent or remote, he will not be able to direct the boy away from the mother. What results is the unfinished business of separation from the mother, and this often leads to deep-seated antagonism toward women later in life. According to this theory, the need of many black men to be dominant in romantic relationships is one of the masks they wear to hide a fear of being controlled by a woman.[47]

Martin Luther King, Jr., is a case in point. It was common knowledge among those active in the civil rights movement that King had problems with black women he considered strong or overbearing (he was conspicuously not alone in having this dilemma). For example, Ella Baker, who served as the executive secretary of the Southern Christian Leadership Conference (SCLC) and the "political and spiritual midwife" for SNCC, could say: "There would never be a role for me in a leadership capacity with SCLC. Why? First, I'm a woman."[48] Andrew Young traced King's discomfort with strong women to his relationship with his mother:

> We had a hard time with domineering women in SCLC, because Martin's mother, quiet as she was, was the really strong, domineering force in the family. She would never publicly say anything but she ran Daddy King, and she ran the church, and she ran Martin, and Martin's problem in the early days of the movement was directly related to his need to be free of that strong matriarchal influence.[49]

The all-powerful mother can leave an indelible imprint on her children, especially her sons. Dr. Ben Carson, an internationally renowned African-American pediatric neurosurgeon, describes growing up in a home with a demanding mother and how his father's absence after his parents' divorce left him without a male role model:

> Sonya Carson has the classic Type A personality—hard-working, goal-oriented, driven to demanding the best of herself in any situation, refusing to settle for less. She's highly intelligent, a woman who quickly grasps the overall significance rather than searching for details. . . . Mother had only a third grade educa-

tion when she married, yet she provided the driving force in our home. She pushed my laid-back dad to do a lot of things. . . . [After my parents' divorce, neither my brother nor I] had a role model of success, or even a respectable male figure to look up to.[50]

The historical issue of father absence in black homes affects daughters as well, but in different ways. Unlike boys, girls do not need to give up their attachment to their mothers in order become autonomous adults. Girls can form a dependent bond on their mothers and retain this close affiliation. If the mother is angry toward men or distrustful of them, however, the daughter may become overly reliant on her mother and also learn to distrust men. One survey of black mothers and daughters revealed that a majority of black mothers gave their daughters negative messages about black men. Many black daughters hear "Never depend on a man to support you" or "You can't rely on men to satisfy your needs or fulfill their responsibility" and carry these negative messages into their own relationships with black men.[51]

Daughters can be affected in yet another way by the absence or emotional distance of their fathers. A father or surrogate father figure is generally the first love in a girl's life, and the one who teaches her about the possibility of trust, emotional intimacy, and tenderness with members of the opposite sex. When daughters are deprived of a loving relationship with their fathers, the effects can be lasting. Iyanla Vanzant, a motivational speaker and best-selling author, is a black woman who was deprived of a loving relationship with her father: "My father died when I was 30. . . . My father never kissed me, never hugged me, never embraced me—never, never, never, never."[52] Once again, the messages carried by early experiences like this can impair a woman's ability to establish an intimate and trusting relationship with a man.

Father absence has thus created different dynamics for black men and women, dynamics that can become a self-perpetuating cycle. Father absence, over time, has created a pattern wherein many black women are excessively self-reliant and unwilling to develop the trust and interdependence that a healthy relationship demands. In contrast, many black men have developed a pattern of simultaneous dependence on women and antagonism toward them. Under the tutelage of their mothers, black women have learned how to exercise optimal control over their environments, while black men have learned to resist this control by any means necessary. The result has been to put into motion a set of forces that generate rivalry, bitterness, rage, and yearning—emotions that are played out in the arena of romantic relationships.

Given the distinctive history of African Americans, it is evident that virtually none of us has managed to reach adulthood unscathed by such injuries. The many strains and instabilities in black family life replicate themselves over time in the emotional baggage we each carry from our families of origin.

To undo the legacy of generations is no easy task, yet some individuals do manage to find a way. Shirlee Taylor Haizlip discusses her mother's family background in her memoir *In the Garden of Our Dreams*. Haizlip notes that her mother was abandoned as a child and grew up in a series of foster homes:

> My mother had no one to teach her to be a mother. Her own mother died when she was four. A series of guardians, one mad, one busy, and one cold, raised her. Somehow, from the deep spaces of her heart, she patched together her own formula of mothering. . . . She extended her maternal wings. With the profound sorrow of her childhood as a subtext, she gathered and nurtured other motherless, wounded children. Although they were not the children of her womb, they were the children of her heart. Our family blossomed as she sheltered, loved, and spoiled five other girls.[53]

Many individual men and women, like Shirlee Haizlip's mother, grew up in family settings that were less than ideal but have found the way to turn the memory of pain into a resolve to find a better way. It has been said that no one has the parents they deserve, but this is no excuse for our not beginning the healing process in our adult lives. The psychic wounds many of us have sustained are not limited to those we received in our families of origin. We may have been deeply injured by teachers, friends, employers, colleagues, and especially lovers. The cycle of pain and conflict repeats itself—until we make the decision to break it.

Breaking the Cycle of Pain and Conflict

When black women organized their "Million Women March" in Philadelphia in 1997, some black men were also in attendance. Kazembe and Farmina Williams, husband and wife, made the nineteen-hour trip from Tulsa, Oklahoma, to participate in the event. Kazembe had attended the "Million Man March" in Washington two years earlier and was so overwhelmed by the love he had experienced that he was determined his wife should be part of a similar event. Kazembe noted, "The world knows that the black woman has been the backbone of every struggle."[54]

Loving relationships like the Williamses' are the place where healing begins. Embarking on such a relationship is always a risk, especially for African Americans who have experienced so much hurt and pain in their past. The first step is to acknowledge and confront the hurtful behavior of the past and to both seek forgiveness and give forgiveness.

One example of such an effort is the group of black men who have started a project called "Sister, I'm Sorry." Building on the theme of "atonement" at the Million Man March, these men are calling for a truce in the battle of the sexes in the African-American community. The group's leader, Reverend Donald Bell, recently appeared on the *Oprah Winfrey Show* along with men and women who had taken part in the group's "apology sessions":

REVEREND DONALD BELL: I want you brothers to go to 'em, take 'em by the hand, look 'em in the eye and apologize on behalf of the brother that abandoned 'em. If we really searched our hearts, we would have to acknowledge that we've created an environment that is hostile towards women.

OPRAH: The apology is for the deep emotional and physical scars that men have inflicted on women. Bell says it doesn't matter that these men and women are strangers. The apology is the first step in healing the wound and bridging the gap between the sexes. . . . Sharon Nash says that years of being lied to and cheated on and betrayed left her bitter and unable to trust men.

SHARON NASH: I didn't value myself at times, and so I was involved with a lot of the wrong people, and they were abusive to me, verbally, emotionally, they hurt me. You know, when I've given my heart to men and they've stepped on it or squashed it or—you know, why?

OPRAH: Sharon says that the apology sessions have been life-changing, like a deliverance. The question I have, and I'm sure so many other people watching have, is, OK, so these are not the men who did this to you. . . . So how do men who didn't do that to you—how does that have any impact on the pain?

SHARON NASH: I think they're like a tool. They're used like a tool. They were used like a tool to damage you, and they're used like a tool to heal.

OPRAH: Terrell Maclin says that seeing the women's pain during the apology session was a powerful slap in the face, because it helped him to realize that he was a cheater. . . .

TERRELL MACLIN: . . . We talked about [how] society teaches us as young men that it's cool, that it's happening, that, you know, you can be the mac daddy, you can be the playboy and it's cool—the fancy cars, the women. And we—we go through this. And it—it's something that is taught. And we have to stop that . . . to listen to that and things that I never thought about that women have been through and things we have done, it just blew my mind. And I—I said, "We, as a—as a generation of men, we got to do something about this, because if we don't fix it, what about the—the ones after us and the ones after them if we don't take a stand today to—to fix this thing?"[55]

Confronting the issue of men's attitudes toward dating and fidelity is important in view of the research cited earlier in this chapter which has shown that, compared to whites, twice as many black husbands acknowledged having been unfaithful to their wives. In contrast to the 44 percent of black husbands who admitted infidelity, only 18 percent of black wives made comparable admissions, or about the same proportion of white married women (15 percent).[56] Ossie Davis, the legendary actor, addressed this issue in his memoirs when discussing his long-term marriage to Ruby Dee:

Fifty years of being married and what have I learned from it all? I say to my fellow husbands—whose eyeballs may be covered with lust—that the way to possess all women is to love one woman well.[57]

The "Sister, I'm Sorry" project is an important step toward healing the relationships between black males and females. But women, too, must confront their past behavior. Many black women have allowed themselves to be used by men—and have used men as well. To begin their healing process, women will need to take responsibility for their own behavior. A recent article in *Essence* entitled "Are You Being Played?" averred, "A woman's intuition is very sharp if she chooses to use it. . . . We ignore the signals because we want to make love work so badly."[58]

A second step on the path to healing is to examine the attitudes and perceptions that underlie our behavior. Although works such as psychologist John Gray's *Men Are from Mars, Women Are from Venus* may contribute to the perennial debates on gender differences, they also highlight the role that stereotyping based on gender plays in our relationships.

For black Americans, history has given gender stereotyping a unique twist. It is not only the man or woman who is stereotyped but the black man and the black woman. This issue surfaced, for example, when in a national sample black women were asked "What stands out in your mind most clearly with regard to what your mother told you about men?" Seventy-seven percent of the women indicated that their mothers gave them negative messages about black men. Some of the responses were as follows:

They're dogs. Always in heat, move from one woman to another without a thought in their minds.

All men are degenerate animals.

That they were no good and they are only after what you have to offer sexually.

You can't depend on them. You have to rely on yourself.

Do not trust any man, not even your brothers.

Never depend on a man to support you.

Always be sure you could take care of yourself, and without the husband's knowledge, have money on the side for yourself.

With these kinds of systematic messages coming from their mothers, it is not surprising that many black women bring so much negativity to their relationships with black men. But black men, too, have stereotyped images of black women as lacking softness and femininity both in personality and appearance.

To begin to confront the stereotypes of the other sex, black women and men must begin to ask themselves questions like these:

What biases and generalizations do I make about black men or women?

What emotional reactions are associated with these generalizations?

How might these generalizations affect decisions I make about working with, interacting with, or dating black men or women?

Is there anything about my behavior that would cause a black man or woman to feel uncomfortable or apprehensive?

Am I significantly more comfortable with people of my own sex than I am with black members of the opposite sex? Why? Am I willing to move beyond my level of discomfort so that I learn to be more at ease with black men or women?

When we perceive others in terms of our stereotypes, we may create self-fulfilling experiences. At the same time, human beings seem to have a built-in mechanism for detecting when we feel safe and when we do not. This applies not just to physical safety but to emotional and psychological safety. In relationships, if we detect a risk of being hurt, ridiculed, or misjudged, our immediate reaction is to become defensive or to shut down emotionally. Many black women send these signals to black men. By the same token, many black men send comparable signals to black women. Their very aggressiveness may mask the fear of being dominated. Asking and answering questions like those listed above can uncover some of these defense mechanisms, but to do so requires the courage to be honest with oneself. A willingness to engage in this process of self-examination is a key step in changing the long-standing patterns that divide black men and women from one another.

If we are to deal effectively with the difficulties that we experience in gender relations, we will need to do even more than acknowledge and seek forgiveness for past actions and combat stereotypes. We will need to go to the root source of destructive patterns in our relationships. That is, we will need to recognize and address the ways in which the dominant culture has systematically supported us in maintaining our separateness and hampering our ability to build effective partnerships.

That is why I have taken such pains in this book to describe the evolution of black family life and relationships between black women and men in America. We are still living out today a story that began in the chains of slavery. It was during slavery that our family lives were broken apart, that our men learned the price of trying to live out their ideas of manhood, and that our women learned both their helplessness in the face of exploitation and their responsibility and power to hold their families together. Though they were given no part in the dominant culture, even then black men and women could not escape the influence of its values. They absorbed the white southern ideal that made the white mistress the paragon of "femininity," at once an object of scorn for black women and a forbidden attraction for black men. They absorbed, too, the very stereotypes that white culture had imposed on them, of coarse and lascivious black women and emasculated black men.

After emancipation, impoverished black husbands and wives tried to reconstitute family life amid a confusion over gender roles and in circumstances that compelled black women to perform the double duty of working long days alongside their husbands in the fields while fulfilling the roles of mother, caregiver, cook, seamstress, and housekeeper. Black women yearned to return to the home; black men yearned to take their "rightful" place at the head of the household. Both sought self-respect while being victimized by a culture that punished black men for achieving and sexually exploited black women, who, in the eyes of southern white men, could be raped with impunity.

Those black men and women who did succeed in advancing to the middle class tended to adopt the same Victorian ideals of family life that were prevalent among white families. This model separated human experience into "the man's world" of governance, power, and control and the "woman's world" of motherhood and homemaker, with women totally dependent on men for financial support. This paradigm has made it difficult for men and women to experience themselves as equal partners in the work of raising children, taking care of the home, generating an income, and building businesses. Moreover, the "ideal" was out of step with black reality. Since very few black women had the opportunity to stay at home and care for their families, many developed a cumulative anger at black men for depriving them of their "rightful" place in the home. Men, in turn, demanded support and submission from women who had earned the right to be strong and whose own issues were eclipsed by the overpowering issue of racism.

The irony is that the cultural values that permeated the consciousness of black men and women not only were ill-suited to the real circumstances of African Americans but were dysfunctional even for the members of the dominant culture. It is not only black men and women who are trying to find their way in today's society, but in their unique circumstances they suffer the consequences of these values more than any other group.

Once we recognize and acknowledge the cultural conditioning that has prevented black men and women from coming together to create synergistic male-female partnerships, we will be ready to begin developing the skills and capabilities for moving beyond our difficulties. The greatest challenge for African-American men and women is letting go of the past. For black women it is letting go of the resentment and anger that have been transmitted from their mothers and grandmothers—the cumulated rage over the lack of support from black men, over the feelings of abandonment and betrayal. Black women will need to learn new ways of building effective partnerships with black men based on trust and mutual respect. Similarly, black men will need to recognize the ways in which they have bought into the cultural myths of femininity and male dominance. If they learn to let go of these myths, to listen and to learn, they may be genuinely saddened to realize how adherence to these myths has led them to harass and abuse black women. Black men will need to learn new relational skills in order to move beyond these biases against women and toward genuine intimacy.

In particular, the issue of male dominance remains one of the primary sources of tension in black marriages, especially when the wife is the principal wage earner. Overcoming the effects of their conditioning on this issue is difficult, but it can hold great rewards.

Consider the case of Monica and Avery, a young black couple who were having financial problems that threatened their marriage. He managed a restaurant, while she was a premed student. The couple was $29,000 in debt when Suze Orman, the best-selling author, showed them how forgiveness could get them past the anger and shame that were keeping them from resolving their difficulties constructively. These conflicts were having some of their most harmful effects on the romantic and sexual aspects of their marriage. After Orman's intervention, the couple shared with a television audience how they both changed. Avery discussed a recent incident:

AVERY: We had a chance just to be out in Chicago, about town, and it was just amazing that every thought about little things, you know, little purchases we wanted to buy, you know, a little small outfit for my son, and I just asked my wife—I said, you know, "Is this something that he needs or something that we want to get?" And it was, for the first time . . .

MONICA: That shocked me.

AVERY: Yeah. Yeah. And it felt really weird, honestly, to ask that question, because, I think, for a lot of men, it—well, I know for me—I'll speak for myself—it seemed to be like breaking out of a bondage that men have about asking permission. There's a stigma that to be a man, you know, you can never ask, you just step out and do. And my wife is just forced to follow and to say, OK, you're the man. I'll just, you know, "tag along." But it was—it was, I guess, a breakthrough, because after I was able to ask, I felt that she appreciated me asking and . . .

MONICA: Not only . . .

AVERY: . . . it made me want to do it more.

MONICA: Not only that, the closeness that we have for each other now, I'm able to enjoy him and . . . to be able to forgive him, because I kept myself in bondage for so long. And then, looking back, if my husband can forgive me some of the choices that I made, the decision that I made that caused us to have problems in our relationship, I should be able to forgive him. And in every aspect, it has changed for the better.[59]

Monica and Avery seem to be finding a new way—a way that breaks the chains of the past.

In her groundbreaking book *Friends and Strangers,* Karen Mains describes the challenge of intimacy:

This is a society where, for the most part, men know only how to use women, control them, or possess them; where women manipulate men. Intimacy seems possible only in the sex act. . . . [But] there's a better way a few of us with strength enough, with wisdom enough must forge. . . . The truth is that we are lonely for each other because we were created to need each other.[60]

This is the challenge we face as black men and women in America. Our survival as a race is predicated upon our ability to relate to each other as equals. We must begin by recognizing and honoring our differences as men and women, and devise ways to use our differences and complementary strengths to enrich our visions and our joint struggles. As Paulo Freire admonished, "The true focus of revolutionary change is never merely the oppressive situations that we seek to escape, but that piece of the oppressor that is planted deep within each of us, and that knows only the oppressor's tactics, the oppressor's relationships."[61]

We have arrived where we are today by traveling on a long, hard road, one that was not wholly of our own choosing. The path ahead is long as well, and the way is steep. But if we choose it, and if we learn to walk together as comrades, we will, at long last, lighten the load.

Let the healing begin.

Appendix

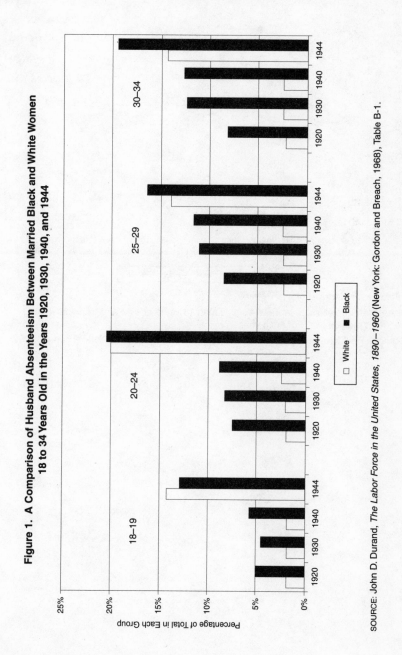

Figure 1. A Comparison of Husband Absenteeism Between Married Black and White Women 18 to 34 Years Old in the Years 1920, 1930, 1940, and 1944

SOURCE: John D. Durand, *The Labor Force in the United States, 1890–1960* (New York: Gordon and Breach, 1968), Table B-1.

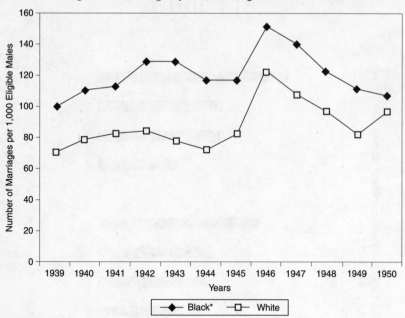

Figure 2. Marriages per 1,000 Eligible Males: 1939–1950

*Figures for blacks are for nonwhites.

NOTE: Marriage eligibles represent single men 15 years or over and all divorced or widowed men as of 7/1 of each year.

SOURCE: Paul H. Jacobson, *American Marriage and Divorce* (New York: Rinehart, 1959).

Figure 3. Education in the United States

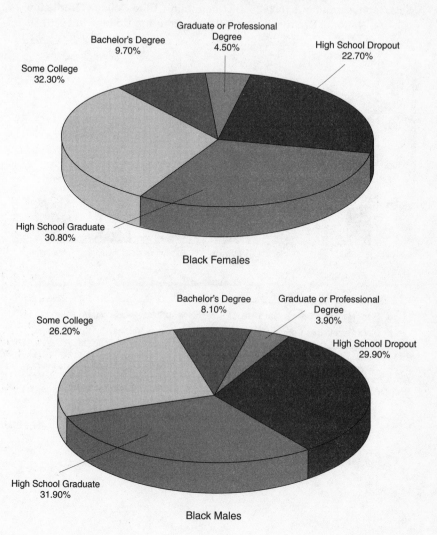

Graduate or Professional
Degree
4.50%

Bachelor's Degree
9.70%

Some College
32.30%

High School Dropout
22.70%

High School Graduate
30.80%

Black Females

Bachelor's Degree
8.10%

Graduate or Professional
Degree
3.90%

Some College
26.20%

High School Dropout
29.90%

High School Graduate
31.90%

Black Males

SOURCE: Education in the United States, U.S. Bureau of the Census, 1990.

Figure 4. Percentage of Black Males and Black Females in Selected Occupations in 1995, by Occupation, Elite College Graduates, and National Graduates (for Students Entering College in 1976)

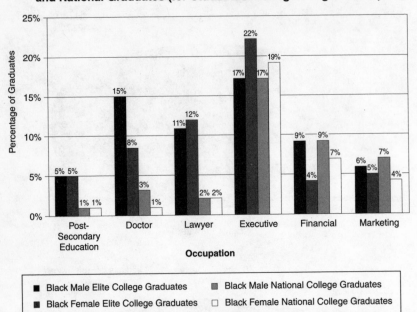

SOURCES: Adapted from William G. Bowen and Derek Bok, *The Shape of the River: Long-Term Consequences of Considering Race in College and University Admissions* (Princeton, NJ: Princeton University Press, 1998); and U.S. Bureau of the Census, 1990.

Figure 5. Mean Earned Income in 1995, by Race and Gender, Elite College Graduates and National Graduates (for Students Entering College in 1976)

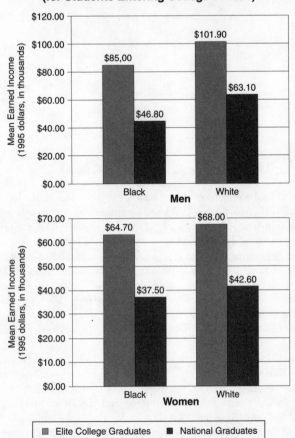

SOURCES: Adapted from William G. Bowen and Derek Bok, *The Shape of the River: Long-Term Consequences of Considering Race in College and University Admissions* (Princeton, NJ: Princeton University Press, 1998); and U.S. Bureau of the Census, 1990.

Notes

1 Breaking the Silence

1. This material was forwarded to the author several times on the Internet.

2. The marital opportunities index was computed for unmarried black men aged 18–44 and for unmarried black women aged 18–42. See Marcia Guttentag and Paul Secord, *Too Many Women? The Sex Ratio Question* (Beverly Hills, CA: Sage Publications, 1983), p. 201. For one of the most rigorous analyses of sex ratios controlling for the black man's labor force participation, see William A. Darity and Samuel L. Myers, "Family Structure and the Marginalization of Black Men: Policy Implications," in M. Belinda Tucker and Claudia Mitchell-Kernan, eds., *The Decline in Marriage Among African Americans* (New York: Russell Sage Foundation, 1995).

3. Tucker and Mitchell-Kernan, *The Decline in Marriage Among African Americans,* p. 12.

4. Michael Lind, "The Beige and the Black," *New York Times Magazine,* August 16, 1998. See also Orlando Patterson, *Rituals of Blood: Consequences of Slavery in Two American Centuries* (Washington, DC: Civitas/Counterpoint, 1998), pp. 128–29.

5. Scott South, "Racial and Ethnic Differences in the Desire to Marry," *Journal of Marriage and the Family* 55 (May 1993): 357–71. See also M. Belinda Tucker and Robert Taylor, "Demographic Correlates of Relationship Status Among Black Americans," *Journal of Marriage and the Family* 51 (1989): 655–65.

6. Pam Belluck, "Study Exposes Domestic Violence as Leading Killer of Women," *The New York Times,* March 31, 1998. See also W. Oliver, "Black Males and the Tough Guy: A Dysfunctional Compensatory Adaptation," *The Western Journal of Black Studies* 3 (1984): 201–12; Murray R. Straus and Richard R. Gelles, *Physical Violence in American Families: Risk Factors and Adaptations to Violence in 8,145 Families* (New York: Transaction Publishers, 1994); and Fox Butterfield, "Study Shows a Racial Divide in Domestic Violence Cases," *The New York Times,* May 18, 2000, p. A16.

7. Richard A. Mackey and Bernard A. O'Brien, "Marital Conflict Management: Gender and Ethnic Differences," *Social Work* 43 (March 1998): 128–40.

8. Paul Amato and Alan Booth, "Consequences of Parental Divorce and Marital Unhappiness for Adult Well-Being," *Social Forces* 69 (1991): 895–914.

9. Gloria I. Joseph and Jill Lewis, *Common Differences: Conflicts in Black and White Feminist Perspectives* (Boston: South End Press, 1981), p. 121. Data from this nationwide survey were collected from 1979 to 1980 and are somewhat dated, but when I surveyed fifty black women in 1999, 68 percent indicated they had received negative messages from their mothers about black men.

10. These trends were documented by Natalie J. Sokoloff in *Black Women and White Women in the Professions: Occupational Segregation by Race and Gender, 1960–1980* (New York: Routledge, 1992), p. 99.

11. Jacqueline J. Jackson, "Black Women and Higher Education," mimeographed (Duke University, 1973).

12. Kent G. Mommsen, "Career Patterns of Black American Doctorates" (Ph.D. dissertation, Florida State University, 1970). See also Shirley Malcolm, "Increasing the Participation of Black Women in Science and Technology," *Sage: A Scholarly Journal on Black Women* 6 (Fall 1989): 15–17.

13. Erma Lawson and Aaron Thompson, "Black Men Make Sense of Marital Distress and Divorce: An Exploratory Study," *Family Relations* 44 (April 1995): 211–19.

14. Darlene Clark Hine, "Rape and the Inner Lives of Black Women in the Middle West: Preliminary Thoughts on the Culture of Dissemblance," in Ellen Carol Du Bois and Vicki L. Ruiz, eds., *Unequal Sisters: A Multicultural Reader in U.S. Women's History* (New York: Routledge, 1990).

2   The Past Is Prologue: Slavery and Its Aftermath

1. Maya Angelou's words are from an interview on the *Charlie Rose* television show, December 25, 1996.

2. Leon F. Litwack, *Been in the Storm So Long: The Aftermath of Slavery* (New York: Vintage Books, 1979), pp. 234–35.

3. George P. Rawick, ed., *The American Slave: A Composite Autobiography*, vol. 2, *South Carolina Narratives*, part 2 (Westport, CT: Greenwood Press, 1972), pp. 235–36.

4. Charles L. Perdue Jr., Thomas E. Barden, and Robert K. Phillips, eds., *Weevils in the Wheat: Interviews with Virginia Ex-Slaves* (Charlottesville: University Press of Virginia, 1976), pp. 33–34.

5. For a more in-depth discussion of the way the concept of manhood was socially constructed in West Africa, see Simon Ottenberg, *Boyhood Rituals in an African Society* (Seattle: University of Washington Press, 1989); Ali A. Mazrui, ed., *The Warrior Tradition in Modern Africa* (Leiden: Brill, 1977); Diane Kayongo-Male, *The Sociology of the African Family* (London: Longman, 1984); Harold K. Schneider, *The Africans: An Ethnological Account* (Englewood Cliffs, NJ: Prentice-Hall, Inc., 1981); Malidoma Patrice Some, *Of Water and the Spirit* (New York: Penguin Books, 1994); and Daniel P. Black, *Dismantling Black Manhood: An Historical and Literary Analysis of the Legacy of Slavery* (New York: Garland Publishing, 1997).

6. John Blassingame, *The Slave Community: Plantation Life in the Antebellum South* (New York: Oxford University Press, 1979), p. 172.

7. Stanley M. Elkins, *Slavery: A Problem in American Institutional and Intellectual*

Life (Chicago: University of Chicago Press, 1959). Elkins's work has been sharply criticized for emphasizing the demoralizing aspects of slavery with little attention to the strengths reported by W. E. B. Du Bois and E. Franklin Frazier. In Elkins's view the slave would be assured of his master's affection only if he conformed to the rules of conduct that governed his relations with his master and carefully observed "the fine line between friskiness and insubordination; between cuteness and insolence. Slavery robbed the slave of his self-confidence and promoted 'infantilization.'" In *The Slave Community,* John Blassingame augmented Elkins's Sambo with two additional personalities, arguing that there were differential reactions to the institution of slavery. Neither Elkins's nor Blassingame's typology included females, and the emphasis in both books is on male influence and leadership.

8. See Alan Kulikoff, *Tobacco and Slaves: The Development of Southern Culture on the Chesapeake, 1860–1900* (Chapel Hill: University of North Carolina Press, 1986). Kulikoff discovered that on the larger plantations about 47 percent of the slaves lived in nuclear households and on smaller plantations only about 18 percent did. Orlando Patterson also discussed the differences between the large and small plantations and made the distinction between the gang systems and other types of slavery in *Slavery and Social Death: A Comparative Study* (Cambridge, MA: Harvard University Press, 1982).

9. Alice Walker, "Coming Apart," in *You Can't Keep a Good Woman Down* (New York: Harcourt Brace Jovanovich, 1981), p. 42. See also Patricia Hill Collins, "The Sexual Politics of Black Womanhood," in *Black Feminist Thought: Knowledge, Consciousness, and the Politics of Empowerment* (New York: Unwin Hyman, 1990), p. 168.

10. June P. Guild, ed., *Black Laws of Virginia: A Summary of the Legislative Acts of Virginia Concerning Negroes from Earliest Times to the Present* (New York: Negro Universities Press, 1969), pp. 26–27.

11. For analyses that controlled for the size of the plantation, see Stephen C. Crawford, "Quantified Memory: A Study of the WPA and Fisk University Slave Narrative Collections" (Ph.D. dissertation, University of Chicago, 1980). See also Richard H. Steckel, "A Peculiar Population," *Journal of Economic History* 46 (September 1986): 721–41; and Richard H. Steckel, "Miscegenation and the American Slave Schedule," *Journal of Interdisciplinary History* 11 (Autumn 1980): 251–63.

12. Milton Meltzer, ed., *In Their Own Words: A History of the American Negro, 1619–1983* (New York: Thomas Y. Crowell, 1984), pp. 142–43.

13. Deborah Gray White, *Ar'n't I a Woman? Female Slaves in the Plantation South* (New York: W. W. Norton, 1985), p. 110.

14. Frances Ann Kemble, *Journal of a Residence on a Georgia Plantation in 1838–1839,* ed. by John A. Scott (New York: Alfred A. Knopf, 1961), pp. 224–41.

15. Richard Sutch, "The Breeding of Slaves for Sale and the Westward Expansion of Slavery," in Stanley L. Engerman and Eugene D. Genovese, eds., *Race and Slavery in the Western Hemisphere: Quantitative Studies* (Princeton, NJ: Princeton University Press, 1975). Sutch has attributed these growth differentials to the influence of the slave breeding practices of planters. He also asserts that the planters' practices "fostered polygamy and promiscuity among slaves" (p. 198). In Stanley L. Engerman's opening chapter, however, he challenges Sutch's analyses and argues that these issues were far more complicated than Sutch realized. See also Robert W. Fogel and Stanley L. Engerman, "Recent

Findings in the Study of Slave Demography and Family Structure," *Sociology and Social Research* 63 (April 1979): 566–89.

16. See Donna L. Franklin, *Ensuring Inequality: The Structural Transformation of the African-American Family* (New York: Oxford University Press, 1997), p. 27.

17. Herbert Gutman, *The Black Family in Slavery and Freedom, 1750–1925* (New York: Vintage Books, 1976). Gutman asserted that the essential value of the slave woman rested on her capacity to reproduce the labor force. A premium was placed on the slave woman who bore the most children. Gutman viewed the early childbearing patterns of African Americans as shaped by slavery when he stated that "much indirect evidence suggests a close relationship between the relatively early age of a slave woman at the birth of her first child, prenuptial intercourse . . . and the economic needs of the slave-owner." For a more in-depth analysis of Gutman's work, see Nathan Irvin Huggins, "Herbert Gutman and Afro-American History," *Labor History* 29 (Summer 1988): 323–337.

18. Narrative of Martha Jackson, born in 1850, *Alabama Narratives,* Federal Works Project, WPA for the State of Alabama, 1939.

19. James A. Rawley, "Slave Trade," in Eric Foner and John A. Garraty, eds., *The Reader's Companion to American History* (Boston: Houghton Mifflin, 1991), p. 995.

20. See Robert Fogel and Stanley L. Engerman, *Time on the Cross* (Boston: Little, Brown, 1974). In this book the Nobel laureate Fogel and his coauthor Engerman argue that the family was the main instrument for promoting the increase of the slave population. Planters believed that the fertility rates would be the highest when the family was the strongest. Planters promoted the stability of the family by providing a system of rewards for marriage and a system of sanction against adultery and divorce.

21. Gilbert Osofsky, ed., *Puttin' In on Ole Massa: The Slave Narratives of Henry Bibb, William Wells Brown, and Solomon Northrup* (New York: Harper & Row, 1969), p. 213.

22. John Hope Franklin and Loren Schweninger, *Runaway Slaves: Rebels on the Plantation* (New York: Oxford University Press, 1999), pp. 209–10.

23. Brenda E. Stevenson, *Life in Black and White: Family and Community in the Slave South* (New York: Oxford University Press, 1996). See especially chapter 7, "Slave Family Structure." For an in-depth discussion of slave family patterns in the Chesapeake Bay Region in Maryland and in South Carolina, see Philip D. Morgan, *Slave Counterpoint: Black Culture in the Eighteenth-Century Chesapeake and Low Country* (Durham: University of North Carolina Press, 1998).

24. Perdue et al., eds., *Weevils,* pp. 149–51.

25. Osofsky, *Puttin' In on Ole Massa,* p. 135.

26. Robin W. Winks, "An Autobiography of the Reverend Josiah Henson," in *Four Fugitive Slave Narratives* (Reading, MA: Addison-Wesley, 1969), pp. 13–15.

27. Milton Meltzer, ed., *In Their Own Words: A History of the American Negro, 1619–1865* (New York: Thomas Y. Crowell, 1964), pp. 5–6.

28. See Linda Brent, *Incidents in the Life of a Slave Girl,* ed. by Lydia Marie Child (New York: Harcourt Brace Jovanovich, 1973). According to Brent, most men slipped away from witnessing attacks on their wives and "feigned ignorance."

29. George P. Rawick, ed., *The American Slave: A Composite Autobiography,* vol. 18 (Westport, CT: Greenwood Press, 1972).

30. James Kirk, "When Love Conquered Slavery," *Negro Digest* 6 (July 1948): 34–35.

31. Stevenson, *Life in Black and White*. In this book Stevenson examines the plantation records and slave registers in Virginia and makes a stronger case than prior historians who have studied slavery that slave families were routinely denied the right to cohabit as husband and wife even when they lived on the same plantation.

32. William Waller Hening, ed., *The Statutes at Large of Virginia (1619–1682)*, vol. 2 (New York: R. & W. & G. Bartow, 1823), p. 170.

33. Perdue et al., eds., *Weevils*, p. 230. See also John Blassingame, ed., *Slave Testimony: Two Centuries of Letters, Speeches, Interviews, and Autobiographies* (Baton Rouge: Louisiana State University Press, 1977).

34. These incidents are reported in Ann Patton Malone's *Sweet Chariot: Slave Family and Household Structure in Nineteenth-Century Louisiana* (Chapel Hill: University of North Carolina Press, 1992), p. 228.

35. For an argument on the occupational differences based on gender, see Fogel and Engerman, *Time on the Cross*. For a conception of the slave family with gender-stratified roles, see also White, *Ar'n't I a Woman?*

36. It should be noted that African-American men attained property and other rights under the law before any women did. When the Nineteenth Amendment was passed, giving women the right to vote, it was rejected by Alabama, Virginia, and Maryland. West Virginia rejected it at first and then, in the most contentious session of its legislature, passed it.

37. For an in-depth discussion of the relationships between slaveholding women and black female slaves, see, for example, Elizabeth Fox-Genovese, *Within the Plantation Household: Black and White Women of the Old South* (Chapel Hill: University of North Carolina Press, 1988), pp. 334–72. See also Perdue et al., eds., *Weevils*, pp. 316–20.

38. Fox-Genovese, *Within the Plantation Household*, p. 32.

39. Harriet Jacobs, *Incidents in the Life of a Slave Girl* (Cambridge, MA: Harvard University Press, 1987), p. 10.

40. Jacqueline Jones, "My Mother Was Much of a Woman: Black Women, Work, and the Family Under Slavery," unpublished manuscript, 1980, pp. 41–42.

41. Ophelia Settle Egypt, J. Masouka, and Charles S. Johnson, "Unwritten History of Slavery: Autobiographical Account of Negro Ex-Slaves," Social Science Documents, no. 1 (Nashville: Social Science Institute, Fisk University, 1945), pp. 284–91.

42. Gerda Lerner, *Black Women in White America: A Documentary History* (New York: Vintage Books, 1972), pp. 50–51.

43. Litwack, *Been in the Storm So Long*, p. 243.

44. Blassingame, *Slave Community*, p. 400.

45. Rawick, *The American Slave*, vol. 16, pp. 46–50.

46. Litwack, *Been in the Storm So Long*, p. 232.

47. Ibid., pp. 233–34.

48. Henry L. Swint, ed., *Dear Ones at Home: Letters from Contraband Homes* (Nashville: Vanderbilt University Press, 1966), pp. 242–43.

49. Litwack, *Been in the Storm So Long*, pp. 246–47.

50. Ibid., pp. 245–46.

51. Ibid.

52. Ira Berlin and Leslie S. Rowland, eds., *Families and Freedom: A Documentary*

History of African-American Kinship in the Civil War Era (New York: The New Press, 1997), pp. 185–87.

53. Refer to pages 31–32 of Donna L. Franklin's earlier book, *Ensuring Inequality,* for a more in-depth discussion on the bureau's role in the subjugation of black women to black men.

54. Ibid.

55. Quotes taken from Leon F. Litwack, *Trouble in Mind: Black Southerners in the Age of Jim Crow* (New York: Alfred Knopf, 1998), pp. 349–51.

56. John Dollard, *Caste and Class in a Southern Town* (Garden City, NY: Doubleday Anchor, 1949), pp. 450–51.

57. Howard Bell, ed., *Proceedings of the National Negro Convention, 1830–1864* (New York: Arno Press, 1969), p. 33.

58. Litwack, *Been in the Storm So Long,* pp. 245–46.

59. Benjamin E. Mays, *Born to Rebel: An Autobiography* (Athens: University of Georgia Press, 1987), pp. 9–10.

60. Theodore Rosengarten, *All God's Dangers: The Life of Nate Shaw* (New York: Vintage Books, 1989), p. 10.

61. Franklin, *Ensuring Inequality,* p. 32.

62. Ibid., pp. 38–42.

3   The Cult of True Womanhood

1. Quoted in Sharon Harley, "Northern Black Women Workers: Jacksonian Era," in Sharon Harley and Rosalyn Terborg-Penn, eds., *The Afro-American Woman: Struggles and Images* (Port Washington, NY: Kennikat Press, 1978), p. 12.

2. James O. Horton, "Freedom's Yoke: Gender Conventions among Antebellum Free Blacks," *Feminist Studies* 12 (Spring 1986): 70.

3. Theodore Rosengarten, *All God's Dangers: The Life of Nate Shaw* (New York: Vintage Books, 1989), p. 9.

4. Benjamin E. Mays, *Born to Rebel: An Autobiography* (Athens: University of Georgia Press, 1987), pp. 9–11.

5. Zora Neale Hurston, *Dust Tracks on a Road: An Autobiography* (New York: Harper Perennial, 1996), p. 10.

6. Donna L. Franklin, *Ensuring Inequality: The Structural Transformation of the African-American Family* (New York: Oxford University Press, 1997), pp. 32–33.

7. Orville Vernon Burton, *In My Father's House Are Many Mansions: Family and Community in Edgefield, South Carolina* (Chapel Hill: University of North Carolina Press, 1985), p. 255.

8. John Dollard, *Caste and Class in a Southern Town* (Garden City, NY: Doubleday Anchor, 1949), pp. 450–51.

9. Leslie Howard Owens, *This Species of Property: Slave Life and Culture in the Old South* (New York: Oxford University Press, 1976), p. 195.

10. W. E. B. Du Bois, *The Philadelphia Negro: A Social Study,* with a Special Report on Domestic Service by Isabel Eaton (Philadelphia: University of Pennsylvania Press, 1899).

11. Jacqueline Jones, *Labor of Love: Black Women, Work, and the Family from Slavery to Present* (New York: Basic Books, 1985), p. 63.

12. Dolores Janiewski, "Sisters Under Their Skins: Southern Working Women, 1880–1950," in Joanne V. Hawks and Sheila L. Skemps, eds., *Sex, Race, and the Role of Women in the South* (Jackson: University of Mississippi Press, 1983), pp. 13–35.

13. Dorothy Sterling, *We Are Your Sisters: Black Women in the Nineteenth* Century (New York: W. W. Norton, 1984), pp. 325–26.

14. Rosengarten, *All God's Dangers*, p. 14.

15. Mays, *Born to Rebel*, p. 8.

16. Hortense Powdermaker, *After Freedom: A Cultural Study in the Deep South* (New York: Viking Press, 1939), p. 154.

17. There are a number of excellent analyses of women's wage-earning history. See Alice Kessler-Harris, *Out to Work: A History of Wage-Earning Women in the United States* (New York: Oxford University Press, 1982); Barbara M. Wertheimer, *We Were There: The Story of Working Women in America* (New York: Pantheon Books, 1977); and Susan Estabrook Kennedy, *If All We Did Was to Weep at Home: A History of White Working Class Women in America* (Bloomington: Indiana University Press, 1979). For a detailed discussion on the meaning of "true womanhood," see Julie Matthaei, *An Economic History of Women in America* (New York: Schocken Books, 1982). For a superb exposition on nineteenth-century independent white women's lives, see Martha Vicinus, *Independent Women: Work and Community for Single Women, 1850–1920* (Chicago: University of Chicago Press, 1985); and Carol Smith-Rosenberg, *Disorderly Conduct: Visions of Gender in Victorian America* (New York: Alfred A. Knopf, 1985).

18. Eileen Boris, "The Power of Motherhood: Black and White Activist Women Redefine the 'Political,'" in Seth Koven and Sonya Michel, eds., *Mothers of a New World* (New York: Routledge, 1993), pp. 233–34.

19. Barbara Welter, "The Cult of True Womanhood: 1820–1860," *American Quarterly* 18 (Summer 1966): 151–74.

20. Ann Firor Scott, *The Southern Lady from Pedestal to Politics: 1830–1930* (Chicago: University of Chicago Press, 1970), p. 122.

21. Jacqueline Jones, *Labor of Love*, p. 62.

22. For a comprehensive discussion on public education in the South during the Reconstruction period, see W. E. B. Du Bois, *Black Reconstruction in America: 1860–1880* (New York: Simon & Schuster, 1935; rep. 1962, 1992), pp. 637–69.

23. Jacqueline Jones, *Soldiers of Light and Love: Northern Teachers and Georgia Blacks, 1865–1873* (Chapel Hill: University of North Carolina Press, 1980), p. 133.

24. Mays, *Born to Rebel*, pp. 35–36.

25. Teresa Amott and Julie Matthaei, *Race, Gender, and Work* (Boston: South End Press, 1991).

26. The following books have addressed the precipitous decline of public education in the South at the end of Reconstruction. See, for example, Henry Allen Bullock, *A History of Negro Education in the South: From 1619 to Present* (Cambridge, MA: Harvard University Press, 1967); Louis Harlan, *Separate and Unequal: Public School Campaigns and Racism in the Southern Seaboard States* (New York: Atheneum, 1969); Robert C. Morris, *Reading, 'Riting, and Reconstruction: The Education of Freedmen in the South, 1861–1870* (Chicago: University of Chicago Press, 1981); Jacqueline Jones, *Soldiers of Light and Love.*

27. Leon F. Litwack, *Been in the Storm So Long: The Aftermath of Slavery* (New York: Vintage Books, 1979), pp. 464–65.

28. Quoted in William Laird Clowes, *Black America: A Study of the Ex-Slave and His Late Master* (Westport, CT: Negro Universities Press, 1971), p. 93.

29. Gerda Lerner, ed., *Black Women in White America* (New York: Vintage Books, 1973), p. 291.

30. Ben Sidran, *Black Talk* (New York: DaCapo, 1981), p. 24.

31. Mays, *Born to Rebel*, p. 4.

32. Lawrence W. Levine, *Black Culture and Black Consciousness: Afro-American Folk Thought from Slavery to Freedom* (New York: Oxford University Press, 1977), p. 262.

33. Ibid., p. 16.

34. Hazel Carby, "It Just Be's Dat Way Sometime: The Sexual Politics of Women's Blues," *Radical America* 20 (June–July 1986): 9. For another revisionist perspective on the blues, see Angela Y. Davis, *Blues Legacies and Black Feminism* (New York: Random House, 1998), p. 4.

35. Frank Wilkeson, *New York Sun,* December 28, 1882; February 9 and March 28, 1883.

36. J. L. Tucker, *The Relation of the Church to the Colored People* (Chicago: Dramatic Publishing Company, 1883), pp. 1–87. It should be noted that although some criticisms were directed at Tucker's assertions, he went on to become an international "expert" on emancipated blacks. The ninth edition of the *Encyclopaedia Britannica* cited Tucker as an expert observer and witness to the "non-moral" behavior of blacks.

37. George Frederickson reviewed Bruce's study and made this declaration in "Black Image in the White Mind," in *The Debate on Afro-American Character and Destiny, 1817–1914* (New York: Harper & Row, 1972), pp. 244–82.

38. Philip A. Bruce, *The Plantation Negro as a Freeman: Observations on His Character, Condition, and Prospects in Virginia* (Williamstown, MA: Corner House Publishers, 1970), p. 83–84.

39. Quoted in Bettina Aptheker, *Woman's Legacy: Essays on Race, Sex, and Class in American History* (Amherst: University of Massachusetts Press, 1982), p. 62.

40. Alexander Crummell, "The Black Woman in the South: Her Neglects and Her Needs," in *Africa and America: Addresses and Discourses* (New York: Negro Universities Press, 1969), p. 65. This paper was originally an address before the Freedman's Aid Society in Ocean Grove, New Jersey, on August 15, 1883.

41. W. E. B. Du Bois, *The Negro American Family* (Atlanta University Publication No. 13, 1908; rep. New York: Arno Press, 1968), p. 41. A study conducted under the auspices of the John F. Slater Fund during this period likewise found that matters of sexual chastity and morality were of great concern to black people. See E. C. Hobson and C. E. Hopkins, "A Report Concerning the Colored Women of the South," John Slater Fund Occasional Papers, No. 9 (Baltimore: 1896). Thirty years after these pronouncements were made, Elsie McDougald was still fighting the stereotype of the black woman's sexual immorality and arguing that there was no proof of inherent moral defect in the women of the race. See Elsie Johnson McDougald, "The Task of Negro Womanhood," in Alain Locke, ed., *The New Negro: An Interpretation* (New York: Albert & Charles Boni, 1925), pp. 379–82.

42. Quoted in Wilson Jeremiah Moses, *The Golden Age of Black Nationalism, 1850–1925* (New York: Oxford University Press, 1978), p. 115.

43. Elizabeth Lindsay Davis, *Lifting as They Climb: The National Association of Colored Women* (Washington, DC: National Association of Colored Women, 1933), pp. 18–19.

44. Ibid., p. 20.

45. The alliance with Booker T. Washington was weakened when he refused to use his influence or take a stand when Ruffin was excluded from the proceedings of the Milwaukee Convention of the General Federation of Women's Clubs in 1900 because she was black.

46. Margaret Murray Washington wrote a letter to Edna D. Cheyney on November 13, 1896, requesting greater support from progressive white women and accusing them of "entirely overlooking" the problems of women of color. See William Jeremiah Moses, *The Golden Age of Black Nationalism* (New York: Oxford University Press, 1978), p. 112.

47. Davis, *Lifting as They Climb*, p. 19.

48. Linda Gordon, *Pitied but Not Entitled* (New York: Oxford University Press, 1978), p. 112.

49. Davis, *Lifting as They Climb*, p. 30.

50. Sharon Harley, "Mary Church Terrell: Genteel Militant," in Leon F. Litwack and August Meier, eds., *Black Leaders of the Nineteenth Century* (Urbana: University of Illinois Press, 1988), p. 311.

51. Ruth Edmonds Hill, ed., *The Black Women's Oral History Project*, vol. 5 (Westport, CT: Meckler, 1991), p. 22. Black men were ambivalent about black women's pursuit of higher education in general but understood its importance in keeping them out of the "white man's kitchen." Mary Church Terrell confirmed this resistance to black women's pursuit of higher education when she stated, "Many of my friends tried to dissuade me from studying for an A.B. degree." One of the things she was told was that "no man would want to marry a woman who studied higher mathematics." In an effort to understand the double bind in which black women were caught, see Jeanne Noble, "The Negro Woman's College Education" (Ph.D. dissertation, Columbia University, 1956), p. 23; and Leon F. Litwack, *Trouble in Mind: Black Southerners in the Age of Jim Crow* (New York: Alfred A. Knopf, 1998), p. 342.

52. Evelyn Brooks Higginbotham, *Righteous Discontent: The Women's Movement in the Baptist Church, 1880–1920* (Cambridge, MA: Harvard University Press, 1993), pp. 213–15.

53. Other black women who founded schools during this period included Charlotte Hawkins Brown, Lucy C. Laney, and Mary McLeod Bethune, but these schools focused on academic subjects and included industrial arts courses. According to Burroughs, what distinguished the National Training School from other schools was that domestic and manual training were the school's most extensive and well-funded programs.

54. Higginbotham, *Righteous Discontent*, p. 291.

55. Phyllis Palmer, *Domestics and Dirt: Housewives and Domestic Servants in the United States, 1920–1945* (Philadelphia: Temple University Press, 1989), p. 147.

56. Litwack, *Trouble in Mind*, p. 351.

57. Fannie Barrier Williams, "The Woman's Part in a Man's Business," *Voice* 1, no. 11 (1904): 544.

58. Higginbotham, *Righteous Discontent*, p. 41.

59. Noble, "The Negro Woman's College Education," p. 45.

60. Quoted in Bert James Loewenberg and Ruth Bogin, eds., *Black Women in Nineteenth-Century American Life: Their Words, Their Thoughts, Their Feelings* (University Park: Pennsylvania State University Press, 1986), p. 327.

61. Benjamin E. Mays, *Born to Rebel: An Autobiography* (Athens: University of Georgia Press, 1971).

62. Higginbotham, *Righteous Discontent*, p. 24. These dramatic shifts in educational achievement for black men and women can be explained by looking at the escalating rates of literacy during this period. While whites were busy spreading their racist "retrogressionist" propaganda, it went unnoticed that blacks were refining and retooling their educational skills in massive numbers. For example, between 1900 and 1920 the illiteracy rates among African Americans dropped from 44.5 to 22.9 percent. One of the reasons for this dramatic reduction was that benefactors contributed funds for the creation of schools for blacks. The Julius Rosenwald Fund alone was responsible for assisting in the construction of 1,523 schools during the twenty-year span of 1900 to 1920.

63. Anna J. Cooper, *A Voice from the South by a Black Woman of the South* (Xenia, Ohio, 1892; rep. New York: Negro Universities Press, 1969), p. 79.

64. Addie Hunton, "Negro Womanhood Defended," *Voice* 1, no. 7 (1904): 280.

65. Sandra N. Smith and Earle H. West, "Charlotte Hawkins Brown," *Journal of Negro Education* 51, no. 3 (1982): 199.

66. Linda Gordon, *Pitied but Not Entitled: Single Mothers and the History of Welfare, 1890–1935* (New York: Free Press, 1994), p. 133.

67. Paul Giddings, *When and Where I Enter: The Impact of Black Women on Race and Sex in America* (New York: Bantam Books, 1985), p. 75.

68. David T. Beito, "Mutual Aid, State Welfare, and Organized Charity: Fraternal Societies and the 'Deserving' and 'Undeserving' Poor, 1890–1930," unpublished paper.

69. Hortense Powdermaker, *After Freedom: A Cultural Study in the Deep South* (New York: Viking Press, 1939), p. 165.

70. Gordon, *Pitied but Not Entitled*, pp. 120–21.

71. Stephanie J. Shaw, *What a Woman Ought to Be and Do* (Chicago: University of Chicago Press, 1996), p. 170.

72. Gordon, *Pitied but not Entitled*, p. 133.

73. Jacqueline A. Rouse, *Lugenia Burns Hope, Black Southern Reformer* (Athens: University of Georgia Press, 1989), pp. 20–21.

74. Ibid., pp. 23–24, 36–37.

75. Interview with Ardie Clark Halyard conducted by Marcia Greenlee in 1978, in *Black Women Oral History Project* (Cambridge, MA: Schlesinger Library), p. 15. Interview with Martha Harrison conducted by Merze Tate in 1979, p. 9.

76. Marion Culbert, "Problems Facing Negro Young Women," *Opportunity* (February 2, 1936): 48. It should be noted that Culbert's concept of "comradeship" did not include the husband's reciprocal assistance with housekeeping or child care.

77. Lawson Andrew Scruggs, *Women of Distinction: Remarkable in Work and Invincible in Character* (New York: Macmillan, 1893), p. 14.

78. Victoria Earle Matthews, "The Awakening of the Afro-American Woman," address delivered at the Annual Convention of the Society of Christian Endeavor, San Francisco, on July 11, 1897 (New York: published by author), pp. 6–7.

79. Ida B. Wells, *Crusade for Justice: The Autobiography of Ida B. Wells,* ed. by Alfreda M. Duster (Chicago: University of Chicago Press, 1970), p. 101.

80. Linda O. McMurry, *To Keep the Waters Troubled: The Life of Ida B. Wells* (New York: Oxford University Press, 1998), pp. 238–39.

81. Ibid., p. 102.

82. Shaw, *What a Professional Woman Ought to Be and Do,* pp. 125–26.

83. Cited in Wilson Jeremiah Moses, *The Golden Age of Black Nationalism, 1850–1925* (Hamden, CT: Archon Books, 1978), p. 123.

84. Lucy Laney, "Address," Women's Meetings, Second Annual Atlanta University Conference, *Proceedings* (Atlanta: Atlanta University Press, 1898), p. 56.

85. Mary Terrell, "Club Work of Colored Women," *Southern Workman* 30 (1901): 438.

86. Bessie Jones, *For the Ancestors: Autobiographical Memories* (Urbana: University of Illinois Press, 1983), p. 40.

87. Fannie Barrier Williams, "The Colored Girl," *The Voice of the Negro* (June 1905): 403.

88. Nannie H. Burroughs, "Not Color but Character," *The Voice of the Negro* (July 1904): 277, 278.

89. Cited in Deborah Gray White, *Too Heavy a Load: Black Women in Defense of Themselves, 1894–1994* (New York: W.W. Norton, 1999), pp. 56–58.

90. E. Franklin Frazier, *The Negro Family in the United States* (Chicago: University of Chicago Press, 1939), p. 102.

4   A Shifting Landscape: The "New Manhood" Movement

1. Mary Ann Shadd Cary, "The Colored Women's Progressive Association," Mary Ann Shadd Cary Papers, Moorland-Spingarn Research Center, Howard University, Washington, D.C.

2. It is important to note that one of the objectives of the organizers of this academy was to enhance the achievements of black men since "there has been a higher attainment of scholarship by our women than by our men." Although George Grisham challenged the exclusion of women and argued for their admission, the bylaws were never changed and black women were not admitted. For an in-depth discussion see Alfred A. Moss, Jr., *The American Negro Academy: Voice of the Talented Tenth* (Baton Rouge: Louisiana State University Press, 1981).

3. Sadie T. Alexander is quoted in Paula Giddings, *When and Where I Enter: The Impact of Black Women on Race and Sex in America* (New York: Bantam Books, 1985), p. 196.

4. Elsa Barkley Brown, "Womanist Consciousness: Maggie Lena Walker and the Independent Order of Saint Luke," *Signs* 14 (Spring 1989): 610–33. See also Elsa Barkley Brown, "Maggie Lena Walker and the Independent Order of Saint Luke: Advancing Women, Race, and Community in Turn-of-the-Century Richmond," in Linda K. Kerber and Jane Sherron De Hart, *Women's America: Refocusing the Past,* 4th ed. (New York: Oxford University Press, 1995), pp. 231–39.

5. A'Lelia Bundles, "Madam C. J. Walker," in *American History* 30 (August 1996): 42. See also Louis R. Harlan, *Booker T. Washington: The Wizard of Tuskegee, 1901–1915* (New York: Oxford University Press, 1983), p. 296.

6. Bundles, "Madam C. J. Walker," p. 45.

7. Kathy Peiss, *Hope in a Jar: The Making of America's Beauty Culture* (New York: Henry Holt, 1999), p. 94.

8. Ibid.

9. It should be noted that many rural women were not open to Madam Walker's hair-straightening techniques. Mamie Garvin Fields, a club woman, learned Walker's hair care methods and tried them on the hair of one of the girls in the rural community where she was working. According to Fields, the mother did not appreciate the "standard of beauty" that she brought to the community. Peiss, *Hope in a Jar*, p. 96.

10. Kathryn M. Johnson, *What a Spelman Graduate Accomplished: Ezella Mathis Carter, a Biography and an Appeal* (Chicago: Pyramid Publications, 1935).

11. Peter Kolchin, *First Freedom: The Response of Alabama Blacks to Emancipation and Reconstruction* (Westport, CT: Greenwood Press, 1972), p. 62.

12. Two excellent biographies of Garvey's life and work include E. David Cronin, *Black Moses: The Story of Marcus Garvey* (Madison: University of Wisconsin Press, 1955), and Theodore Vincent, *Black Power and the Marcus Movement* (New York: Ramparts Press, 1972). See also Robert A. Hill, ed., *Marcus Garvey and the Universal Negro Improvement Association Papers*, 7 vols. (Berkeley: University of California Press, 1984–1991).

13. John Hope Franklin and Alfred A. Moss, Jr., *From Slavery to Freedom: A History of African Americans*, 7th ed. (New York: McGraw-Hill, 1994), p. 357.

14. Theodore Vincent, *Black Power and the Marcus Movement* (New York: Ramparts Press, 1972), p. 114.

15. Percival Burrows, *Negro World*, June 9, 1923.

16. Marcus Garvey cited in Barbara Bair, "True Women, Real Men: Gender, Ideology, and Social Roles in the Garvey Movement," in Dorothy O. Helly and Susan Mo Reverby, eds., *Gendered Domains: Rethinking Public and Private in Women's History* (Ithaca, NY: Cornell University Press, 1992), pp. 155, 159.

17. Bair, "True Women, Real Men," p. 157.

18. "Obligations of Motherhood," *Negro World* (March 29, 1924); and "Emancipated Womanhood" *Negro World* (April 29, 1924).

19. Eunice Lewis, *Negro World*, April 19, 1924.

20. Bair, "True Women, Real Men," p. 158.

21. Mrs. Scott is cited in Bair, "True Women, Real Men," pp. 160–61.

22. Maymie Leona Turpeau De Mena, "World Echo," *Ethiopian World* (April 19, 1924).

23. Marcus Garvey is quoted in E. David Cronin, *Black Moses: The Story of Marcus Garvey* (Madison: University of Wisconsin Press, 1955), pp. 192–93.

24. Quoted in Rupert Lewis and Patrick Bryan, eds., *Garvey: His Work and Impact* (Trenton: African World Press, 1991), p. 75.

25. Amy Jacques Garvey is cited in Deborah Gray White, *Too Heavy a Load: Black Women in Defense of Themselves, 1894–1994* (New York: W.W. Norton, 1999), p. 138. For a more in-depth analysis of Amy Jacques Garvey's life and work, see Ula Yvette Taylor's Ph.D. dissertation titled "The Veiled Garvey: The Life and Times of Amy Jacques Garvey" (Santa Barbara: University of California, 1992).

26. Taylor, "The Veiled Garvey," p. 329.

27. Franklin and Moss, *From Slavery to Freedom,* p. 359.

28. For biographical information on "Anthony Overton," see Arnett G. Lindsey, "The Negro in Business," *Journal of Negro History* 32 (April 1929): 156–201.

29. Anthony Overton, "Largest Negro Manufacturing Enterprise in the United States," in National Negro Business League, "Report of the Thirteenth Annual Convention," pp. 96–100.

30. Ibid., p. 113.

31. Ida B. Wells, *Crusade for Justice: The Autobiography of Ida B. Wells,* ed. by Alfreda M. Duster (Chicago: University of Chicago Press, 1970), p. 102.

32. Rosalyn Terborg-Penn, "Black Male Perspectives on Nineteenth-Century Women," in Sharon Harley and Rosalyn Terborg-Penn, eds., *The Afro-American Woman: Struggle and Images* (Port Washington, NY: Kennikat Press, 1978), p. 42.

33. Chandler Owen, "Good Looks Supremacy," *Messenger* 6 (March 1924): 80.

34. L. R. Stephens, "Black Girl," *Messenger* 8 (December 1926): 381.

35. George Schuyler, "Unnecessary Negroes," *Messenger* 8 (1926): 307; "Shafts and Darts: A Page of Calumny and Satire," *Messenger* 9 (July 1927): 230.

36. George Schuyler, *Black No More* (1931; rep., Boston: Northeastern University Press, 1989).

37. Anna Julia Cooper, *A Voice from the South* (1892; rep. New York: Negro Universities Press, 1969), p. 75.

38. Fannie Barrier Williams, "The Colored Girl," *Voice of the Negro* (June 1905): 402.

39. T. Thomas Fortune is quoted in Alfred A. Moss, Jr., *The American Negro Academy: Voice of the Talented Tenth* (Baton Rouge: Louisiana State University Press, 1981), p. 55.

40. Nannie Burroughs, "Not Color but Character," *Voice of the Negro* 1 (July 1904): 278.

41. Peiss, *Hope in a Jar,* p. 97.

42. John H. Adams, Jr., "Rough Sketches: A Study of the Features of the New Negro," *Voice of the Negro* 1 (August 1904): 323–26. Also see Henry Louis Gates, Jr., "The Troupe of the New Negro and the Reconstruction of the Image of the Black," *Representations* 24 (Fall 1988): 129–55.

43. *Pittsburgh Courier,* April 7, 1923; editorial.

44. *Messenger,* August 2, 1920.

45. Claude Barnett would later become the head of the Associated Negro Press and went on record as opposing articles from sororities that detailed only social events when he declared "old social cliches which made oganizations slightly snobbish are passe." Quoted in White, *Too Heavy a Load,* p. 187.

46. Peiss, *Hope in a Jar,* p. 221.

47. Burroughs, "Not Color but Character," p. 277. For more on beauty standards during this period, refer to the following articles: "Beauty Synonym," *Messenger* 6 (August 1924): back cover; "Men Prefer Beauty," *Messenger* 9 (September 1927): 51.

48. Paul Jacobson, *American Marriage and Divorce* (New York: Rinehart, 1959), p. 102.

49. For an analysis of the transformation that was occurring in this country with regard to sexual values, see John D'Emilio and Estelle B. Freedman, *Intimate Matters: A History of Sexuality in America* (New York: Harper & Row, 1988).

50. For an excellent discussion of women's blues culture, see Hazel Carby, "It Jus Be's Dat Way Sometime: The Sexual Politics of Women's Blues," *Radical America* 20, no. 4 (1986): 22; Angela Y. Davis, *Blues Legacies and Black Feminism* (New York: Random House, 1998); and Daphne Duval Harrison, *Black Pearls: Blues Queens of the 1920s* (New Brunswick, NJ: Rutgers University Press, 1988).

51. Mrs. Joe Brown, "Negro Woman's Greatest Needs: A Symposium," *Messenger* (June 1927): 30–36.

52. In spite of the decline in their influence, the club women retained their numerical vitality. According to historian Darlene Clark Hine, the NACW became the "largest and most enduring protest organization in the history of African-Americans." What is unclear, however, is whether or not they continued as a protest organization. To support her argument, Hine uses the example of the Detroit association of colored women's clubs. According to Hine, this association boasted 73 member clubs with nearly 3,000 individual members in 1945. See Darlene Clark Hine, "Rape and the Inner Lives of Black Women. Women in the Middle West: Preliminary Thoughts on the Culture of Dissemblance," in Beverly Guy-Sheftall, ed., *Words of Fire: An Anthology of African-American Feminist Thought* (New York: New Press, 1995), p. 384.

53. Gloria Hull, *Color, Sex, and Poetry: Three Women Writers of the Harlem Renaissance* (Bloomington: Indiana University Press, 1987), pp. 10–13.

54. Franklin and Moss, *From Slavery to Freedom*, pp. 390–93.

55. For an in-depth analysis of FDR's legacy to African Americans, see Donna L. Franklin, *Ensuring Inequality: The Structural Transformation of the African-American Family* (New York: Oxford University Press, 1997), pp. 63–65.

56. The lack of leadership roles for black women apparently was not unique to White House planning sessions. When the White House conference on the Moynihan Report was planned, the only black woman invited was Dorothy Height, and she did not challenge Moynihan's thesis. See Franklin, *Ensuring Inequality*, pp. 166–68.

57. Franklin, *Ensuring Inequality*, pp. 163–65.

58. White, *Too Heavy a Load*, pp. 196–97.

5   The Allure of Miss Anne

1. The term "Miss Anne" is a colloquial expression that emerged during slavery. In that slaves were not allowed to address whites by their first names, "Mr. Charlie" and "Miss Anne" were used within the slave community to refer to all white men and women, especially the master and mistress of the plantation. After the slaves were freed and discrimination against blacks persisted, so did the use of these terms to describe white men and women.

"Miss Anne" is disparaging in the sense that it conveys an alliance of white women with men in their oppression of African Americans. Catherine MacKinnon has challenged the categorization of white women as oppressors in that they themselves are oppressed: Catherine MacKinnon, "From Practice to Theory, or What Is a White Woman Anyway?" *Yale Journal of Law and Feminism*, vol. 4, no. 13 (1991). For a thoughtful reaction to MacKinnon's analysis, see Martha Mahoney, "Whiteness and

Women, in Practice and Theory: A Reply to Catherine MacKinnon," *Yale Journal of Law and Feminism,* vol. 5, no. 217 (1993).

2. Alexander C. King, "Race Problems of the South," in Leon F. Litwack, *Trouble in Mind: Black Southerners in the Age of Jim Crow* (New York: Alfred A. Knopf, 1998), p. 212.

3. Philip A. Bruce, *The Plantation Negro as a Freeman: Observations on His Character, Condition, and Prospects in Virginia* (Williamstown, MA: Corner House Publishers, 1970), pp. 83–84, 129, 130.

4. Francis Butler Simkins, *Pitchfork Ben Tillman: South Carolinian* (Baton Rouge: Louisiana State University Press, 1944), p. 397.

5. Litwack, *Trouble in Mind,* p. 303.

6. Felton quoted in Litwack, *Trouble in Mind,* p. 197; Northern quoted in Litwack, *Trouble in Mind,* p. 305.

7. Quoted in Albert D. Kirwan, *Revolt of the Rednecks: Mississippi Politics, 1876–1925* (Lexington: University of Kentucky Press, 1951), pp. 146–47.

8. Kelly Miller, "Possible Remedies for Lynchings," *Southern Workman* 28 (November 1899): 421.

9. Sutton E. Griggs, *The Race Question in a New Light* (Nashville: Orion Publishing, 1909), pp. 23–25.

10. Richard Wright, *How "Bigger" Was Born* (New York: Harper & Row, 1940), pp. 3–6.

11. The most comprehensive accounts of Jack Johnson's life are Randy Roberts, *Papa Jack: Jack Johnson and the Era of White Hopes* (New York: Free Press, 1983); Finis Farr, *Black Champion: The Life and Times of Jack Johnson* (Greenwich, CT: Fawcett Publications, 1969); and his autobiography, *Jack Johnson: In the Ring and Out* (New York: Citadel Press, rep. ed. 1992).

12. Farr, *Black Champion,* p. 197.

13. Benjamin Mays, *Born to Rebel: An Autobiography* (New York: Scribner's, 1971), p. 19.

14. Lawrence W. Levine, *Black Culture and Black Consciousness: Afro-American Folk Thought from Slavery to Freedom* (New York: Oxford University Press, 1977), p. 433.

15. Louis R. Harlan and Raymond W. Smock, eds., *The Booker T. Washington Papers,* vol. 10 (Urbana: University of Illinois Press, 1972), pp. 75–76.

16. Ida B. Wells, *Crusade for Justice: The Autobiography of Ida B. Wells,* ed. by Alfreda M. Duster (Chicago: University of Chicago Press, 1970), pp. 64, 72.

17. Ibid., p. 128.

18. Quoted in William Jeremiah Moses, *The Golden Age of Black Nationalism: 1850–1925* (Hamden, CT: Archon Books, 1978), p. 109.

19. Ibid., pp. 25–26.

20. James H. Robinson, *Road Without Turning: The Story of Reverend James H. Robinson, An Autobiography* (New York: Insight Books, 1950), p. 21.

21. Ida B. Wells, *On Lynchings: Southern Horrors* (New York: Arno Press, 1969), p. 6.

22. Walter F. White, *Rope and Faggot: A Biography of Judge Lynch* (New York: Viking, 1929), pp. 56–57.

23. Ibid., pp. 35–36.

24. National Association for the Advancement of Colored People, *Thirty Years of Lynching in the United States, 1889–1918* (New York: Negro Universities Press, 1919), pp. 29–30. See also W. Fitzhugh Brundage, *Lynching in the New South: Georgia and Virginia,*

1880–1930 (Urbana: University of Illinois Press, 1993); and Stewart E. Tolnay and E. M. Beck, *Festival of Violence: An Analysis of Southern Lynchings, 1882–1930* (Urbana: University of Illinois Press, 1995).

25. Walter F. White, "The Work of a Mob," *Crisis* 16 (September 17, 1918): 221–22.

26. Herbert Gutman, *The Black Family in Slavery and Freedom, 1750–1925* (New York: Pantheon Books, 1976), p. 437.

27. Calvin C. Hernton, *Sex and Racism in America* (Garden City, NY: Doubleday, 1965, rep. 1988), pp. 57–59.

28. Jacqueline Rouse, *Lugenia Burns Hope: Black Southern Reformer* (Athens: University of Georgia Press, 1989), pp. 32–33.

29. Ralph Ellison, *Shadow and Act* (New York: Random House, 1964), p. 90.

30. Hylan Lewis, *Blackways of Kent* (Chapel Hill: University of North Carolina Press, 1955), p. 155.

31. W. E. B. Du Bois, *The Autobiography of W.E.B. Du Bois: A Soliloquy on Viewing My Life from the Last Decade of Its First Century* (New York: Viking, 1968).

32. Stephen J. Whitfield, *A Death in the Delta: The Story of Emmett Till* (New York: Free Press, 1988), pp. 48–49.

33. Maria Diedrich, *Love Across the Color Lines: Ottilie Assing and Frederick Douglass* (New York: Hill & Wang, 1999).

34. Wells, *Crusade for Justice*, p. 73.

35. Rouse, *Lugenia Burns Hope*, p. 53.

36. Deborah Gray White, *Too Heavy a Load: Black Women in Defense of Themselves, 1894–1994* (New York: W. W. Norton, 1999), p. 57.

37. For an interesting perspective on black men's view of black women see Roi Ottley, "What's Wrong with Negro Women?" *Negro Digest* (December 1950): 71–75.

38. "80,000 Negro Girls Will Never Go to the Altar," *Ebony* (June 1947): 4.

39. Langston Hughes, "Mellow," *Montage of a Dream Deferred* (New York: Holt, 1951), p. 35.

40. Anonymous, "I Want to Marry a Negro," *Negro Digest* (August 1948): 12–13.

41. Anonymous, "Are White Women Stealing Our Men?" *Negro Digest* (April 1952): 52–55.

42. E. Franklin Frazier, *The Black Bourgeoisie* (rep., New York: Free Press, 1997), p. 180.

43. Lyrics by "punster" cited in C. Eric Lincoln, "Color and Group Identity in the United States," in John H. Franklin, ed., *Color and Race* (Boston: Houghton Mifflin, 1968).

44. Michael Lind, "The Beige and the Black," *New York Times Magazine*, August 16, 1998.

45. M. Belinda Tucker and Claudia Mitchell-Kernan, "New Trends in Black American Interracial Marriage: The Social Structural Context," *Journal of Marriage and the Family* 52 (February 1990): 209–19.

46. Willie's remarks can be found in an interview with Isabel Wilkerson, "Black-White Marriages Rise, but Couples Still Face Scorn," *New York Times*, December 2, 1991, B6.

47. For a comprehensive analysis of black divorce rates during this period, see Phillip Cutright, "Components of Change in the Number of Female Family Heads Aged 15–44: United States, 1940–1970," *Journal of Marriage and the Family* 36 (November 1974): 714–22.

48. St. Clair Drake, "Why Negro Men Leave," *Negro Digest* (April 1950): 25–27.

49. Gwendolyn Brooks, "Why Negro Women Leave Home," *Negro Digest* (March 1951): 26–28.

50. Pauli Murray, "Why Negro Girls Stay Single," *Negro Digest* (July 1947): 4–8.

51. Calvin C. Hernton, *Sex and Racism in America*.

52. Hernton, *Sex and Racism in America*, p. 247. See also Richard Wright, "The Ethics of Living in Jim Crow," in Sterling A. Brown, Arthur P. Davis, and Ulysses Lee, eds., *The Negro Caravan* (New York: Arno Press, 1941).

53. William H. Grier and Price M. Cobbs, *Black Rage* (New York: Bantam Books, 1968), pp. 41, 50.

54. Thomas Pettigrew quoted in Daniel Patrick Moynihan, *The Negro Family: The Case for National Action* (Washington, D.C.: Office of Policy Planning and Research, U.S. Department of Labor, 1965), p. 34.

55. Thomas F. Pettigrew, *A Profile of the Negro American* (New York: D. Van Nostrand, 1964), pp. 15–16. See also Richard Wright, *Black Boy: A Record of Childhood and Youth* (New York: Harper & Row, 1966), pp. 45–47.

56. Whitney Young quoted in Moynihan, *The Negro Family*, p. 34.

57. Eldridge Cleaver, *Soul on Ice* (New York: McGraw-Hill, 1968), p. 162.

58. Ibid., p. 6.

59. Nathan Hare and Julia Hare, *The Endangered Black Family: Coping with the Unisexualization and Coming Extinction of the Black Race* (San Francisco: Black Think Tank, 1984), pp. 94–96.

60. Alice Walker, *In Search of Our Mothers' Gardens* (New York: Harcourt, Brace & World, 1984), p. 62.

61. For two excellent analyses of the trial, see Darnell M. Hunt, *O. J. Simpson Facts and Fictions: News Rituals in the Construction of Reality* (New York: Cambridge University Press, 1999); and Jewelle Taylor Gibbs, *Race and Justice: Rodney King and O. J. Simpson in a House Divided* (San Francisco: Jossey-Bass, 1996).

62. E. R. Shipp, *Columbia Journalism Review* (November-December 1994): 41.

63. Ibid., pp. 55–56.

64. Sheila Weller, *Raging Heart: The Intimate Story of the Tragic Marriage of O. J. and Nicole Brown Simpson* (New York: Pocket Books, 1995), p. 62.

65. Amiri Baraka appeared on CNN News coverage of the Simpson verdict on October 5, 1995.

66. Poll results reported by Mark Whitaker, "Whites vs. Blacks," *Newsweek* (October 16, 1995): 29.

6   Does Race Trump Gender?

1. Nathan Hare quoted in Hollie I. West, "Sexual Politics and the Afro-American Writer," *The Washington Post*, May 8, 1978.

2. Ida B. Wells, *Crusade for Justice: The Autobiography of Ida B. Wells*, ed. by Alfreda M. Duster (Chicago: University of Chicago Press, 1970), pp. 229–31.

3. Ibid., p. 232.

4. Ibid., p. 230.

5. Aileen S. Kraditor, ed., *Up from the Pedestal: Selected Writings in the History of American Feminism* (Chicago: Quadrangle Books, 1968), p. 246. It should be noted that in a speech Anthony delivered in June 1873 in upstate New York, she asserted, "I stand for universal suffrage; and as a matter of fundamental principle, do not recognize the right of society to limit it on any found of race or sex." And although she publicly stated her commitment to not limiting a person's rights on the basis of race, at this same conference she would go on record as saying that woman suffrage and the race question were completely separate causes.

6. Susan B. Anthony and Ida Husted Harper, eds., *History of Woman Suffrage,* vol. 4 (Rochester, NY: 1902), p. 343. It should be noted that a similar resolution was placed on the Council for Interracial Cooperation agenda by Charlotte Hawkins Brown. Margaret Murray Washington reportedly presented the resolution to the National Federation of Afro-American Women (NFAAW) at the 1896 Atlanta congress. See William Jeremiah Moses, *The Golden Age of Black Nationalism, 1850–1925* (New York: Oxford University Press, 1978), pp. 125–26.

7. Susan B. Anthony is quoted in Angela Y. Davis, *Women, Race, and Class* (New York: Random House, 1981), p. 118.

8. Herbert Aptheker, ed., *The Correspondence of W.E.B. Du Bois,* vol. 1 (Amherst: University of Massachusetts Press, 1973), p. 127.

9. For more information on black women's activism for woman suffrage, see Dorothy Salem, *To Better Our World: Black Women in Organized Reform, 1890–1920* (Brooklyn, NY: Carlson, 1990).

10. Adelle Hunt Logan is quoted in Paula Giddings, *When and Where I Enter: The Impact of Black Women on Race and Sex in America* (New York: Bantam Books, 1985), p. 121.

11. Bert James Lowenberg and Ruth Bogin, eds., *Black Women in the Nineteenth Century, Their Words, Their Thoughts, Their Feeling* (University Park: University of Pennsylvania Press, 1976), pp. 243–44.

12. Anna Julia Cooper, *A Voice from the South* (rep., New York: Oxford University Press, 1988), pp. 138, 140.

13. R. E. Wall, "Shall Our Girls Be Educated?" *The A.M.E. Church Review* (April 1888): 45.

14. Editorial in *The Women's Era* (September 1894): 8.

15. Mary Church Terrell, "The Justice of Woman Suffrage," *The Crisis* (September 1912): 243.

16. Wells, *Crusade for Justice,* pp. 345–47.

17. T. J. Woofter, Jr., "The Negroes of Athens, Georgia," Phelps-Stokes Fellowship Studies no. 1, *Bulletin of the University of Georgia* 14 (December 1913): 43.

18. "A Southern Domestic Worker Speaks," *The Independent* 72 (January 25, 1912): 46.

19. Mary Ovington, *Half a Man* (1911; rep. New York: Hill & Wang, 1969), pp. 56, 57, 149. David M. Katzman found that in 1920 the percentage of black women in domestic service occupations exceeded 60 percent in Chicago, 70 percent in New York City, and 80 percent in Philadelphia, and the percentage had increased by the 1930s. Katzman reported this in *Seven Days a Week: Women and Domestic Service in Industrializing America* (Urbana: University of Illinois Press, 1978), pp. 219–22.

20. Claudia Goldin, *Understanding the Gender Gap* (New York: Oxford University Press, 1990), pp. 213, 249.

21. Vivian Morris, "Bronx Slave Markets," December 6, 1938; Federal Writers Project, Negro Folklore Division, Archive of Folk Song, Manuscript Division, Library of Congress, Washington, D.C.

22. Roper-Fortune Poll 35, Map 1943, Roper Center, Williams College. According to this poll, factory work was also acceptable to those with only an elementary education (37 percent), in contrast to its rejection by better-educated women (2 percent). Education and socioeconomic/racial status clearly overlapped, in that most black women had attained less education than their white counterparts. Both race and class had strong independent effects.

23. A domestic quoted in Howard W. Odum, *Folk, Region, and Society* (Chapel Hill: University of North Carolina Press, 1964), p. 63.

24. Susan M. Hartman, *The Home Front and Beyond: American Women in the 1940s* (Boston: Twayne Publications, 1982), p. 90.

25. Charles S. Johnson quoted in Philip S. Foner, *Women and the American Labor Movement: From World War I to Present* (New York: Free Press, 1980), p. 344.

26. Jacqueline Jones, *Labor of Love, Labor of Sorrow: Black Women, Work, and the Family from Slavery to the Present* (New York: Basic Books, 1985), p. 208.

27. Hartman, *The Home Front and Beyond*, pp. 5–6. For more about employment opportunities during the war years, see also August Meier and Elliott Rudwick, *Black Detroit and the Rise of the UAW* (New York: Oxford University Press, 1979); Allan Nevins and Frank Ernest Hill, *Ford: Decline and Rebirth, 1933–1962* (New York: Charles Scribner & Sons, 1963); and Joe Trotter, Jr., *Black Milwaukee: The Making of an Industrial Proletariat* (Urbana: University of Illinois Press, 1985).

28. A domestic quoted in John Langston Gwaltney, *Drylongso: A Self-Portrait of Black America* (New York: Random House, 1980), p. 171.

29. Toni Morrison, "What Black Women Think About Women's Lib," *New York Times Magazine*, August 22, 1971.

30. For an in-depth discussion of gender politics in the civil rights movement, see Giddings, *When and Where I Enter*, chapter 17; also Donna L. Franklin, *Ensuring Inequality: The Structural Transformation of the African-American Family* (New York: Oxford University Press, 1997), chapters 7, 8; Deborah Gray White, *Too Heavy a Load: Black Women in Defense of Themselves, 1894–1994* (New York: W. W. Norton, 1999), chapters 6 and 7; Jones, *Labor of Love, Labor of Sorrow*, chapters 7 and 8; and Michele Wallace, *Black Macho and the Myth of the Superwoman*, 2d ed. (New York: Verso, 1999).

31. For an analysis of the effect these relationships were having on the organization and on white women, see Alvin Poussaint, M.D., "The Stresses on the White Female Workers in the Civil Rights Movement in the South," *American Journal of Psychiatry* 123 (April 1966): 401–5.

32. Sara Evans, *Personal Politics: The Roots of Women's Liberation in the Civil Rights Movement and the New Left* (New York: Vintage Books, 1979), pp. 78–79.

33. Ibid., p. 80.

34. Ibid., p. 81.

35. Ibid. For a different historical perspective on the emergence of SNCC, see Clayborne Carson, *In Struggle: SNCC and the Black Awakening of the 1960s* (Cambridge, MA: Harvard University Press, 1981).

36. Evans, *Personal Politics,* p. 87.

37. Ibid., p. 88.

38. Betty Friedan, *It Changed My Life: Writings on the Women's Movement* (New York: Random House, 1963), p. 96.

39. Aileen Hernandez, "Money: Small Change for Black Women," *Ms.* (August 1974): 18.

40. Quoted in Cellestine Ware, *Women's Power: The Movement for Women's Liberation* (New York: Tower Publications, 1970), p. 81.

41. For example, in 1963, Height was the only woman to attend the organizing sessions for the March on Washington.

42. Poll results were reported in Jo Freeman, *The Politics of Women's Liberation* (New York: Longman, 1975), p. 38, and in Gloria I. Joseph and Jill Lewis, *Common Differences: Conflicts in Black and White Feminist Perspectives* (Boston: South End Press, 1986), p. 59.

43. Women's Bureau, U.S. Department of Labor, *Handbook on Women Workers* (Washington, D.C.: Government Printing Office, 1969), pp. 33–35; U.S. Department of Commerce, *United States Summary: Detailed Characteristics, 1970 Census of the Population.* It should also be noted that black women had the lowest median income of any group in the population.

44. Morrison, "What Black Women Think About Women's Lib," p. 15.

45. Quoted in Freeman, *The Politics of Women's Liberation,* pp. 156, 157.

46. Carol Kleiman, "When Black Women Rap, the Talk Sure Is Different," *Chicago Tribune,* June 1, 1975.

47. White, *Too Heavy a Load,* pp. 251, 252.

48. This survey was conducted June 20–25, 1989, and was analyzed by Gerda Lerner. In her view, black women "do not necessarily expect black men to support them and their children"; thus, their attitude toward feminism "is more positive than that of white women." Quoted in Gerda Lerner, *Why History Matters: Life and Thought* (New York: Oxford University Press, 1997), p. 142.

49. This scale was developed by Otis Duncan. See "A Socioeconomic Index for All Occupations" in A. J. Reiss, ed., *Occupations and Social Status* (New York: Free Press, 1961).

50. For a critical analysis of the Moynihan Report, see Franklin, *Ensuring Inequality,* chapter 7.

51. Jessie Bernard, *Marriage and Family Among Negroes* (Englewood Cliffs, NJ: Prentice-Hall, 1966).

52. Andrew Hacker, *Two Nations: Black and White, Separate, Hostile, and Unequal* (New York: Ballantine Books, 1992), p. 120.

53. Bernard, *Marriage and Family,* pp. 68–70. The weaknesses of Bernard's analysis were documented by Julianne Malveaux; she noted that researchers have turned a major disadvantage of being a black women—that is, the labor market disadvantage of black men—into an advantage. See Julianne Malveaux, "Gender Difference and Beyond: An Economic Perspective on Diversity and Commonality Among Women," in Deborah L. Rhode, ed., *Theoretical Perspectives on Sexual Difference* (New Haven, CT: Yale University Press, 1990), pp. 226–38.

54. The two surveys were conducted by J. S. Fichter, "Career Expectations of Negro Women Graduates," *Monthly Labor Review* (November 1967): 36–42; and by W. P. Kuv-

lesky and A. S. Obordo, "A Racial Comparison of Teenage Girls' Projection for Marriage and Procreation," *Journal of Marriage and the Family* 34 (1972): 75–84.

55. B. F. Turner, "Socialization and Career Orientation Among Black and White College Women." Paper presented at the annual convention of the American Psychological Association, Honolulu, 1972.

56. Patricia Gurin and Edgar Epps, *Black Consciousness, Identity, and Achievement* (New York: John Wiley, 1975).

57. E. Wilbur Bock, "The Farmer's Daughter Effect: The Case of Negro Professional Women," *Phylon* (Spring 1969): 39–48.

58. These trends were documented in the following studies: Natalie J. Sokoloff in *Black Women and White Women in the Professions: Occupational Segregation by Race and Gender, 1960–1980* (New York: Routledge, 1992), p. 99. A. L. Sorkin, "Education, Occupation, and Income of Nonwhite Women," *Journal of Negro Education* 41 (1972): 343–351. Nonwhite women were mainly black, and that is the designation I use in the text. Patricia Gurin and E. Katz, "Motivation and Aspiration in the Negro College," Final Report, U.S. Department of Health, Education, and Welfare (Washington, D.C.: Government Printing Office, 1966). For findings on higher confidence levels, see Fichter, "Career Expectations of Negro Women Graduates," pp. 36–42; Elizabeth Higginbotham, "Employment for Professional Black Women in the Twentieth Century," in Christine Bose and Glenn Spitz, eds., *Ingredients for Women's Employment Policy* (Albany: State University of New York Press, 1987), pp. 73–91; Malveaux, "Gender Difference and Beyond," pp. 226–38.

59. Jacqueline J. Jackson, "Black Women and Higher Education," mimeographed (Duke University, 1973).

60. Kent G. Mommsen, "Career Patterns of Black American Doctorates" (Ph.D. dissertation, Florida State University, 1970).

61. Shirley Malcolm, "Increasing the Participation of Black Women in Science and Technology," in *Sage: A Scholarly Journal on Black Women* 6 (Fall 1989): 15–17.

62. Sokoloff, *Black Women and White Women in the Professions,* pp. 98–99.

63. Ari L. Goldman, "Black Women's Bumpy Path to Church Leadership," *New York Times,* July 29, 1990. The ministry has historically been a place of professional concentration for black men. See Marion Kilson, "Black Women in the Professions, 1890–1970," *Monthly Labor Review* 100 (May 1977): 38–41.

64. John Hope Franklin and Alfred A. Moss, Jr., *From Slavery to Freedom: A History of African-Americans,* 7th ed. (New York: McGraw-Hill, 1994), p. 409.

65. Jonathan Leonard, "The Impact of Affirmative Action on Employment," *Journal of Labor Economics* (October 1984).

66. Dorothy J. Gatter, "The Gender Divide: Black Women's Gains in Corporate America Outstrip Black Men's," *Wall Street Journal,* March 8, 1994. See also Keith Alexander, "Minority Women Feel Racism, Sexism Are Blocking Path to Management," *Wall Street Journal,* July 25, 1990; and Lori Silver, "Few Women, Minorities at the Top," *Washington Post,* August 14, 1990.

67. Bari-Ellen Roberts, with Jack E. White, *Roberts vs. Texaco: A True Story of Race and Corporate America* (New York: Avon Books, 1998), pp. 147–48.

68. Gatter, "The Gender Divide." For a comprehensive explanation on why black women have been more successful in the professional arena, see Cynthia Fuchs Epstein,

"Positive Effects of the Multiple Negatives Explaining the Success of Black Professional Women," *American Journal of Sociology* 78 (January 1973): 912–35.

69. Gatter, "The Gender Divide." In contrast, 22.7 percent of white women in the labor force held a minimum of a bachelor's degree, while 26.2 percent of white males had similar credentials. A recent report found that these patterns are now emerging among whites. See Tamar Lewin, "U.S. Colleges Begin to Ask, 'Where Have the Men Gone?'" *New York Times,* December 6, 1998. Similar patterns have recently emerged among whites, and by the year 2007 the U.S. Department of Education projects that 9.2 million women and only 6.9 million men will be enrolled in colleges.

70. Harry J. Holzer, *What Employers Want: Job Prospects for Less-Educated Workers* (New York: Russell Sage Foundation, 1996), pp. 80–105.

71. National Association of Women Business Owners, 1996; black men owned 405,200 businesses whereas black women owned 172,200.

72. The twenty-eight colleges and universities included in the database are as follows: liberal arts colleges Barnard, Bryn Mawr, Denison, Hamilton, Kenyon, Oberlin, Smith, Swarthmore, Wellesley, Wesleyan, and Williams; research universities Columbia, Duke, Emory, Miami, Northwestern, Pennsylvania State, Princeton, Rice, Stanford, Tufts, Tulane, Michigan, North Carolina, Pennsylvania, Vanderbilt, Washington, and Yale.

73. William G. Bowen and Derek Bok, *The Shape of the River: Long-Term Consequences of Considering Race in College and University Admissions* (Princeton, NJ: Princeton University Press, 1998), pp. 122–25.

74. Ibid., pp. 370–73.

75. For a critical analysis of this report, see Franklin, *Ensuring Inequality,* pp. 153–66.

76. Nathan and Julia Hare, "Black Women, 1970," *Trans-action* 8 (November-December 1970): 66.

77. Pauli Murray, "The Liberation of Black Women," in Beverly Guy-Sheftall, ed., *Words of Fire: An Anthology of African-American Feminist Thought* (New York: W. W. Norton, 1995), p. 196.

7   The Path to Healing

1. Kimberle Crenshaw quoted by Andrea L. Mays in *USA Today,* October 18, 1995.

2. Felicia R. Lee, "Thousands of Women Share Wounds and Celebrate," *New York Times,* October 26, 1997.

3. M. Belinda Tucker and Claudia Mitchell-Kernan, "Trends in African-American Family Formation: A Theoretical and Statistical Overview," in *The Decline in Marriage Among African-Africans* (New York: Russell Sage Foundation, 1995), p. 12. For further information on marriage and African-American divorce patterns, see also Andrew J. Cherlin, *Marriage, Divorce, and Remarriage* (Cambridge, MA: Harvard University Press, 1992); Scott South, "Racial and Ethnic Differences in the Desire to Marry," *Journal of Marriage and the Family* 55 (May 1993): 357–71; and M. Belinda Tucker and Robert Taylor, "Demographic Correlates of Relationship Status Among Black Americans," *Journal of Marriage and the Family* 51 (1989): 655–65.

4. For a black male's response to black feminists, see Robert Staples, "The Myth of Black Macho: A Response to Angry Black Feminists," *Black Scholar* (March–April 1979):

24–32. For black journalists' analysis of these issues see Donna Britt, "What About the Sisters? With All the Focus on Black Men, Somebody's Getting Left Out," *Washington Post*, February 2, 1992; and Mel Watkins, "Sexism, Racism, and Black Women Writers," *New York Times*, June 15, 1986.

5. Jose Torres, *Fire and Fear: The Inside Story of Mike Tyson* (New York: Warner Books, 1989), p. 74.

6. Commentary in two different newspapers points to this kind of thinking in the black community. See Kimberle Crenshaw, "Perspective on the Simpson Case: Racism Ploy Can Only Hurt Blacks," *Los Angeles Times*, July 24, 1994; and Glen Frankel, "O.J., O.J., on the Wall, Who's the Most Divided, Anxious, and Fearful of Them All?" *Washington Post*, June 4, 1995.

7. For details of the planned event and the organized response, see Jill Nelson, *Straight, No Chaser: How I Became a Grown-up Black Woman* (New York: G. P. Putnam's Sons, 1997), pp. 160–69.

8. Bob Herbert, editorial, *New York Times*, June 10, 1995.

9. Although these hearings were the catalyst for this discussion, in the ensuing period this discussion has remained both a sensitive and a sometimes volatile issue between black men and women, and four books have been published about these hearings: Toni Morrison, ed., *Race-ing, Justice, En-gendering Power: Essays on Anita Hill, Clarence Thomas, and the Construction of Social Reality* (New York: Random House, 1992); Robert Chrisman and Robert L. Allen, eds., *Court of Appeal: The Black Community Speaks Out on the Racial and Sexual Politics of Thomas vs. Hill* (New York: Ballantine Books, 1992); Anita Faye Hill and Emma Coleman Jordan, eds., *Race, Gender, and Power in America: The Legacy of the Hill-Thomas Hearings* (New York: Oxford University Press, 1995); and Geneva Smitherman, ed., *African-American Women Speak Out on Anita Hill–Clarence Thomas* (Detroit: Wayne State University, 1995). See also Beverly Guy-Sheftall, "Breaking the Silence: A Black Feminist Response to the Hill/Thomas Hearings," in *Black Scholar* (1992).

10. These poll figures are taken from Kimberle Crenshaw's excellent essay "Whose Story Is It Anyway? Feminist and Antiracist Appropriations of Anita Hill," in Morrison, ed., *Race-ing, Justice, En-gendering Power*, p. 417.

11. In the transcript of the Thomas hearings, Senator Orrin Hatch noted that Hill had expressed concern about Thomas's "repeated public criticism of his sister and her children for living on welfare" and Thomas responded that he had "no recollection of ever making a statement about my sister in any speeches."

12. Karen Tumulty, "Sister of High Court Nominee Traveled Different Road," *Los Angeles Times*, July 5, 1991. For another perspective, see also Joel F. Handler, "The Judge and His Sister: Growing Up Black," *New York Times*, July 23, 1991 (letter to the editor).

13. Kimberle Crenshaw, "Roundtable: Doubting Thomas," *Tikkun* 6 (September–October 1991): 27–28.

14. Felicity Barringer's article in the *New York Times* titled "The Drama as Viewed by Women," October 18, 1991, surveyed women who disagreed with Anita Hill's testimony, and here's a sampling of their comments: "You have to make sure you get across that you're a professional. If someone isn't willing to accept that, you make sure you're not in a room alone with him." Another one asserted, "Wouldn't you haul off and poke a guy in

the mouth if he spoke in that manner?" And yet another one averred, "It's unbelievable that a woman couldn't stop something like that at its inception."

15. James Cox, "Harassment Furor Still Brews at *Washington Post*," *USA Today* (November 4, 1991). According to this report, there were allegations by at least seven women at the *Washington Post* that Williams harassed them with lewd remarks. Williams wrote an open letter of apology and the letter was posted on a newsroom bulletin board. In addition, Williams met with a group of female staff in the presence of a counselor. The women who made the charges objected to the *Post*'s decision not to disclose the disciplinary action it took against Williams.

16. Nathan and Julia Hare's article appeared in the November 18, 1991, issue of *Final Call*. The headline in the newspaper read "Thomas Survives High-Tech Lynching."

17. M. Belinda Tucker and Claudia Mitchell-Kernan, "Marital Behavior and Expectations: Ethnic Comparisons of Attitudinal and Structural Correlates," and K. Jill Kiecolt and Mark A. Fossett, "Mate Availability and Marriage Among African Americans: Aggregate- and Individual-Level Analyses," in Tucker and Mitchell-Kernan, eds., *The Decline in Marriage Among African Americans*. For one of the early analyses of sex ratio see Marci Guttentag and Paul F. Secord, *Too Many Women? The Sex Ratio Question* (Beverly Hills, CA: Sage Publications, 1983).

18. Arlene F. Saluter, *Marital Status and Living Arrangements: March 1993*, U.S. Bureau of the Census, Current Population Reports, Series P20-478 (Washington, D.C.: Government Printing Office, 1994). See also U.S. Bureau of the Census, 1995. *Statistical Abstract of the United States: 1995* (Washington, D.C., Government Printing Office, 1995).

19. Cherlin, *Marriage, Divorce, and Remarriage*, pp. 94–95. Another study, also reported by Cherlin, estimated 75 percent.

20. One of the most comprehensive analyses can be found in Tucker and Mitchell-Kernan, eds., *The Decline in Marriage*.

21. Lynn C. Burbridge, "Policy Implications for a Decline in Marriage Among African Americans," in Tucker and Mitchell-Kernan, eds., *The Decline in Marriage*, pp. 323–44.

22. The analysis that found diminished employment for black men explained only 20 percent of the decline in marriages was reported in Robert D. Mare and Christopher Winship, "Socioeconomic Change and the Decline in Marriage for Blacks and Whites," in Christopher Jencks and Paul E. Peterson, eds., *The Urban Underclass* (Washington, DC: Brookings Institution, 1991), pp. 182–87. The finding that young men delay marriage when they are unemployed was reported in T. M. Cooney and Dennis H. Hogan, "Marriage in an Institutionalized Life Course: First Marriages Among American Men in the Twentieth Century," *Journal of Marriage and the Family* 53 (1991): 178–90. Other empirical studies that have analyzed the relationship between men's employment and marriage rates include Mark Testa, Nan Marie Astone, Marilyn Krough, and Kathryn Neckerman, "Employment and Marriage Among Inner-City Fathers," *The Annals of the American Academy of Political and Social Sciences* 501 (1989): 79–81; Randall J. Olsen and George Farkas, "The Effect of Economic Opportunity and Family Background on Adolescent Cohabitation and Childbearing Among Low-Income Blacks," *Journal of Labor Economics* 8, no. 3 (1990): 341–62; Robert I. Lerman, "Employment Patterns of Un-

wed Fathers and Public Policy," in Robert I. Lerman and Theodora Ooms, eds., *Young Unwed Fathers: Changing Roles and Emerging Policies* (Philadelphia: Temple University Press, 1993); and Robert J. Sampson, "Unemployment and Imbalanced Sex Ratios: Race-Specific Consequences for Family Structure and Crime," in Tucker and Mitchell-Kernan, eds., *The Decline in Marriage*, pp. 229–60.

23. Stewart E. Tolnay, "The Great Migration and Changes in the Northern Black Family, 1940–1990," *Social Forces* 75 (June 1997): 1213–38.

24. Tucker and Mitchell-Kernan, "Marital Behavior and Expectations," pp. 160–61.

25. Scott South, "Racial and Ethnic Differences in the Desire to Marry," *Journal of Marriage and the Family* 55 (May 1993): 357–71. Black women were also less likely to desire marriage than their white counterparts, but these differences were attributable to smaller gender differentials in the wages between black men and women. See, for example, F. K. Goldscheider and Linda J. Waite, "Sex Differences in the Entry into Marriage," *American Journal of Sociology* 92 (July 1986): 91–109. A seminal research study, although somewhat dated, compared the heterosexual social development of prepubescent black and white boys ages ten to thirteen and found that black boys had a "progressive disenchantment with marriage": Carlfred B. Broderick, "Social Heterosexual Development Among Urban Negroes and Whites," *Journal of Marriage and the Family* 27, no. 2 (1965): 200–203.

26. From *Oprah Winfrey Show*, "Men Apologize to Women," August 17, 1998, Harpo Productions, Inc. Transcript produced by Burrell's Information Services, pp. 1–3.

27. bell hooks, *Wounds of Passion: A Writing Life* (New York: Henry Holt, 1997), pp. 163–64.

28. Ibid.

29. C. Wright Mills, *The Sociological Imagination* (New York: Oxford University Press, 1959).

30. William G. Bowen and Derek Bok, *The Shape of the River: Long-Term Consequences of Considering Race in College and University Admissions* (Princeton, NJ: Princeton University Press, 1998), pp. 175–76. It should be noted that the divorce rate for both blacks and whites who graduated from the more elite universities was lower, and the authors explain these trends in the following statement: "They may be too busy to get divorced, while still others made too much money to be able to afford divorce."

31. The wage gap between white college-educated women and their spouses is narrower than it is between white college-educated men and their spouses.

32. See, for example, Kingsley Davis, "Intermarriage in Case Societies," *American Anthropologist* 43 (1941): 376–95; and Robert K. Merton, "Intermarriage and Social Structure: Fact and Theory," *Psychiatry* 4 (1941): 361–74. A cost-benefit analysis of marriage was also set forth in Nobel laureate Gary S. Becker's *Treatise on the Family* (Cambridge, MA: Harvard University Press, 1982).

33. Bowen and Bok, *The Shape of the River*, pp. 176–78.

34. Figures taken from Orlando Patterson's *Rituals of Blood: Consequences of Slavery in Two Centuries* (Washington, D.C.: Civitas/Counterpoint, 1998), pp. 63–64.

35. The Harvard/*Washington Post*/Kaiser Foundation Survey, 1997. Tabulated by Patterson, in *Rituals of Blood*, pp. 105–106.

36. R. A. Bulcroft and K. A. Bulcroft, "Race Differences in Attitudinal Motivation in the Decision to Marry," *Journal of Marriage and the Family* 55 (1993): 338–55. Com-

pared to white women, black women placed greater "emphasis on economic support" and were more resistant to marrying someone with fewer economic resources. This apprehension on the part of black women regarding the financial stability of their spouse is more than likely an extension of the legacy in the black community wherein black men with few economic resources exchanged romance for monetary benefits. For more about these historic patterns, see Franklin, *Ensuring Inequality,* pp. 78–81.

37. Mark R. Rank and Larry E. Davis, "Perceived Happiness Outside of Marriage Among Black and White Spouses," *Family Relations* (October 1996): 435–42. See also Annie S. Banes, "Black Husbands and Wives: An Account of Marital Roles in a Middle-Class Neighborhood," in Constance Obudho, ed., *Black Marriage and Family Therapy* (Westport, CT: Greenwood Press, 1983), pp. 55–73.

38. Shirley Hatchett, Joseph Vernoff, and Elizabeth Douvan, "Marital Instability Among Black and White Couples in Early Marriage," in Tucker and Mitchell-Kernan, eds., *The Decline in Marriage,* pp. 177–218.

39. Shirley J. Hatchett, "Women and Men," in James S. Jackson, ed., *Life in Black America* (Newbury Park, CA: Sage Publications, 1991), pp. 90–103. Hatchett's findings indicated that marriages were unstable if black men felt their wives had equal power in the family. See also Sandra DeJarnett and Bertram H. Raven, "The Balance, Bases, and Modes of Interpersonal Power in Black Couples: The Role of Sex and Socio-Economic Circumstances," *Journal of Black Psychology* 7, no. 2 (1981): 51–66. DeJarnett and Raven found that black men of both classes, especially the middle class, continued to hold sexist views about male dominance and women's place in the home. Seventy-one percent of middle-class black men believed that husbands should have the final say in all matters. Black women strongly rejected these sexist views.

40. Tucker and Mitchell-Kernan, "Marital Behavior and Expectations," pp. 145–71.

41. Paul Amato and Alan Booth, "Consequences of Parental Divorce and Marital Unhappiness for Adult Well-Being," *Social Forces* 69 (1991): 895–914.

42. John M. Gottman, *The Seven Principles for Making Marriage Work* (New York: Crown, 1999).

43. Erma Lawson and Aaron Thompson, "Black Men Make Sense of Marital Distress and Divorce: An Exploratory Study," *Family Relations* (April 1995): 211–19.

44. Julia Boyd, *Embracing the Fire: Sisters Talk About Sex and Relationships* (New York: Penguin Books, 1997), pp. 78–79.

45. Carolyn Pape Cowan and Phillip A. Cowan, *When Partners Become Parents: The Big Life Change for Couples* (New York: Basic Books, 1992), pp. 137–49.

46. Quote taken from Barbara Ransby and Tracye Matthew, "Black Popular Culture and the Transcendence of Patriarchal Illusions," in Beverly Guy-Sheftall, ed., *Words of Fire: An Anthology of African-American Feminist Thought* (New York: The New Press, 1995), p. 530.

47. For a more in-depth discussion of this theoretical perspective, see Nancy Chodorow, *The Reproduction of Mothering: Psychoanalysis in the Sociology of Gender* (Berkeley: University of California Press, 1978).

48. "Interview with Ella Baker," Civil Rights Documentation Project, Moorland-Spingarn Collections, Howard University, pp. 34–35.

49. Quoted in Nick Kotz and Mary L. Kotz, *A Passion for Equality: George Wiley and the Movement* (New York: W. W. Norton, 1977), p. 252.

50. Benjamin S. Carson, *Gifted Hands* (New York: Zondervan, 1997). One could argue that his brother, Curtis, served as his "male figure" or role model whereas Curtis was more sensitive because he didn't have an older brother to "look up to."

51. Gloria I. Joseph and Jill Lewis, *Common Differences: Conflicts in Black and White Feminist Perspectives* (Boston: South End Press, 1981). Chapter 3, titled "Black Mothers and Daughters," focuses on data collected from black mothers and daughters.

52. "Can You Love God and Sex?" was the topic of a roundtable discussion with eight distinguished religious leaders, facilitated by Marcia Dyson, *Essence* (February 1999). Vanzant is currently married to a caring man, which is one more testament that a person can overcome his or her fears and heal the wounds of the past.

53. Shirlee Taylor Haizlip and Harold C. Haizlip, *In the Garden of Our Dreams: Memoirs of a Marriage* (New York: Kodansha America, 1998).

54. Lee, "Thousands of Women Share Wounds and Celebrate."

55. From *Oprah Winfrey Show,* April 10, 1998. Harpo Productions, Inc. Transcript produced by Burrell's Information Services, pp. 4–6.

56. Figures taken from Orlando Patterson, *Rituals of Blood: Consequences of Slavery in Two American Centuries* (Washington, D.C.: Civitas/Counterpoint, 1998), p. 130. See also Claire Sterk-Elifson, "Sexuality Among African-American Women," in Alice S. Rossi, ed., *Sexuality Across the Life Course* (Chicago: University of Chicago Press, 1994), p. 112.

57. Ossie Davis and Ruby Dee, *With Ossie and Ruby: In This Life Together* (New York: William Morrow, 1998), p. 435.

58. Clare McIntosh, "Are You Being Played?" *Essence,* February 1999.

59. *Oprah Winfrey Show,* March 16, 1999. Transcript produced by Burrell's Information Services.

60. Karen Mains, *Friends and Strangers* (Dallas: Word Publishing, 1990), p. 127.

61. Paulo Freire, *Pedagogy of the Oppressed* (New York: Seabury Press, 1970), p. 104.

Index

245

About the Author

Donna L. Franklin is the author of *Ensuring Inequality: The Structural Transformation of the African-American Family,* which won the American Sociological Association's Goode Distinguished Book Award for "outstanding contribution to family scholarship." She has held faculty appointments at the University of Chicago, Howard University, Smith College, and the University of Southern California. She currently lives in Los Angeles, California.